MAY I HAVE A WORD WITH YOU?

MAY I
HAVE A WORD
WITH YOU?

BY

Rabbi Morris Adler

COMPILED BY

Goldie Adler

AND

Lily Edelman

A B'nai B'rith Book

CROWN PUBLISHERS, INC.

BM
45
.A33

• *Acknowledgments*

THE ESSAYS AND SHORT PIECES making up this volume were culled from *The Shaarey Zedek Recorder* and from addresses and printed articles by Rabbi Morris Adler over the years. Except in the case of the latter, dates and exact sources are included only when necessary to the context.

Grateful acknowledgment is given herewith for permission to reprint essays from the following publications: *Bulletin of Sinai Hospital*, Detroit; *Congress Bi-Weekly* (formerly *Congress Weekly*); *Harper's Magazine; Jewish Frontier; Jewish Heritage; Jewish Heritage Reader; Physical Therapy Review* (journal of American Physical Therapy Association); *The Reconstructionist.*

We wish also to express appreciation to Rabbi Irwin Groner of Shaarey Zedek for his wholehearted cooperation in making available file copies of Rabbi Adler's speeches and articles; to Herbert Michelman and Nathan Lyons of Crown Publishers, Inc., for their sensitive editorial guidance in giving final shape to this volume; and to Mrs. Beatrice Shere, of B'nai B'rith's Commission on Adult Jewish Education, for her devoted assistance in readying the manuscript for publication.

• Contents

• Introduction

THIS BOOK IS OVERDUE. It was in the making long before the black February Shabbat on which Rabbi Adler was fatally wounded by a deranged student, under the very eyes of the Detroit congregation he had so vigorously led over twenty-five years. Rabbi Adler himself had been assembling favorite pieces, under assorted headings and in multiple notebooks, in order to meet repeated requests from farflung colleagues and friends and occasional feelers from would-be publishers.

May I Have a Word With You?, the humorous, humane rabbinic chats appearing weekly in his synagogue *Recorder* and widely reprinted, were familiar to thousands of readers beyond the confines of Shaarey Zedek. So too were many of his sermons and public addresses, famed for their energetic amalgam of passion and prophecy, wisdom and wit. Selections from all three sources make up this book. While this present compilation of "stray leaves" can be only a partial fulfillment of their author's promise, its aim is simple and single: to be worthy of the living memory of Morris Adler.

Who, after all, was Morris Adler that fifteen thousand mourners—Jew and Gentile, Negro and white, leader and led, worker and employer, religionist and nonbeliever—should have converged, from near and far, on the Detroit suburb of Southfield on March 13, 1966, to pay their last respects? What manner of man was he that so many should continue to remember?

"I have a feeling of love and tenderness for words," Rabbi Adler confesses. "They are among the greatest gifts the past has given us." In his memorial essay on Hayim Greenberg, he lists a cluster of Hebrew words which can unlock the legacy of that ardent Labor Zionist and secularist who remained for the younger man, despite their differing approaches to Jewish life, a personal hero of immeasurable impact, and on whose biography he was working before his own premature death.

Similarly, a select list of phrases with which to interpret Morris Adler, the man and his message, would have to lead off with "being a *mentsh*" and "doing justly." Other key concepts, Anglicized but deeply rooted in their Biblical origins—like Rabbi Adler himself, for whom Judaism was "bone of his bone, flesh of his flesh"—must of necessity include: "man's cosmic dignity," "social justice," "equality and freedom," "compassion," "brotherhood." First, last, and always: "choose life."

Of vibrant voice and massive physique, Morris Adler seemed, with every energetic step and gesture, to attack the world-as-it-is. For him, nothing human was alien. Unlike many professing men of faith, he really did believe, with every fiber of his being, that man is created in the image of God and as such has the potential and the obligation to do good and "to act brotherly." Children, family, the home; friends, conversation, debate, and mutual criticism; reading, meditation, study; involvement in the world's work and business; the self-renewing wonders of God's universe and the daily miracles of man's individual acts of generosity or courage—these he extolled.

Not that Morris Adler was naïve. His ever-ready wit let no foible pass. He lashed out, sometimes bitterly, against the weaknesses to which man and society are heir. With courage and conviction he denounced evil and injustice wherever they reared their heads, often espousing unpopular causes and lonely positions. Pain, suffering, and death were daily companions; he spent an inordinate proportion of his waking hours counseling the disturbed, visiting the sick, burying the dead, comforting the living.

Man's main task, in Rabbi Adler's view, was so to live that his presence made a difference in the lives of other men and in human society. By engaging in the task of building a better world—from which no one is exempt—man makes himself worthy, raises himself Godward.

In the work of enhancing this world, Judaism, Rabbi Adler emphatically believed, has a special contribution to make. As a rabbi, he devoted most of his effort to teaching Jews the nature

of their Jewish difference and how to give it a human meaning.
Fundamentally an optimist and convinced that the modern Jew
has opted to remain Jewish—at least not to be non-Jewish—
Rabbi Adler, from his pulpit and before the numerous religious
and secular organizations he so frequently addressed as a most
sought-after public speaker, posed the same question again and
again: "How can we make Judaism function so that our people
derive strength and guidance from it?" What he called "the
Jewish lag" or discrepancy between modern intelligent Jews and
their Jewish illiteracy disturbed him profoundly.

In the final analysis, Rabbi Adler was himself the most complete and persuasive example of what he was talking about—
a Jew so rooted in Judaism that his every word and deed
reflected its teachings. Late in 1965 he penned an answer to the
question put him by a young sophisticate: "How can you
believe?"

"Judaism opens wide the door that leads me into the heart
of all mankind," Morris Adler affirmed. "Judaism teaches me
to appropriate as my own the pain and suffering of all men who
live under the shadow of sorrow and oppression. . . . It leads
me out of self into the broad places where all men live and into
the high places where abide truth, justice, and glory."

Far from being a narrow faith, Judaism invited him to "a
broad adventure in human ideals, hopes, and values." The good
life was for him one that put Judaism into action for the service of
all mankind.

Many tributes have been paid Morris Adler. He has been
called by some the most outstanding rabbi of our day, the
quality of whose thirty years of ministering to the Jewish people
shall not soon be matched. His leadership in Conservative
Judaism left its impact on that major movement. The late
Stephen S. Wise, recognizing a kindred mover and shaker of
men, affectionately dubbed him "Bishop of Detroit," mindful of
Rabbi Adler's enormous contribution to the communal life of
that city—its interfaith and interracial movements, its cultural
and educational enrichment activity.

On the national scene, also, Rabbi Adler cast a long shadow,
not only on Jewish life, whose multiple purposes he served in

many capacities and whose collective goals he helped to elevate, but also on the larger America which he so loved. He was summoned on occasion to White House and other major national conferences involving religious leadership. From its inception in 1957, he served as Chairman of the Review Board of the United Automobile Workers, pioneering new methods of out-of-court arbitration of labor-management disputes.

Perhaps the most profound tribute is that Morris Adler was "a vessel of Torah." His words and deeds, born of his integrity as a Jew and a human being, healed the wounds of many, brightened the lives of multitudes, opened to view the possibility of a better tomorrow.

L. E.

MAY I HAVE A WORD WITH YOU?

~ PART I ~

MAN AND SOCIETY

IN *The World of the Talmud** *Rabbi Adler points out that the modern Jew is the inheritor of a long tradition that ensures "his generally liberal position on social questions" and "his sensitivity to human need." The Rabbis of the Talmudic period were more than teachers and religious leaders. Intimately involved in the life of the community, they arbitrated disputes according to prescribed Jewish law. They were also men of affairs (most of them earned their livings as workers or merchants) who wielded great influence in shaping community action and policy. Rabbi Akiba, one of Rabbi Adler's great personal favorites, led the Jewish rebellion against the Romans and died a martyr's death.*

A loyal Jew and consciously "the proud descendant of patriarchs and prophets," Morris Adler was equally dedicated to his adopted country, to which his immigrant parents had brought him from Russia in 1913, at the age of seven. A serious student of American history and civilization, he felt very much at home both as an American and as a Jew.

Because of this dual heritage, Rabbi Adler regarded it as his duty to bring the teachings of Judaism to bear on the larger social issues of the day. He cautioned against the dangers threatening America's pluralistic society and urged the need to safeguard or "put fences around" the rights and freedoms of all its citizens. As a chaplain in the United States Army who rendered distinguished service during World War II in the Southwest Pacific and Japan, he concurred in the need to fight for democracy. But, immediately after the war, Rabbi Adler was unrelenting in urging Americans to continue to wage war—not against foreign enemies but in defense of peace, human rights for all, and cooperation and peaceful coexistence among the faiths. He saw the struggle for freedom as never-ending, one which has to be rewon in every generation.

* Hillel Little Book, Washington, D.C., 1959; Schocken paperback.

I

1 • *Freedom and Law*

CHOOSING LIFE

ONE OF THE MOST profound convictions in Biblical doctrine is that which relates to man's basic freedom. To man is given the freedom to chart his path in life, and his is the responsibility for the choice he makes. If man were bereft of such freedom of choice, righteousness and wrong, good and evil would have no essential meaning, and morality would be an empty phrase. In the absence of the freedom to determine the kind of life he shall lead, man would be nothing more than the fettered slave of circumstance, acting solely in compulsive conformity with its dictates or with the imperious and undeniable impulses of his flesh.

Holy Writ eloquently enunciates man's basic freedom. In the Law of Moses and in the words of his successor, Joshua, the view is affirmed and reiterated that man can choose between good and evil, life and death. In doing so he assumes responsibility for the consequences of his choice. To be sure, the freedom man enjoys is neither absolute nor unlimited. True freedom has its bounds and can be experienced only within the area thus restricted. The Rabbis, for all their belief in man's freedom of choice and freedom of will, remind us "for perforce thou wast formed, and perforce wast thou born, and thou livest perforce and perforce thou wilt die."

The very facts of life and manhood impose limitations that none can set aside. We are born to a particular set of parents and thus become the products of a specific stream of heredity and the objects of specific influences and conditions. We are born into a definite period or age and cannot escape the forces that prevail at that particular point in time's unending flow. We are raised in a specific society and its environmental influences im-

2

pinge upon us to shape and direct our lives. We become, willingly or not, heirs of the culture patterns of the group into which we are born and the target of its pressures. We find ourselves male or female, Jew or Christian, white or black, brown or yellow, American or French, Chinese or Greek. Yet religion unhesitatingly and with complete assurance proclaims that the sovereign choice is man's. It is he who within the framework of inevitable restriction determines the quality of his life, whether it be, as the Bible puts it, "for life and good," or "for death and evil," whether it be for a blessing or for a curse. "Choose ye this day whom ye will serve," says Joshua to the assembled multitude.

Everything, say the Rabbis, is in the power of God except the fear of God. It is man who independently decides what shall be the quality and essence of the life he wishes to lead. External conditions and forces beyond man's control, the Rabbis declare, may conspire to determine whether one be strong or weak, wise or foolish, rich or poor. But man and man alone makes the free and decisive choice that determines whether he be wicked or righteous, good or evil. "Behold I set before you this day, a blessing and a curse." Man possesses the deepest freedom, stamping him as unique among the creatures of the earth, namely, the freedom to choose between spiritual and moral life and death, between humanity and beastliness.

That man possesses this vital freedom, which is at the heart of all freedom, needs to be stressed in our day. For man today all too often sees himself as the creature of circumstance, the puppet of fate, the victim of impersonal forces, buffeted about by the storms and pressures that arise outside of him. We seek to escape the responsibility for the character of our lives by pointing to the outer forces that play upon us.

Each generation, including our own, which has been placed by destiny in an atomic age, hears the echo of the Biblical words, "I call heaven and earth to witness against you this day, that I have set before thee life and death, the blessing and the curse; therefore choose life that thou mayest live, thou and thy seed." Man must take into his own hands the freedom to live nobly, creatively, usefully.

THE FREEDOM OF FREE MEN

FREEDOM IS A CONCEPT in the tradition of the Jew that has been sired by experience, nurtured by doctrine, and lovingly tended by great and constant concern. Judaism is, therefore, incomparably rich in insights about this basic value which it has enwreathed with numberless rites, comments, and parables. One of the recognitions to which the Jew early rose was that freedom requires eternal vigilance and struggle, and that in the process of this incessant attempt to safeguard it, its meanings deepen and multiply. The Haggadah, read at the Seder, reminds us that "in every generation oppression is wont to raise its head." The tradition, likewise, speaks of the ultimate, lasting freedom which will complete and fulfill the *Pesah Mizraim,* the partial liberation from Egyptian bondage.

Freedom is an expanding concept. It grows from generation to generation. It enlarges with the experience and wisdom of mankind. At one time, freedom meant the ability to wrest from the reluctant soil more than a meager and minimal subsistence. This achievement released human energy from enslavement to survival and freed man for a life beyond physical existence.

At another stage, freedom meant the banding together of men and families into a clan or tribe giving the individual the assurance of some measure of collective protection. It brought emancipation for many from the fears that assail him who is doomed to solitariness. At another level, freedom spelt cooperation through alliance or covenant of several groups or clans or states, thus enabling tribes and nations to find release from the perpetual fear of attack by the neighbors outside its immediate borders.

Science brought liberation to man in many areas where he had hitherto either wallowed in ignorance or lay chained by helplessness. Understanding more fully the world of nature about him and achieving greater control over his environment, man could breathe more easily and enjoy a higher degree of freedom. Public education increased liberty through literacy, and enlarged the scope of man's awareness even as it widened his horizons of experience and understanding.

Religion, when true to its noblest purposes, extended man's liberty by the knowledge that he stands in a wholesome and benign relationship with the universe in which he must perforce live. It unshackled him from dark superstition and from the fear that malignancy and terror crouch at the center of life. Freedom came to man through the conception of the moral dependability of the universe which religion stressed, and from the discovery of the world's integrity and coherence, which science presented to him.

Man's political freedom became more assured when, in relatively recent times, the rights and dignity of man inhering in him were given political status, and were thus made independent of the will or whim of those who ruled him. This is the profound significance of that inspired concept so integral to the American tradition suggested by the term "inalienable rights."

History is, in a major sense, the record of the growth of human freedom. Liberty expands in time and redeems more and more of man's life from oppression, illness, ignorance, statuslessness and powerlessness. Hence, man must not cease from a continuing exploration both of life and the meanings of liberty still imbedded in it and not yet brought to light. Is not this the deep intent of the statement of the Haggadah, "he who persists in the investigation and recital of man's liberation is praiseworthy"?

The ultimate goal can be nothing less than that none shall be deprived, dispossessed, or disinherited. We mark Passover yearly and participate in its moving rites, lest we become complacent and acquiescent to our situation before we shall have achieved the time when "all who are hungry have been fed" and "all who are dependent have been freed."

The progression in freedom applies to groups no less than to individuals. It is not achieved at one swoop in the collective life. Nor is it won once for all time. The process of emancipation is a continuing one. The struggle for greater freedom cannot end. The aspiration to liberty must look beyond present attainments else advance is impossible and the freedom seemingly already secured endangered. Nations settled on their own soil, proud in the possession of their sovereignty, cannot afford to rest by calling a truce to the unending struggle for freedom.

The confidence in our liberty today cannot be purchased at the expense of unconcern about the morrow. Liberty is endangered when apparent security throttles a people's alertness, even as it is imperiled when men give to security priority over freedom. Communists have known how to exploit the tragic weakness of those who are ready to purchase security or its counterfeit at the cost of their liberty. In the long run, and indeed in the short too, security divorced from liberty is as insecure as it is unfree. Tyrants and dictators believe that people will content themselves with the illusions they offer them or else will early become weary in battling for freedom and will resign themselves to the low status which such regimes impose upon them.

This is true in the case of nations at home within their own borders and invested with sovereignty. A lax contentment with partial freedom all too often sets in. How much more exposed to surrender are minorities which lack the shelter which the possession of one's own territory affords a group, and who must live constantly in the presence of a large and overshadowing majority. How perilously tempting it is for a minority to resign itself to an uneasy peace with a condition that is less than free or just. There is the fear of becoming conspicuous in the eyes of the group which so vastly outnumbers it and in the midst of which it must live. There is the tendency to talk in muted whispers and to tread softly. There is the real danger that self-esteem and dignity will be sapped under the ever-present pressure of forces created by the massive, overt, and subtle power of the majority.

Decades ago the great modern Jewish thinker Ahad Ha'am pointed out that self-depreciation eventuates in assimilation and absorption. Minorities must, therefore, constantly reevaluate their position, reaffirm their rights, and reinvigorate their spirit. This is true even of minorities living in the lands of freedom. The pressures for conformity are ever present to attack that individuality which the few wish to preserve.

The Jew is the classic minority of mankind. Perhaps more than other people he must be unslumberingly aware of the dangers to freedom and unambiguously lucid in his own mind about the character of the freedom which he, like all men, merits.

In his case, too, no less than in that of the majority, liberty is a right with a dynamic need for constant enlargement.

With the coming of the Emancipation, which conferred civil rights on him, the Jew was content to think of freedom as synonymous with equality. He had been an outsider so long, an alien living on the outermost fringes of society that his great yearning was to be permitted to live within the framework of citizenship. For centuries the Jew was a vague and marginal figure haunting the borderline of the states, an all but invisible figure. Indeed, one can read many standard histories of Europe and not suspect that a single Jew inhabited that continent. Hence, the Jew thrilled to the slogan which one of the fighters for emancipation inscribed on his banner, "To the Jews, as men, everything." In it he saw the promise of equality which would forever remove from him the oppressive and humiliating stigma of alienism and refugeeism. He wearied of being mankind's displaced people. No wonder that the Jew hurled himself into the struggle for equality with a passion intensified by centuries of repression.

But the dream soon dissolved in the face of an undercurrent of uneasiness and unhappiness. Even when some degree of equality was granted the Jew, he began to feel that something was wrong, even false, about his new position. He recognized that equality was not enough. One can have equality and yet be far from free. Equality that withholds the freedom to remain true to one's individuality does not yet spell freedom. This is the kind of "liberty" that the Emancipation conferred. The same leader who said "To the Jews, as men, everything," had gone on to say, "To Jews as Jews, nothing."

Here was the Achilles' heel of a liberation that promised much and gave little. In a profound sense, the modern movement of Zionism was Jewry's answer to an Emancipation that failed to emancipate. Liberty means the right of an individual to share in the collective life of his ancestral group and to live in terms of its tradition without penalty and without displacement from the common life in which all men in a free land share. This is the fuller meaning of the freedom which is a minority's right. It is the corollary of the freedom a democracy extends the majority. There are Jews in America who have not yet risen to this higher and nobler conception. There are Jews who fear that our public concern about the State of Israel violates the caution and discretion with which a minority ought to bear itself even in a free land. Many organized Jewish activities have been established and are maintained as nonsectarian programs, as if it were wrong to label them Jewish.

What then is the nature of our liberty as a Jewish group within the fabric of the American community? Freedom for the American Jew means the participation on the basis of equality in the concerns, duties, and interests common to all Americans. It assures the full right to him of self-expression as the inheritor and bearer of a specific tradition. The Jew who did not exist as an individual before Emancipation must not now disappear in our democracy. America does not wish us to become nondescript, characterless adherents of a nonsectarian persuasion. Freedom should mean for the Jew the right and opportunity to strengthen those areas in Jewish life which most authentically and profoundly reflect the specific character and genius of his tradition. Then he will be entering upon the fuller freedom which is his due and will add substance to American culture in place of mere difference.

We have thus far defined the freedom of a minority within the larger society as comprising both equality and identity or group individuality. True freedom also implies responsibility, a responsibility not imposed by external sanctions but assumed willingly and graciously by the spirit of free men. The minority within a democratic order should utilize the position it occupies and the vantage that position gives it to enlarge the view of the majority and thus aid it in attaining a better perspective from which it may more wisely form its policies and arrive at its decisions. We are not accustomed to think of a minority as assisting a majority. We are more prone to consider the protections with which a majority should surround a minority.

Yet the theory of democracy implies that the dissenter or nonconformist has a role to play in perceiving and refining those truths by which all men may more nobly live. A member of the minority should regard it as his obligation to present his convictions clearly and responsibly so that out of the meeting of differing outlooks a wiser decision may result than would have been possible in a monolithic society. None can see the whole picture in connection with any of the complex social and political issues that agitate our times. The majority, too, sees the scene from a partial and limited view. It is always in danger because of the strength that inheres in its numbers and the influence it wields by its power. The very presence of a minority is a constant reminder of the relative character of our formulated answers to the questions of our day.

When is the Jew free? When he is unconstrained in speaking out of his particular vantage in the interests of the common good. When is the Jew free? When he feels free as man and as Jew—as a citizen of America and as a member of a minority group—the one not in conflict with the other, the one not apart from the other, but both fused into a single undivided personality. When is the Jew free? When he voices his view unintimidated by the non-Jewish demagogue and undeterred by the frightened within the Jewish fold.

Then will his voice be doubly authentic and, therefore, doubly resonant. He will speak simultaneously in the loftiest accents of the American tradition and in the truest spirit of his Jewish heritage. Side by side with all America, partner yet individual, merged yet distinct, the free Jew will be at one with all free men in the continuing struggle for freedom for all.

FREE SPEECH*

FELIX FRANKFURTER, answering a question at a hearing before a Senate Committee, vigorously affirmed his readiness to defend even a Nazi group in America should its civil rights be involved. Associate Justice Frankfurter is not the man to speak casually, nor was the occasion one which invited an opinion lightly given. The substance of his remarks, the form in which they were cast, the emphasis placed upon them were undoubtedly

*Religion: A Digest, August, 1939; condensed from The Reconstructionist, April 7, 1939.

the result of long and judicious deliberation. And there was reason too why he should at this time reiterate with considerable forcefulness this view, which proposes to safeguard the freedom guaranteed by democracy, even to the most outspoken and violent enemies of freedom and democracy.

For some time there has been considerable discussion in various circles, and not by any means in circles that could be described as reactionary, about the proper limits of freedom of speech. Interested believers in democracy have been asking: "Is it the better part of wisdom to allow the many raucous and undemocratic voices and viewpoints a public arena for their opinions, and unrestrained opportunity to enlist adherents for their program?"

Are there not times when the common good counsels restriction upon free expression? Some have assumed that the advisability of such limitation cannot be questioned. Being essentially believers in democratic forms, they have asked themselves: "What bounds may be set upon freedom of speech without endangering the basic principle of free speech?" Many Jews, too, alarmed by the unprecedented dissemination of anti-Semitic propaganda, and fearful of the poisoned voices which in our day ride the airwaves, have been casting about for a legal way by which to curb them without simultaneously weakening the fundamental guarantee of freedom of opinion established by the Bill of Rights.

Democracy, however, is based not on a theory of the suppression of minorities, but of their cooperation and interrelation. Variations of view and program are an indispensable element in the social climate. There can be no democracy where there is no freedom for diversity of opinion. The first of the articles of the Bill of Rights, ratified at the very beginning of our national government, states in unambiguous language that "Congress shall make no law respecting the establishment of religion, or prohibiting the free exercise thereof, or abridging the freedom of speech, or of the press, or the right peaceably to assemble, and to petition the government for a redress of grievances."

That this right is the very foundation of free government was recognized at the outset. As Benjamin Franklin pointed out, "Whoever would overthrow the liberty of a nation must begin by subduing the freeness of speech." Jefferson called it the liberty which "guards all other liberties." The first casualty of war, it has been said, is truth. The first casualty of dictatorship is freedom of speech.

The present-day restrictionists of that right correctly state that free speech has never been an absolute and unqualified privilege. Seven years after the adoption of the Bill of Rights, Congress, without any consciousness of contradicting, abrogating, or circumscribing its original intent, passed a series of sedition laws which restricted freedom of expression. Laws pertaining to libel and slander have been in effect in the United States since colonial times.

Even under freedom of speech, one is liable to lawsuit and punishment should he transgress its definite bounds. One may not send obscene literature through the mails and claim immunity from restraint on the basis of free speech. In time of war stringent limits are placed upon the latitude usually granted citizens. Pacifists who then take the right of freedom of opinion too seriously soon find themselves behind bars, deprived of all freedom. The unanimity of attitude reflected by press, platform, and pulpit during World War I was, even in democracies, not the result of chance.

There is thus incontrovertible proof that freedom of opinion always had its limits. These traditional limitations, it is argued, are not sufficiently strong in the face of the powerful forces arrayed against democracy today, and therefore further limitations are urged.

For we are passing through a period when the differences of opinion which rend our national life no longer revolve exclusively about methods and policies within the framework of democratic government. We are faced with divergent views which repudiate both the assumptions and objectives of our democracy. Political parties have always differed in method, in practical policy, in personnel. They did not differ as to the desirability of free government, nor as to the basic principles of democracy. In our day, however, many of the opinions articulated endanger the very fabric of our society.

The American scene is full of panacea peddlers, Utopia salesmen, salvation mongers, wild-scheme brokers—all serving as the "pied pipers of hysteria" to befuddle and befoul democracy.

Never was there such a flood of words in behalf of what are basically undemocratic doctrines. No scheme is too dangerous, no proposal too fantastic, not to appeal to many and seduce them. And all these schemes are assured a hearing by the very democracy they seek to undermine.

No wonder many liberals are concerned and look to a means of curbing the opportunity enjoyed by these antidemocratic voices to gain an audience. The Jew, too, under the compulsion of tragic experience, has had occasion to ponder ways to check this Niagara of evil propaganda. The Jew's interest in the preservation of democracy has something of the desperation of a biologic struggle for self-preservation. He falls socially, politically, and economically when democracy falls. The hostile campaign carried on against the Jew is so often the smoke screen behind which the suppression of all citizens follows.

If formerly our government made a clear distinction between subversive deeds and subversive words, banning only the former, can it afford to continue to do so? We live in an age in which propaganda has become both art and science. Such a division therefore is hopelessly academic, it is argued. Words have power. Words *are* deeds. The most dangerous of opiates is the word, the most deadly of weapons is the idea. And ideas develop prestige and power and gain recruits, not necessarily in proportion to their validity and truth, as the rise of totalitarian states abundantly proves. Hitler states in *Mein Kampf* that if a lie, no matter how impudent, is stated and restated with unflagging emphasis, something of it remains with the auditors. Words thus become the very dynamite which may blow democracy to pieces. Hamlet's uncle poured poison into the king's ear while the latter slept. Demagogues distill bewitching poisons into the minds of great numbers, when hunger and fear lull the consciences and the critical faculties of multitudes to sleep.

The advocates of further restriction of freedom of expression argue therefore that democracy had better awaken, and forcibly still the voices and pens of its enemies within its borders. Several suggestions have been made. We are asked to join in the demand for a law which would ban all undemocratic organizations and movements. An attempt is being made to win support for the inclusion, in our libel law, of a clause which would make the slander of a group a punishable misdemeanor. It is also recommended that we close the radio by law to all who speak in terms inimical to the spirit of Americanism.

Can we fight these movements by suppression? Will that method succeed? History will testify that movements are rarely suppressed. The law succeeds only in driving them underground. Czarist Russia, for all its stringent and inhuman treatment of those whom it regarded as political heretics, did not extirpate the revolutionary movement. It compelled it to move in secret, and a large proportion of the leadership of Russia's Communist party are graduates of that underground movement. Though banned by law, it did not cease. Though secret, it was not ineffective.

Suppression even of the mildest sort not infrequently leads to results opposite to its intent. Many a propagandist needs only a seeming martyrdom to be lifted from obscurity to the headlines. His martyrdom becomes of itself a powerful means of winning converts.

If suppressive laws are passed, it should not be hard for the organizations affected by them to hide behind all kinds of "neutral" fronts and façades. They could pose as innocuous social clubs or athletic organizations and continue to carry on their nefarious propaganda. It would require a vast government espionage system to ferret them out. Is there not more ground to fear the espionage system, which, in the long run, may prove more dangerous than the evil it will seek to cure?

Nor could any law making the defamation of a group illegal possibly defy all evasion. One could slander without specifically mentioning Jew or Catholic or Negro, and yet leave no doubt in the minds of the hearers as to the identity of the objects of the attack. The proposed law might give us a false sense of security, without affording us additional protection.

Nor must we forget that suppression begets suppression. Ban the Communist or the Nazi, you say, yet the definition of who should be so labeled rests with the administrators of the law. The definition of "Red," for example, becomes so flexible as to include all who hold to opinions contrary to the speaker. The Dies Committee heard solemn testimony which branded Albert Einstein, Thomas Mann, and Eleanor Roosevelt as Communists.

Communists have a habit of including, under the name of fascist, all who differ with them. I am not sure that these laws would not serve to give a great deal of power to local authorities who cannot be trusted with such power. An illiberal administration could exploit these laws, or similar proposed legislation, to gag unfriendly newspapers and critical voices.

We must tread a harder and longer road than that of summary suppression. We must not fall easy victims to the popular reliance on "there ought to be a law" as of itself solving the problem. A suppressive law deals with effects, not causes, with manifestations, not roots. The causes of the growth of the present antidemocratic front lie too deep to be reached merely by a censorious law.

We start at the wrong end when we seek to curb the voices and pens of propagandists. We ought to think in terms of the audience, and concern ourselves with the conditions that make people willing listeners and converts.

We must, as citizens of this democracy, advocate those measures which attempt to grapple with our economic problems realistically. We must fight for a broadening base of economic protection and security. It is a long-range struggle, an extended program—but nothing less than that can save democracy. As we spread jobs and security we shall be reducing the number of people who have ears for the ranting of demagogues. No simpler plan will be effective.

We must keep that eternal vigil which is the price of liberty. We must seek to keep inviolate the rights that tradition has extended to the citizens of democracy. The curbing of the civil rights of any group presages a decline of freedom, which cannot leave the rest untouched. Together with our fellow Americans we must counter the propaganda of reactionaries.

We must keep alive and intense our faith in democracy. G. K. Chesterton has said that "a despotism may almost be defined as a tired democracy."

The problems with which our generation must grapple are severe. What is required is a great reserve of faith in and enthusiasm for democracy, so that we seek to solve them within our democratic framework rather than take the shortcut other forms seem to offer.

Freedom with its manifold dangers is to be preferred to suppression with its inescapable evils. It is a long way—but the only safe way.

WHAT IS REQUIRED

THE GREAT EVENT IN the history of the Jewish people, which *Pesah* commemorates and exalts, is the Exodus, the emancipation from the Egyptian house of bondage. Monumental as that achievement was, it does not begin to tell the entire story. When Moses appeared before Pharaoh, he did not plead for release as such. He asked that the Hebrews be permitted to go forth and serve the Lord, that is, to substitute for the serfdom they had endured in Egypt the freedom that comes from serving God. They wanted to overthrow a degrading yoke and accept a nobler discipline. In a short sentence in the Bible, Moses suggests the nature of freedom more incisively than a hundred volumes devoted exclusively to the subject. In a word, freedom means discipline.

Paradoxically, the truly free man is not free to do many things that the slave of ambition, passion, and greed has no compunctions about doing. The free man is not free to oppress or debase another, for he is not fully free till he recognizes that he has the right to enjoy freedom only because freedom is the right of all men. The free man is not free to distort or trifle with the truth. There is no greater tyranny than error, and tyrants have invariably used the "big lie" as a chain with which to bind the multitude.

The free man is not free to be haughty, for pride divides people into classes and violates the fundamental equality of all mankind. The free man is not free to hate, for hatred blinds and imprisons its subject even more than its object. The hate-filled man surrenders his freedom to think clearly, to act justly, to feel humanely. The free man is not free to sit by while others hunger and are homeless, for the need that darkens the life of many throws its shadow upon the freedom of any who live by its light. The fruit of freedom is responsibility for our fellowman.

The free man is not free to scorn the past, but for whose sacrifices and struggles he would not have come into his heritage of freedom. Nor is the free man at liberty to shirk all obligation to the future, since none is entitled to receive who is not prepared to give

LAW DAY*

IT IS PROPER THAT we mark Law Day. Many things have gone into the greatness that is America: its Founding Fathers; the bountiful resources with which a generous Creator dowered this continent; the courage and determination of generations of pioneers; the devotion and diligence of many who spent their lives building it; the broad diversity of the immigrants who came in quest of freedom and opportunity; the idealism of those who, believing in God, were inspired to put their faith in man's endless potentialities; its writers and poets, its painters and sculptors; its houses of prayer and its shrines. But no single factor has contributed more to the molding of American character than the law. No other element helped more in enabling the far-ranging variety of peoples, races, and religions to dwell together in mutual respect and common purpose.

They who stood at the cradle of America's birth said that this was to be a government of laws, not of men. Crises challenged but were not able to shake the enduring stability of the law through the nearly two centuries of America's existence.

The law protected the rights of each religion, giving preeminence to none. It made the inherent dignity of each man the basis of his rights, not the class into which he was born, the altar at which he bowed or the color of his skin. It set up a system which limited the men and mechanisms of government, restraining them from an undue exercise of power.

The law established procedures so that no man need fear summary imprisonment or be deprived of the right to defend himself before an impartial court. It recognized an authority

*Talk delivered at Ford Auditorium, May 2, 1960.

greater than itself when it affirmed the inalienable rights of every man. It protected the weak against the aggressiveness of the strong, the humble against the highborn. It wiped away the boundaries of class, caste, and station and united people of every color and creed into a universal fraternity of equality.

The law is more, however, than procedure or document or statute—important as these are. It is alive with the sensitivities and ideals of the people at their highest. It opens frontier after frontier of social responsibility, and extends communal concern to embrace more and more of the people. It is the bulwark of freedom, the bastion of progress.

But law cannot function if it possesses only those coercions which justice requires—namely, police, prisons, and the power of the courts. Its greatest source of strength lies not in its judges, lawyers, learned interpreters or enforcement agents. Its greatest source of strength lies in the respect which American citizens accord it, the esteem in which they hold it, the recognition that it is the guarantor of their freedom. Whenever a legal enactment or a judicial decision rendered by properly constituted authority is scorned or disobeyed, a blow is struck at the law itself and at the freedom which it guards.

On this Law Day, we pledge ourselves to that respect for an appreciation of the law as will enable it to remain the guardian of our freedom and the protector of our rights.

2 • War and Peace

WHY WE FIGHT*

THE BIBLE TELLS US that when Nehemiah and his followers sought to rebuild the collapsed walls of Jerusalem, there were in the land enemies who sought to prevent the reconstruction of the holy city. Nehemiah, therefore, placed in the hands of his loyal men a sword and a spade: a sword with which to fend off the attack of the enemy should it be made; a spade to continue building the wall of the rebuilt city.

We are a Nehemiah-like generation. A sword has been thrust in our hand, for a mighty and determined foe seeks to batter down the walls of civilization and to destroy the citadel of freedom. However, even as we hold the sword in one hand, the spade must be firmly grasped in the other.

We are fighting to achieve more than the defeat of the enemy. That is the requisite first step. But we look beyond. We are fighting on a hundred fronts to achieve the victory not merely of our military forces but of peace, freedom, justice. The immediate goal of crushing the enemy achieves meaning, significance, and sanctity only as it clears the path for those ideals of human rights which Americanism at its noblest represents. If we bring the enemy to his knees and permit the conditions out of which he has arisen to continue, we shall have won not a peace but an armistice. Then will future historians describe this war as the most futile, tragic, and suicidal enterprise in which man, in his collective folly, has ever engaged.

What are the objectives not of our military operations but of the greater victory we seek?

First, we are fighting for the rights of individuals. The President has said that we are fighting to uphold the story in Genesis

*From *Why We Fight; Minister, Priest, Rabbi, Discuss Values at Stake*, National Conference of Christians and Jews. Though undated, it was obviously issued in the early 1940's.

that man was created in the divine image. Man, every man, is endowed with cosmic dignity and on the human level is entitled to social dignity. He is not a pawn of the state; he is not the tool of a system; he is not a cog in a machine. To reestablish what the founding fathers of our country called man's "inalienable rights" the boys from the cities and farms of New York, Kansas, Idaho, Maine, and California are now on the battlefields of Tunisia, Sicily, Asia, and in the Pacific.

Second, we are fighting for the rights of peoples. Little nations are not simply to be regarded as the prey of big nations. The smaller peoples and states have their place in the economy of the world. The Belgiums, Czechoslovakias, and Abyssinias of the earth must be made secure from aggression, and must be given the opportunity to develop their national culture and genius.

Third, we are fighting for total freedom. The Civil War in our own history grew out of a recognition that this nation could not continue half-slave and half-free. The interrelated character of the world makes it impossible to have the world half-slave and half-free. Freedom in our day cannot be inalienable unless it is universal. Unless the present *total* war leads to *total* freedom it will prove to be a *total* failure.

Fourth, and last, we are fighting to achieve that kind of international organization which shall introduce law and order in the arena of international affairs. We cannot tolerate "outlaws" among states as we do not permit individuals to violate our laws and go unpunished.

This is a war between ditchdiggers and bridge-builders. The enemy seeks to dig ditches between one man and another, between one church and one race and another. America must remain the great bridge-builder of history, throwing across the chasms of difference of race, color, and creed the bridges of sympathy, understanding, and brotherhood.

OCCUPIED TERRITORIES*

ONE OF THE IMMEDIATE results of the Allied victory was the liberation of millions held captive in territories occupied by the

*Radio address as chaplain in the U.S. Army, Tokyo, fall, 1945.

enemy. Whole populations in Austria, Czechoslovakia, Poland, Holland, Korea, China thrilled with new hope and new life as the yoke of death and oppression was lifted from them. The stories of cruelty of the barbarians continue to shock a world that has lost much of its sensitivity. Hundreds of thousands were buried in anonymous graves. Slave labor was forced upon millions. Starvation was the lot of untold numbers. Neither children nor women nor the aged were spared.

The term "occupied territory" will long remain associated with infamy and brutality. It also suggests another phenomenon too. This war has been more than a military conflict. We have been fighting not only on the field of battle, tank against tank, ship with ship, plane versus plane. We mobilized our strength because the new order which our enemies sought to establish aimed to destroy the ideas and principles which as free men we cherish. The enemy's aim was to banish freedom and equality and blot out our civilization. He sought to eliminate justice and democracy and abolish human rights. In a Nazi primer used in the schools children were taught: "The teaching of mercy and love of one's neighbor is foreign to the German race—and the Sermon on the Mount according to Nordic sentiment is an ethic for cowards and idiots."

One of the foundations of fascist teaching was hate. Insisting on the superiority of their race, they classified all others as inferior and subhuman, and condemned them to extermination or enslavement. Have we won the war of ideas as fully as we have won the war of weapons? I challenge you, as I challenge myself, with the question "Are there still occupied territories of the spirit in our midst?"

Prejudice and discrimination are Nazi attitudes and policies. Whenever an American betrays prejudice, be it to the Negro, the Jew, the Catholic, the Protestant, he gives evidence that there is a Nazi-occupied territory in his outlook. To the extent that the Negro is denied equality, America—the true America—has not been liberated. To that extent we have lost the war.

Let us speak frankly and call things by their right name. Whenever an American denies a man a job because of the applicant's color or creed, the Nazis have won a victory. Whenever an American uses a foul word to designate a section or

group of his fellow citizens, he is infusing new vitality into
naziism. Whenever one of our countrymen gives his support
to a demagogue who has nothing to sell but hate and suspicion,
he is helping the enemy invade America. Whenever a class of
people is denied its right to vote or a fair trial in a court of
justice, a mockery is made of the death of Americans at Nor-
mandy, North Africa, Luzon, and Okinawa. The hand of the
enemy is being upheld, the American ideal is being sabotaged
and betrayed. Whenever we make any group of Americans the
scapegoat of our fears and frustrations, we are resurrecting Hitler
and renewing Hitlerism. Are there occupied territories in your
life?

But we are not only defeating America; we are also crucify-
ing the religious tradition of our fathers. Be we Protestant, Catholic, Jew, a basic teaching of our church is the equality of all men
before God. Our common heritage begins with the story of the
creation of the ancestor of mankind. You cannot believe in the
Fatherhood of God if in your behavior you deny the brotherhood of all people. Worse than atheist by profession of mouth
is the atheist by act. Are there enemy-held positions in your
daily life?

Yesterday afternoon I was called to officiate at the burial of
a soldier. Before me were rows of Christain crosses and Jewish
Stars of David. Under the sod, united in a common heroism, lay
Catholic and Protestant and Jew, black and white. When the
call to battle came, no lines between races were drawn. The
casualty lists know no Jim Crow policy, no anti-Semitism. Read
the lists and you will find that all the varied faith and ethnic
origins pass before you—Pole and German, Russian and Frenchman, Swede and Hungarian—different in name, background,
religion; one in Americanism, and one in their love of freedom.

He who hates builds a Nazi pillbox in our midst. The group
that preaches bigotry and practices exclusiveness is trying to
build a Siegfried line within our land. Such men constitute
fascism's fifth column. Earnestly and honestly let us probe into
our hearts, and ask ourselves, "Are we who helped win the war
on the battlefield now helping to lose it in the realm of ideas and
spirit? Are there occupied territories in our midst?"

THE SOLDIER COMES HOME*

FOR WEEKS BEFORE YOU sailed, one intimate thought and desire above all others beat high within you—the longing to return home. Your separation from your families dramatized for you in the most vivid fashion the significance and sanctity of those personal felicities which for long you had previously accepted as matter-of-fact routine. The warmth and congeniality of the home atmosphere, its privacy and individuality appeared to you, when overseas, transfigured by a rare radiance, formed by a union of wistful remembrance and intense longing.

It was right and proper that you should feel thus. One of the great hungers of man is for roots, for a particularity of place or tradition to which he can be bound by the strongest of ties and which stimulate within him the tenderest of responses. Perhaps the most pathetic of all beings in our time are the spiritual and psychological refugees, without roots, without specific attachments, wandering in a vast amorphousness.

Army life, too, spells uprootedness, march, movement, striking of tents, living in isolated and alien places. Therefore it was natural that you should so strongly desire to join yourselves once again to the roots of your lives, to return to the normal simplicities of your home. That is why for many weeks your conversation revolved exclusively upon the points necessary for redeployment. "How many points have you?" became the customary greeting at every overseas base and camp, and on every ship in foreign harbors. Wherever men met, on the chow-line, in the movies, at the PX, in chapel, their eyes sparkled as they spoke of the possibility of their return home.

No, there was nothing reprehensible in all this. And now that you have returned, though you still feel the ecstasy of your reunion with those who are dear to you, I wish to challenge you, as I challenge myself, with a significant and searching question. Let us ask ourselves: "*What have we brought home with us?*"

We have seen comrades killed and have marched through

---

*Published for Jewish men and women in the Armed Forces by the National Academy for Adult Jewish Studies, Jewish Theological Seminary of America.

cities reduced to ruins and shambles. We have seen world capitals
like Berlin, Manila, Tokyo, London, and Paris, become immense
haunted houses filled with the ghosts of poverty, destruction,
and confusion. Who better than the veteran realizes the demoniac
forces of brutality and desolation which war lets loose? And we
know what it has done or tried to do to us—how it has torn us
away from our families and careers; how it has sought to make
a fighting machine out of us, barren of individuality and sentiment, possessed only of a precise ability to kill and maim. We
know that it has sought to drown the person in the mass, and
steam-roll all that is distinctive and unique into solid uniformity.
We know the hardships it has forced upon us and the perils to
which it constantly exposed us. These have been the daily familiar
routine of our lives as soldiers.

Yet I dare ask "What has the war done *for* you?" For man
possesses within him a divine capacity which can transform darkness into light and draw from sorrow new insight and understanding. A rabbinic legend tells how fire came to the world.
The Jews did not picture life as did the Greeks as a strife between
God and man in which the latter storms the citadels of Olympus
and steals fire from the reluctant hands of the "deities." God, say
the Rabbis, presented Adam with two stones, one the stone of
gloom and darkness, the other the stone of the shadow of death.
When the first man rubbed one stone against the other, fire
leaped forth. This is man's divine gift, to change by a process of
spiritual alchemy suffering into knowledge, pain into appreciation. In the dregs of bitterness he finds the seeds of growth.
Jewish history knows of many instances when in ages dark with
suffering and oppression there flowered an outburst of creativity
and intellectual illumination by whose light we still live.

That the war has had coarsening effects upon some cannot
be denied. The war touched off deep corrosions in the souls of
the sufferers and also of the participants. War works havoc with
men's sensibilities. It dehumanizes, vulgarizes, and rides roughshod
over refinements and gentilities which civilization has been long
in cultivating. The barracks are not noted for delicacy. Living
in a world of violence, in which success in killing is rewarded
with social approval and military recognition; removed from the
graces of social intercourse and the influences of art, literature,

books, and ideas—some suffered a debasing of values and a cal-
lousing of sympathies. Perhaps all of us would be wise to take
precautions to immunize ourselves against the germs of deterioration that may have lodged within us.

But the greater number of us fortunately escaped the worst
effects of these brutalizing forces. Whether by reason of strength
of character or the persistence of home influence, we were able
to resist the environmental pressures which sought to lower our
moral and mental sights. Our experience simultaneously opened
to us, if we but knew, gateways to new appreciation and insights.
What special contribution can we make to a society in confusion
by virtue of what we have seen and felt? As veterans of the
holocaust, is there a specific function which we can fulfill in our
communities so that our usefulness does not end with the war?

I would like to enumerate several attitudes and viewpoints
which, I believe, yesterday's soldiers are best qualified to interpret
and to represent.

First is a hatred of war. I mean not simply the rational recognition of its irrationality and futility; nor even a religious condemnation of this, man's ultimate sin and denial of God. I mean
a determined, impassioned fury, a deep, implacable hatred. Never
again must we permit it to be pictured in romantic or glamorous
fashion. We should give the lie to every poet who casts a halo
of beauty over its grime and blood, and nail to the pillar of shame
every pseudophilosopher who extols its virtue. If as the days pass,
the movies or the magazines picture war in an attractive manner,
we should raise our voices in pained resentment and protest.
There is nothing beautiful in destruction, nothing heroic in a
man crouching behind a gun whose mouth spouts death, or in
a flyer dropping ruin from the skies. Foxholes, sinking ships, dis-
figured bodies, gaping wounds, burning cities are the epitome of
cruelty and ugliness. This note is singularly minor in the literature of Western civilization which has, through the centuries,
extolled war and glorified the warrior. Would that from our
midst there may arise poet, novelist, painter, musician, teacher to
portray the degradation that is war. Each of us can become in
our community a nucleus of truth and reality touching the
character of war.

But our contribution must not be permitted to exhaust itself in hatred. We are qualified to inspire faith that war need not be, that it can be eliminated. A noted American sociologist once said that nothing has retarded human progress as much as a low estimate of human possibilities. One of the factors in our situation is the fatalistic belief held by many that since war has always been with us, it must inevitably continue to be. What is needed is a deep and abiding faith in man's ability to rid himself of this immemorial scourge and to live with his fellowmen midst unbroken peace. You and I have been witnesses to the monumental skill and ingenuity which our civilization possesses. The very instruments of death which we have been taught to operate were produced by a vast knowledge of the forces of nature, and a remarkable and precise ability to exploit them. Radio, radar, and the mountains of machinery of the most complex and intricate kind with which we came in contact are undeniable evidences of a high order of human skill and capacity. Where there is so much skill there is no room for despair nor for wavering in the conviction that it will and can be turned exclusively to wholesome and constructive endeavors.

But we have seen exhibited on the field of battle other qualities which bid us hope. In the midst of the savagery we have seen evoked admirable and lofty traits. We have seen men sacrifice their lives that others might be saved. We have seen men ungrumblingly suffer privation and discomfort. We have seen men selflessly identifying themselves with the larger purpose they believed that they were serving. We have seen men perform feats of endurance which they would normally believe to be beyond their powers. We have seen men overcome fear and with unblanching courage face danger. We know of men who suffered lash and torture yet their lips remained closed and gave no information to their captors which would imperil their comrades. Men who are possessed of such funds of unselfishness and decency can be brought to place them upon the altar of the common weal.

And we, who have lived in the crucible of an epoch's tragedy, should have brought back with us a keen and profound knowledge of the interdependence of all human life. We have been to distant places of the globe and have lived in areas the very names of which were unknown to us but a short time ago.

The bomb that was loosed in Berlin and Tokyo burst upon our own threshhold. Veins and arteries intimately join the world organism into an indissoluble unit. Poisons that gather in one focal point are immediately transmitted to all points.

The prophets long ago taught the interrelationship of all men and the singleness of the human family. The idealism of the ancestors should now become the realism of the descendants. We will be not less but more American as we broaden our vision to embrace the interests and needs of all the world. There can be no peace for any unless there is peace for all. Freedom will perish everywhere if oppression be permitted to live anywhere. Such a world-view you and I should be peculiarly fitted to bring to bear upon the decisions which as American citizens we shall be called upon to make.

Perhaps too more than others we have had impressed upon us a sense of the pathos of the life of the common man. An internationale of destiny binds together the anonymous, obscure little people everywhere. They are remarkably similar, the John Does of Europe, the Philippines, Japan. They seem to want so little. What the man in the street the world over seeks is a job, a home, security, a measure of opportunity for his children. Give him the freedom to enjoy the love of wife and family, to gain a modest livelihood, to have a humble roof overhead, and he moves forward to contentment. He is heir to all the ills of human fortune, disappointment, illness, death of dear ones, the common frustrations of all men. Quiet, unknown, unpublicized, his number is legion. He is son, husband, father; merchant, laborer, clerk, teacher, peddler. We have seen him everywhere the carrier of burdens, the seller, the tiller of the soil, the servant, the employee.

And in our day there is a hauntingly frightened look in his eyes, for the horizon he looks out upon is a huge question mark of uncertainty and confusion. Periodically there break over his head tidal waves of war and panic, hunger and unemployment. His sons are torn from his side, his home is burned, his job is gone. We have seen him sitting dazed among the ruins. We have met him clogging the roads, pushing a pathetic little wagon containing all his worldly goods, his roving eyes searching . . . searching for rest and peace. World forces tear into his life, be he Japanese or American, Frenchman or Englishman, to uproot and

destroy the little stake he has driven into the ground in the tiny
plot of land he calls home.

We, of all people, should be in the forefront of the movement to secure the rights of the average man in society. Here
we have a fine criterion for estimating the value of any policy
proposed. "Does it advance the welfare of the little people? Does
it give them greater access to the opportunities which are to be
found in our world? Does it afford them greater protection
against social cataclysms and disasters?" That is the way of
democracy, the democracy we were told we were fighting for.

"What have you brought home?" I pray that you returned
matured by experience and elevated by the great insights which
that experience afforded to you. May you serve humanity as a
heroic warrior for peace, righteousness, and freedom.

> Blessed wert thou in thy going.
> May God bless thee in thy coming.

ALTERNATIVES TO THE ATOM*

EVERY AGE IN HISTORY is in a sense a "crucial" age and every epoch
a time of "transition." For life is dynamic and flows restlessly
from level to level. The present unites the past with the future.
We are the children of our ancestry and the fathers of our posterity—biologically, socially, and culturally. The decisions any
one age makes are crucial since they have consequences far beyond its own duration. Every period is a transition, since society,
ever in flux, moves from stage to stage of development.

The crucial and transitional character of an era has rarely
expressed itself in such explosive and global manifestations as in
our own. We have experienced the most extensive war of all
times. The discovery of the secret of utilizing atomic energy
brings to the fore a desperate danger which threatens a larger
segment of humanity than has ever before been exposed to a

*Variations of this address were delivered before many churches and civic
organizations in Michigan in late 1946 and 1947.

single danger. The economic and political dislocations and insecurity encompass all of civilization in their vastness and possible
effects. The fact that society must move onward to a new level
of organization and understanding is writ large in unmistakable
and oft ominous signs all about us. The problem is global, the
challenge international. The opportunity given to us matches the
challenge. Our understanding and achievement can and must
likewise be global and international.

In my tradition there is an account of a Roman matron who
challenged the sage Rabbi Jose ben Halafta with the question:
"What strange praise do you bestow upon your God saying,
'He giveth wisdom to the wise' (Daniel 2:21). That He maketh
wise the unwise would have been a much better declaration of
His power." Whereupon Rabbi Jose answered, "Would you hand
one of your costly and delicate ornaments to any ordinary
person you meet and not rather lend it only to one who knows
how to handle it well? It takes the wise man to make good use of
his wisdom." The question of questions for us today is: have we
the divinely blessed wisdom to make good use of our wisdom,
of the wisdom we have developed in our understanding and
exploitation of the great natural forces?

We shall miss the point if we think that man now simply
has the key to greater power than ever before. He has uncovered
a new dimension of destructiveness. The power that is his to
demolish is now possessed of a new and frightful quality. In a
sense it is a new kind of power—the power of total destruction.
When I was in Hiroshima I felt myself in the presence of a fury
and a doom which filled me with foreboding and fear. I know
what one of the great scientists meant when he said: "I am a
frightened man."

However evil men's designs may have been in the past, the
evil they were able to perpetrate was limited. All their fury and
the diabolic purposes they served could express themselves only
in a limited area. The instruments at their disposal could not
measure up to the evil they might have planned. We now have
the skill and genius to realize the most satanic machination, the
most dread holocausts. By a thrice-tragic circumstance we have
discovered the most potent source of destructiveness in that
period when events have shown the unredeemed brutality of

which man at his blackest could be capable. We who have held to liberal and generous philosophies have not made sufficient allowance in our conceptions for the depths of degradation to which man in his savagery and folly could descend. We have been so busily engrossed in pondering man's benign possibilities for good that we have left out of our reckoning his terrifyingly malignant potentialities for evil. To some of us, that which transpired in Europe came as a shocking revelation of the level of evil to which man could descend.

Basically our problem is not of the instrumentalities at our beck and call, but of the inadequate purposes by which we are motivated. When I was in high school, we were taught about the miraculous balance which prevails in nature among the elements required for life and which makes it possible for the cycle of existence to continue. Into our life has now come a new disproportion between our skill and our wisdom, our means and our ends, our instruments and our goals, our power and our motivations.

Human history advances through the extension of human power. It is not an ignoble chronicle which records man's progress in the control of environment and in defense against the contingencies to which life against the physical background of the universe exposes us. By extending our sway over nature, by ever deeper penetration into the secrets of the universe allowing us to bend the forces of life to our needs, by ever refining our skill, we have been released from those pressures and perils which would have made civilization impossible. Every extension of power, however, is unfortunately not an unmixed blessing. For it adds simultaneously to the forces for domination, exploitation, and universal destruction which exist in our day. Achieving new power does not automatically confer upon us new wisdom with which we may deal with that power.

We have been intoxicated with the power that we have succeeded in amassing. We have defined progress in terms of the greater authority over nature which for the past century and a half or more we have been so remarkable in achieving. We have literally remade the physical aspect of our existence and have multiplied innovation, skill, and comfort. A new level to which we must rise is now indicated. We cannot measure our success in a purely *quantitative* manner in terms of the power that is ours. The new quality of demolition which we now can wield requires a new *quality* in our social life—wisdom of control, insight of objective, vision of use, goodness of purpose.

What is required is a redirection and enlargement of our human loyalties. The basic unit of human society claiming our allegiance cannot be any smaller than the civilized world. The physical contraction of the globe which we have achieved through our means of communication must be matched by a corresponding sense of intimacy and community. In the mathematics of human emotions the larger loyalty does not cancel out the smaller—it deepens it. We are now realizing that America is engaged in a far nobler experiment than that represented by the metaphor "melting pot." Loyalty to America does not require that each ethnic group fuse with the general pattern by the total elimination of its own distinctive culture. The danger to peace is not in cultural diversity any more than the threat to order is in the development of human personality and individuality. It is in the institutional frame of nationalism—the state—that the greatest source of conflict is to be found. The enlarged loyalty to a world order is in conflict only with the anachronistic concept of state sovereignty. World order does not require the destruction of the social and cultural independence of a nation. When Sir Alfred Zimmern, a renowned student of international affairs at Oxford, was asked some time ago: "What in your opinion is the greatest obstacle to enduring world peace?," his answer was simple and direct: "The small-scale individual." The small-scale individual and the small-scale state are social atomic bombs which imperil the world.

World stability, however, is not assured by the absence of armed hostility. The antithesis of peace is more truly injustice than war. Where men cannot satisfy their rightful needs, their demands for status, recognition, and security, there is created a subsoil of unresolved aggression and frustration which help to form a climate congenial to war and social upheaval.

What is needed is more than the absence of injustice—desirable and infinitely valuable though that is. What is needed is education for living. A commission of scholars and thinkers set up by the United Nations issued a remarkable statement which opened with the words, "War begins in the mind of man." Peace likewise begins in the mind of man and thus imposes a great responsibility on education.

We must teach ourselves and our children to be socially alert and informed. Social maturity must be one of our primary goals. We must combat social illiteracy as we once fought the inability to read and write. Social maturity consists of two elements: knowledge and civic responsibility. Too many of us live by outmoded patterns of social thinking. There are many social facts at our disposal which we must absorb and which must become the basis of our views. The problem of the place of government in our life and the areas in which it should operate, foreign affairs, the forces at work in our economy and labor-capital relationships—these should be required subjects in the curriculum for intelligent citizens. Our thinking must be geared to the realities of the world situation.

The Hebrew sages speak of knowledge that must issue in action. Forty years ago James Bryce listed the "Hindrances to Good Government" as indolence, self-interest and party loyalty which replaces loyalty to the nation. We have not yet been cured of these symptoms of a national ailment. The percentage of people who exercise their franchise on election day is dangerously inadequate. We Americans are prone to express our interest in political questions only during the first week in November. Good, respectable, and educated citizens often manifest a curious aversion to political affairs and activity and abdicate their opportunity to others less qualified. We must raise the *social quotient* of our people.

And into our thinking there must be infused a moral quality and a sense of adventure. We are a Columbus-like age before whom stretches an uncharted sea of world cooperation and progress. We must learn to find deeper satisfactions in the non-competitive areas of our group life, build and forge stronger links between men, teach ourselves to find high compensations in our daily lives at our jobs, at home, in leisure, and in the community.

And we must be possessed by the conviction that world

peace is no fantasy. It can be fact. "Nothing has so retarded human progress," said the eminent American sociologist Giddings, "as a low conception of human possibilities." He who says of international cooperation that "it is too good to be true," or of a warless society that it is a Utopian dream, is a dangerous saboteur. There is an "easy defeatism" as there is an "easy optimism."

We can do it. We must do it. For until we are well on the road to world understanding we are "dead men on a furlough." To use C. E. Montague's vivid phrase, we are "playing golf across the burned hills of hell." We can and must achieve the constructive wisdom to use the new power at our command for human betterment.

NONE TO SEEK PEACE*

One of the most distressing stories in the news of the day comes from Oslo, where the five-man Nobel Prize Committee met and decided to withhold the Peace Prize for the year 1960. In the view of this group, no individual in any of the nations, large or small, had devoted himself so conspicuously to the cause of peace as to merit the recognition which a Nobel Prize confers.

One might imagine a modern prototype of Abraham the patriarch pleading with the Creator.

"PERADVENTURE THERE BE FIFTY leaders, diplomats, officials in the world intent upon peace; dedicated to its pursuit, seeking by every conventional and novel means to achieve it—wilt Thou yet allow the world to be destroyed?"

And the Lord said, "If I find fifty men in high office sincerely placing the attainment of peace above every other political aim, then will I spare the world for their sake."

And Abraham answered and said, "Behold now, I have taken upon me to speak unto the Lord, and I am but dust and

Recorder, November 11, 1960.

ashes. Peradventure there shall lack five of the righteous leaders, seekers of peace, wilt Thou destroy all the world for lack of five?"

And He said, "If there be forty and five, I will not destroy it."

And he spoke unto Him yet again, and said, "Peradventure there shall be forty found there?"

And He said, "I will not do it for forty's sake."

And he said, "Oh, let the Lord not be angry and I will speak: Peradventure there shall be thirty found there?"

And He said, "I will not do it, if I find thirty there."

And he said, "Behold now, I have taken upon me to speak unto the Lord: peradventure there shall be twenty found there?"

And He said, "I will not destroy it for ten's sake."

More than Sodom and Gomorrah were involved in this intervention by Abraham, for a whole world and all life in it were hanging in the balance. Hence, this modern heir of Abraham presumed to press his plea further than did his Biblical ancestor.

And he said, "Peradventure there be found one alone, sitting in the councils of the great, putting every other matter aside and bending his mind, heart, and will to the prevention of war and the establishment of peace, wilt Thou destroy all the world?"

And God answered, "I will not destroy it for the sake of one."

No human being survived to write the epilogue. But in some distant heaven, beyond the reach of bomb and radiation, a sad angel recorded these words—"There not being one leader who placed peace above all else, the world was destroyed. But it was man and not God who pushed the button that sent it to its destruction."

DAG HAMMARSKJOLD—CITIZEN OF THE WORLD*

THE LOSS OF DAG HAMMARSKJOLD weakens the forces in the world working for peace at a time when mankind can ill afford to

*Memorial Service, Mariner's Church, September 21, 1961.

suffer such a loss. We have been accustomed to think of casualties of war. Dag Hammarskjold was a casualty for the peace. He lost his life on a mission dedicated, as his public life was dedicated, to prevent peace from becoming a casualty.

The loss of this great man is incalculable. He lived near the very center of the international crisis, and no man was closer to the wounds, dangers, and fears of our time—and, paradoxically, to the hopes and aspirations of our time.

But the world has lost far more than an outstanding civil servant of humanity, a high official of mankind, a skilled and brilliant negotiator, pacifier, and stiller of troubled waters. Dag Hammarskjold was all of these and more.

In his death, the world has lost a symbol of that world community which must come into being if the last syllable of recorded time is not to be ashes and desolation. More eloquent than his words was the fact of his being.

Dag Hammarskjold stood before the world in a way that no other public figure does, namely, as a citizen of the world. By virtue of his office and the dignity and stature his eminent personal qualities imparted to it, he gave a reality to an idea which still has to be realized. People talk of a world community and it is good that they should. Writers and students of world affairs point out with irrefutable logic the necessity of a world order in which the diversities and antagonisms of our segmented globe could be reconciled and harmonized. The alternative is chaos and death.

But it must be said that "One World" inhabits the universe of our mind rather than the center of our motivations. It is a concept which we have not yet translated into vivid emotional experience. Though our thought has recognized it, our senses have not given it reality. The world community figures as a hope, and still has about it something of the unreality of a dream. What we do see and experience as real are the divisions, the barriers, the hostilities, the competitiveness, the jealous sovereignties that crisscross and convulse the world. And, alas, even that great instrumentality of world cooperation, the United Nations, more often than not gives us a picture of many nations in their separate and individual aspects rather than of the world

unity which it was founded to achieve. Dag Hammarskjold lived
in terms of a world community that was actual, tangible, invested
with reality, and in personifying it he gave to it a concreteness
it would otherwise not have achieved. In tribute to him, we must
see the world community not as a dream and far-off hope but as
the fundamental reality which is the very condition of life.

Dag Hammarskjold was also a man of superb and exquisite
courage, a prime requisite for the establishment of peace and
stability. His was not only the courage which took him to some
of the most dangerous and explosive areas of the world; but
what is even perhaps more admirable and notable, his was the
courage that withstood the frustrations and disillusionments
which long fruitless negotiations and deliberations stimulated.
His was the courage of patience. His the courage of resolve,
stubbornness, persistence. His the courage that never admits
failure—the courage required by day-by-day undramatic and
routine activity. His the courage of a hope that could not be
downed. He once quoted as part of his credo the words from
Shelley's *Prometheus Unbound* which state that one should
"hope, 'til hope creates from its own wreck the thing it con-
templates." How we need the courage to persist despite setback
and obstacle, despite a fallout in the world's atmosphere of
cynicism, apprehension, and despair!

Dag Hammarskjold looked at every issue from the perspective of the peace and welfare of mankind. He was not neutral,
unrooted in particular convictions and opinions. His was the
large view which embraced the world; his the concern from
which no part of the globe was excluded. He saw in the light
of the perspective out of which he habitually approached every
problem that ours is an age which must set an unbalanced world
aright. We must achieve a balance between our power and our
human purposes; our machines and our morality; our shrunken
world and a broad global understanding and sympathy.

Dag Hammarskjold fell as a martyr to a world community
not yet born and to world peace not yet assured. In our dedication to the achievement of these goals we shall set up the noblest
and most enduring monument to this great servant of the world.

SHALOM, SHALOM

SHALOM IS THE WORD one most commonly hears in Israel. It falls
softly and gently on the ear, for it is always spoken in quiet and
kindly tones. Despite the fact that this land is ringed by four
countries—Lebanon, Syria, Jordan, and Egypt—which are still
not reconciled to its existence, *Shalom* or "peace" is the most
frequently heard of words.

Shalom for the Jew is more than pious rhetoric or ritualistic
formula, more than a convenient bridge between the initial meeting of two persons and the conversation in which they engage.
It is prayer, affirmation, conviction. *Shalom* is one of the central
and luminous terms both in Hebraic thought and vocabulary.
Its cadence immediately suggests rich, deep, and emotion-laden
associations. It recalls prophet and sage, sweet singer and thinker,
even as it invokes the benediction which the priests confer upon
the congregation. The tradition does not hesitate to say that
Shalom is one of the synonyms for God Himself.

The meeting of two human beings is a drama of significance.
Even as each person is an event in the cosmos, so the encounter
of two persons is an experience that registers upon the mind and
personality of each. Perhaps it is an exaggeration to say that man
is the sum total of all whom he has met and known. Yet it
remains true that we do not emerge from any meeting with
another untouched and unchanged. Not only has another human
come into the ken of our small individual universe, but, being
human, he has added to our humanity and has thus enriched and
broadened our domain and sphere as a single being. His voice
echoes in deep chambers of our consciousness. When that voice
is warm and friendly, it increases our warmth and helps us to
realize a greater portion of our inherent, though never fully
expressed, goodness and gentleness.

Two people meeting and saying *Shalom* to each other immediately calls into being a small "minyan" engaged in prayer.
The peace that "in the end of days" will prevail in the entire
world already exists in that minute part of time and space represented by the two who make *Shalom* their greeting. Conflict is
rebellion against the God whose seal is truth and whose name is

peace. The ability to have peace reign at all, in however limited
a dominion, gives the lie to all who say that war is inevitable and
that conflict is inherent in human nature. It is a challenge to and
a reproof of every armed border, every military zone, every
frenzied and idolatrous leader whose policy is based on the
"inescapable" fact of war.

Shalom does not send mushrooming clouds into the air; it is
not marked by loud detonations; it does not project rockets into
outer space. It is only a prayer on the lips, a fervent greeting,
a powerful yearning. Neither yesterday nor today belong to it.
Yet the morrow may be a time of peace—if man is to live at all
on earth and if, through his deepest religious insights and highest
spiritual aspirations, he has caught something of the truth about
the ultimate reality of life and the universe.

Not far from Israel's border are men in trenches, armed
with guns, their finger on the trigger awaiting the command.
Only meters from them men meet on the street, friends greet
one another at home, children greet teachers, and even strangers
passing one another say *Shalom*. It is their faith and hope that
will prevail. Some day a historian will record, "*Shalom, Shalom,*
and there was *Shalom*."

3 • *Negro and White*

I AM IN THIS FIGHT*

I AM IN THIS fight with you because my tradition teaches that none can deny the brotherhood of his neighbor without first rejecting the Fatherhood of God. It thus becomes a religious imperative for me to resist every condition or group which reduces my neighbor to a status less than brother.

I am in this fight with you because as a Jew I am familiar through long experience with the evils of oppression and bigotry. Throughout our entire tradition and in our daily prayers there is repeated emphasis on the liberation of my ancestors from Egypt. No other event in the millennial history of my people is as frequently evoked. On one of the major festivals in our calendar (*Pesah*), we are bidden to proclaim that we are descended from slaves. We place a bitter herb on our tongue so that our body as well as our spirit may never forget the bitterness of enslavement. We still bear upon our flesh scars inflicted by hate-driven tormentors. Awareness of the hurt suffered by the rejected, the harassed, the downtrodden impels me to make my fight the fight of all who are denied equality and justice.

I am in this fight with you because I know that since freedom is indivisible, its curtailment anywhere curtails and threatens my freedom. A democracy that supports the suppression of one group of its citizenry is weakened at its very foundations and renders all others insecure in their liberty. Where a class or race is subjected to second-class citizenship, the first-class citizenship of the rest is impaired, uncertain, and incomplete. A new Pharaoh may arise who will extend the existent pattern of oppression and denial to all.

I am in this fight with you because I want to liberate men

---

*Sunrise Service, Detroit Church, October 4, 1963.

38

from the dark passions of bigotry and hostility. I want to heal
the sickness of those who are obsessed with a hate which drives
them to bear down evilly upon others. If these are beyond healing and therapy, I want their children to grow up in a climate
of freedom in which men of differing faiths and color live in
equality and dignity. Thus will the atmosphere about them not
infect them with the moral and psychic sickness of their parents.

I am in this fight with you because as one who believes in
God, I can do no other. I am in this fight with you because my
tradition and my experience as a Jew have sensitized me to the
deprivations imposed upon you. I am in this fight because I
cannot be fully free until all are free.

VICARIOUS GUILT

AN apparently inexplicable ritual is described in Scripture. If a
man is found slain in an open field and his murderer is unknown,
the elders of the nearest community are required to testify that
their hands have not spilled his blood. In addition, a sacrifice of
expiation is to be made. To which the Rabbis ask, "Did suspicion
fall on the leaders of the community? Why are *they* required
to exonerate themselves?" The answer given is that they are
called upon to testify that the victim had not gone hungry,
neglected, and disregarded because of their indifference or
callousness.

A powerful and significant insight is to be found behind this
ancient rite. As the Talmud says elsewhere, the righteous are
implicated in the misdeeds of their age. All society, including its
elite, its leaders, and the body of its law-abiding citizenry, shares
a degree of culpability for the eruptions of evil and crime.

Long before the phenomenal advances in communication
tangibly bound all peoples, however physically remote, in a
unity of destiny, Judaism recognized and taught the interdependence of all lives—the shared responsibility of all men and the
inescapable guilt which taints all, whenever and wherever violence, hunger, ignorance, hate, and injustice are present. Though

it does not accept the idea of vicarious atonement, Judaism does teach vicarious guilt.

When brutal and bestial men beat others with clubs, water hoses, guns, and set ferocious dogs upon them, it is because savagery and sadism reside in the hearts of the many who regard themselves as respectable. When a group within society is denied its human rights, it is because something of the oppressor lives in the majority. When doors are closed in the faces of certain men, women, and children because of color or creed, it is because large numbers disdain those who are rejected and wish to exclude them.

Through many invisible channels, the mild hates, superiorities, and spiritual corruptions of the "good people" course into society at large and become part of its climate. Sickly people with twilight minds breathe the tainted air and are stimulated to express in primitive and violent form what the generality of the population feels calmly. The action of the "extremists" provides a magnified mirror for the moderate and controlled sinfulness of the majority. Hence when prejudice and injustice convulse any part of the land no one can exonerate himself by saying, "I would never do anything like that." At a dinner table, in the club, in business—by a small act or comment or jest—we may have unloosed a bit of radioactive slander or hate into the atmosphere. We are all of us accomplices in the sins of our times.

WHAT BROTHERHOOD REQUIRES*

THE BIBLE SERVES NOT only as a great bridge between man and God, but also between man and his brother. For true religion casts its eyes not only heavenward but also upon the human scene. He who has no eyes for his fellowman cannot hope to glimpse God or His providence. For religion ever seeks to link man and man in a common family, the expression of our unity as the children of One God. One world is the inescapable

---

*Radio Address, February 8, 1953.

corollary of One God. Man is related to his neighbor not by the
accident of birth, nor by the proximity of dwelling, nor by a
shared danger, nor by an identity of citizenship or color. Man
is more than fellow citizen, coreligionist, classmate, partner,
neighbor. He is brother.

Out of that relationship flow great opportunities and great
responsibilities. The Biblical injunction to "love thy neighbor as
thyself: I am the Lord" derives not merely from the Biblical
view of society but more fundamentally from Scripture's conception of God. No more revolutionary principle of social relations has ever been advanced, no firmer basis for the concept of
human interdependence devised.

The character of what we call today social service, as it is
reflected in the Bible and in rabbinic law, can be suggested most
concisely and accurately by a single phrase, "act brotherly," in
order that, as Scripture expresses it, "thy brother may live with
thee."

This is no abstract concept. Its concrete connotations shine
clearly through Biblical legislation dealing with our duties to our
fellowmen, which in turn are a most significant aspect of our
duties to God. If one's brother chances upon difficult times and
stands in need of assistance, then it must be understood and
remembered that his low estate in no way affects his rights
under God or his basic equality with other men. It cannot be
pointed out too often, for it is a fact that serves as a clue to the
entire range of Biblical law, that the Hebrew word *zedakah*,
usually translated "charity," literally means righteousness or justice. To help our fellowman in need is not to do that which is
beyond the call of duty. It is not an act that should inspire in
us inflated feelings of self-righteousness and self-glorification. It
is but an elementary rendering of justice. Have we not given to
another of God's children that which God has given to us?

But, Jewish teaching continues, justice requires not only that
we come to the assistance of our fallen brother, but also that we
have due regard for his sensibilities. Our aid must never be at
the expense of his human dignity. It must not result in humiliation for him even as it should not lead to self-exaltation by us.
"Better," say the Rabbis, "no giving at all than giving that brings
the blush of shame to the recipient." He who speaks kindly to

the needy, who uplifts the impoverished through brotherly interest and understanding, has done more nobly and meritoriously than he who gives nothing but alms. Talmudic teaching stresses that if a man is too sensitive or bashful to take charity, he should be given money as a loan, though it be for an undefined period, in order to spare him feelings of shame. The self-respect of the dependent must be preserved. A man's fortunes and his need should not become the occasion for the humbling of his spirit. A rabbinic passage proclaims that "better than giving is lending, better than lending is setting up in business." Nine centuries later, the great medieval Jewish philosopher and teacher Maimonides drew up in ascending order eight degrees of charity. Upon the topmost rung of social assistance he placed that kind of helpfulness which provides the opportunity for an individual to become independent and self-supporting. The greatest of all charity is to free man from the need of charity. The most charitable society is that in which none requires charity.

We are brothers and hence as brothers we should share one with the other. This kind of sharing is a reciprocal process. Say the Rabbis, "more than one does for the poor man, does the poor man do for his benefactor." Through brotherly acts of helpfulness we strengthen our character, elevate our humanness, deepen our sensitivity, and permit the divine image in which we are formed to shine through more clearly and brightly. We cannot raise up our brother without simultaneously raising ourselves.

ABSENTEE EDUCATION*

MANY WHITE PARENTS IN New Orleans have joined in organizing a boycott of the public schools in which, by a Federal Court order, two, three, or four Negro children are enrolled in the classes. I suppose some of these parents are thinking that their children are merely missing several sessions of school in the interests of the great and noble goal of keeping the schools lily white.

*Recorder, December, 1960.

By the very absence from school the parents have imposed upon their children, however, the youngsters have learned a lesson which will always remain. A lesson has been impressed upon them more vividly and more lastingly than any which they were taught when they went to class. They are being taught contempt for the law. A deep strand of anarchy and rebelliousness is being woven into the emerging personalities of these boys and girls, who are hardly unaware of the reasons for their absence.

They are also being taught a religion which runs counter to the one they and their parents formally profess. The ideas that not all men are God-created, that neighbor need not be loved, and that indeed it is proper and moral to hate one's fellowmen are being ground deep into the spirit and consciousness of the white children, and no subsequent instruction in the creed and doctrines of their avowed religion will completely dislodge this pagan substratum.

Some of these young people will one day be doctors, engineers, architects, and scientific men of research. They will be well versed in modern technical knowledge and skilled in the use of the most up-to-date mechanisms and procedures. Yet, at the very roots of their being, there will persist a growth of primitive ideas and ancient attitudes. They will be men of today whose outlook will be rooted in the soil of distant and outlived yesterdays. They will be spiritual and social cavemen in the twentieth century. In "one world," they will live behind the vulnerable barricades of their imaginary superiority. In an integrated society (which no willful group can prevent from coming into being) they will be people wearing blinders, shut out by their pathetically segregated minds from free and creative participation in the large areas of an unhampered common life. Halting of tongue, for there will be gaps in their vocabulary where such words as "brotherhood," "equality," "dignity of all men," "liberty for all" would normally be found; paralyzed in the outflow of affection and handicapped in their full adjustment to the better day—they will lead only a husk of their life, as shadows of their potential selves.

No, dear parents of New Orleans, your children have not really missed school. On the contrary, you have taught them all too well a lesson in hostility, divisiveness, fear, and bigotry.

TO A WHITE HIGH-SCHOOL GIRL
IN LITTLE ROCK, ARKANSAS

I DO NOT KNOW your name or your address, and I know nothing of your family background. Yet I feel impelled to write you.

A month ago I saw your picture in the newspaper. You were one of a group of white students standing behind a Negro girl who was carrying books and was evidently making her way to the high school building where you attend classes. An expression of both dignity and determination was on her face. Your mouth was open and one could recognize from the hate with which your face was contorted that you were shouting harsh, if not vile, words at her. She, meanwhile, looking straight ahead, tried to remain oblivious to your unfriendly comments.

My first reaction was one of anger. You probably never had any personal association with the fellow student whom you were insulting, yet you presumed to curse and mock her because her color was other than yours.

My anger soon dissolved, giving way to deep sadness. Young and attractive though you appear, your face shows much ugliness of feeling and spirit. In our civilization, we associate delicacy and tenderness with womanhood, qualities completely absent from your hate-ruled look.

In your hands you carried books, indicating that you are a student, a member of a great community in quest of knowledge and wisdom. Through schools and books we enter the universe of human ideas and ideals and are privileged to become acquainted with the greatest and noblest men and women of all ages. There is no more democratic society than that represented by the world of art, literature, science, philosophy, history—the world of human culture. Perhaps you are diligent, do your lessons faithfully, and receive the approval of your instructors. Your expression, however, shows that you are not qualified to join the body of students who, through knowledge, deepen their humanity, refine their attitudes, and broaden their interest. The books and subjects you have studied have never really entered your mind or your heart. You must keep these bolted against any ideas of human equality, determined as you are to live in a small, darkened ghetto of inherited prejudices and hates.

You are, of course, an American—a claim I am sure you proudly make. If America is only a geographical term or a matter of formal citizenship, then your claim cannot be disputed. But if, as millions of Americans believe, America means freedom and human rights; and if America guarantees, as we say in our Pledge of Allegiance, "liberty and justice for all," then I wonder how American you really are. You and your family are undoubtedly affiliated with a church. Perhaps you even attend its services regularly. But the expression on your face repudiates the most fundamental beliefs of religion and makes you closer to the ancient tribal heathen than to adherents of a monotheistic faith of love and justice.

You offend your femininity, your character, your Americanism, and your religion by that disgraceful incident which a camera has recorded and spread over the world. Some day you will be married. A new generation will spring from you. The feeling of sadness you arouse in me embraces the child you will mother one day. What a sorry heritage of hostility, fury, and hate you will pass on. You will try, I am certain, to provide for all of his necessities and comforts. Yet at the same time you will be pouring poison into his system—the poison of prejudice, the poison of un-American and irreligious hate, the poison that will stunt his growth as a citizen and man. You have my profound sympathy.

PROCLAIM LIBERTY

The Emancipation Proclamation issued in 1863 by Abraham Lincoln was a momentous and moving document on the agenda of our national concern and responsibility. In it flowed, through the mediation of a great and humane spirit, many of the finest traditions and insights that motivated men through the centuries in their bitter, sacrificial struggle for freedom.

Chief among the many influences that united to give birth

to that pronouncement was the religious conscience which, though often permitted to rest dormant, asserted itself in its substance. For though Lincoln was not an orthodox believer, he was a profoundly religious man. He had a deeply rooted awareness of the indivisible unity of mankind. He understood that degradation of any section of mankind is an assault upon the freedom of all men, a Satanic rebellion against the divine law. This is what prompted Lincoln to say: "Slavery was a foul lie that could never be consecrated into God's hallowed truth."

Another basic religious insight involved in his Proclamation was unfaltering faith in the dignity of every human individual—a dignity integral and inalienable; a dignity beyond the right of government or society to assail or reduce. Slavery, a brutal denial of these truths, subjugated and condemned an entire race, on the one hand, and sought to dehumanize every person of that race, on the other. More than any other phenomenon, slavery was the great heresy of American life—the antireligion which existed in the midst of a land professing faith in religion and avowing devotion to freedom.

The struggle the Emancipation Proclamation dramatized is not over, and we who live a century later are not free to desist in vigilance or effort in carrying forward to fulfillment its explicit and implicit ideals of equality, freedom, and human dignity. The progress that has been made, particularly in the past decade and a half, should not stimulate complacency but should rather invigorate us in our work to validate the great Proclamation by translating it into political, social, educational, and economic fact.

When the Negro shall take his full and rightful place as citizen, neighbor, and brother in our midst, it will mean not alone the liberation of one race but the elevation of all America to a new status as the "land of the free." It will be a beacon of promise, hope, and assurance to all those living under oppression anywhere in the world. Our accomplishment may well serve as a global Emancipation Proclamation, casting its light upon all corners of the globe darkened by tyranny, fear, and servitude. We shall honor our destiny as a nation by giving force to the Biblical injunction: "Proclaim liberty throughout the land unto all the inhabitants thereof."

IF I WERE CHRISTIAN*

I HAPPEN TO BE a Jew. That is the most incidental and accidental fact about me. I did not make that choice. Had I been born into another home I would have been the follower of another faith. Given the same personal inclinations but placed in another environment from birth I might have been a Moslem teacher or a Christian minister. I must therefore not impart to my Jewishness and to the accident of birth an absoluteness from which all others are shut out. I must live my Jewish life with the humility that derives from the knowledge that it was neither my choice nor my insistence which determined my Jewishness.

I am a Jew. That is one of the most basic facts about me. It is a strand that colors the whole pattern of my life, the whole texture of my being. By virtue of my training, my conditioning, my environment, my social inheritance, the fact of my Jewishness penetrates every fiber, determines my feelings and reactions, and has contributed largely to the creation of the man that I am. It is so integral to myself that to seek to suppress my Jewishness would mean to tear out a significant part of me, and to present to my fellowmen a partial, fragmentary, and therefore distorted and crippled personality.

If I were a Christian, I would similarly recognize the accident of my Christian birth and would therefore not give to that fact such an exalted importance as to make those seem inferior who are not as "fortunate" as I in the matter of accident of birth. I would realize that that strange and uncontrollable series of circumstances which dictated that I come into being through the medium of white Christian parents likewise dictated that my neighbor be born to a Jewish pair, and another neighbor to a

---

*Brotherhood Week Address. Central Methodist Church, February 18, 1940.

Negro couple. I would not make of that chance occurrence the reason for a basic absolute claim upon superiority.

But as a Christian I would likewise realize that the Christian tradition is of the very essence in the formation of my being. The Christian spirit of my parents and home would be rooted in the deepest soil of my life. I would therefore become aware of the fact that my full self-realization and development, the complete unfolding of my personality would be impossible without the Christian sentiments and values bequeathed me.

If I were a Christian, I would therefore seek to come into my full Christian heritage. I would seek to claim all that its rich history and tradition can give to me. I would trace Christian thought back through the centuries, seeking to acquire the significant deposits which each age and generation of forebears made in the ever widening stream of the Christian experience.

I would journey back through the years and come back to Him who is regarded as the Saviour. I would sympathetically study His day and the society in which He chose to appear in earthly form. I would scrupulously seek to separate the misunderstanding with which obscurity always seeks to screen the truth. I would realize that His appearance, like His crucifixion, was part of a great divine plan, and that the one without the other would not have permitted the full unfolding of that sacred and significant drama. I would then realize that the Jews are the Christ-bearing and not the Christ-killing people.

And I would go back behind the earthly appearance of the Saviour to study the history and forces which dictated the choice of Judea as the site of His advent. I would see that in that environment there lived ideas and memories, traditions and beliefs most akin to the Master's message. From Abraham the patriarch through Moses—and Elijah and Amos and Isaiah and Jeremiah and Ezekiel—there was a direct path leading to the words of Him I call Teacher and Saviour. There is divine law in the physical life of the universe—law and order and regularity—and the fact we live in the cosmos is eloquent testimony to the presence of a Creator. In the moral realm, too, there is law, and it was the expression of such a divine law that Jesus appeared not in Greece or Egypt or Rome, but in Judea. Then I would realize that the Jewish people has played a high part in the drama of Christianity's origin and development. I would make my ears sensitive to the accents of Israel in my creed and prayers. A new sense of kinship would fill me, and I would realize that the Jew is my brother in the high adventure of establishing the Kingdom of Heaven on earth.

And as I looked with my Christian eyes at the world about me, I would see with new vividness the plight of the descendants of my Saviour's forebears. I would realize that the "people of Christ has become the Christ of the peoples," subjected to prejudice and hate and persecution. From across the seas I would hear cries of Jewish oppression, and in our very midst I would hear poisoned voices, and see the performance of poisoned deeds of unbrotherly feeling and discrimination.

With a sudden insight I the Christian would realize that here was a problem, a problem not alone for the Jew, a problem too for me the Christian because it is my tradition that is attacked in the person of my brother the Jew. It is not only his safety that is imperiled but the power and validity of everything I the Christian hold sacred. The Fatherhood of God, the brotherhood of man, dignity of the individual, sanctity of life, love, justice— these are under heavy attack.

It is also my problem because it is never the Jew alone who is attacked. The concentration camps of the oppressors of men are choked with Christians as well as Jews, with liberals, pacifists, idealists, democrats of all denominations. The Jew may be the first but he is never the sole victim.

I would humbly and penitently bear my share of the blame. I would understand that the seeming readiness of people to believe the most fantastic absurdities about the Jew is the out-growth of centuries of my misunderstanding. I have allowed ominous associations to gather about the word "Jew." I have helped circulate myths about him, and give currency to un-founded accusations. I, the member of the majority taking over the history of the majority, must share the responsibility for clearing away the debris of the ages. I would say, in the words of a Christian minister,* to my Jewish brother:

---

*Conrad Henry Moehlman, *The Christian-Jewish Tragedy:* A Study in Religious Prejudice, Rochester, 1933.

We have damned you for the very attitudes which we ourselves have made inevitable. We have robbed you and now criticize you for being secretive. We have driven you together like sheep in a storm and now call you clannish.

We have accused you of materialism because you have been successful in business. Your prosperity has been an evidence of a mercenary mind, ours an evidence of the favor of God.

We have taken your Bible and made it ours and said never a word of appreciation of the genius of the God which produced it. Through all the Christian centuries our ritual has rested upon yours and in these days of enrichment of worship we discover how rich yours is—but no intimation of thanks.

We have called peace a Christian attitude forgetting that it was a Jew who first used those words, which now belong to humanity, about beating swords into plowshares and spears into pruning hooks.

I would first seek deliberately and religiously to purge my spirit of any inherited prejudices, of dark thoughts. I would seek to clear the environment of the imponderable influences for evil and misunderstanding. I would reexamine the story of my faith that I teach my child at home and in the church school to see if it contains aught that can fall like a blight upon his impressionable mind. I would seek to acquire greater knowledge of the contemporary Jew, his life, his problems, his aspirations, his synagogues and communal endeavors.

I would continually ask myself whether I know as much about the great and rich achievements and personalities of the modern Jew as I do about the failings and crudities to which all mortals are heir.

I would try to help the Jew be as Jewish as I the Christian would wish to be Christian. I would say to the Jew: Be Jewish, gloriously, positively, affirmatively, wholesomely Jewish. For this society we must together build, lest paganism and brutality drive out all decency, and God become the greatest refugee of all, we want of you, the Jew, not alone your brawn and the sweat of your brow, but also the distilled wisdom of the centuries, the precious insights of your history, the accumulated riches of your experience, the understanding and tenderness born of your suffering. Give your whole self, as I would give my whole self, so that on the firm Gibraltar of brotherhood we may together build the good life, the city of God, the Kingdom of Heaven.

ANTI-SEMITISM: AN ANALYSIS

ANTI-SEMITISM IS A comparatively new term in the lexicon of nations and men, first coming into use in Germany in the seventies of the last century. It represents, however, an old fact in human society.

Anti-Semitism may be defined as a doctrine or theory which seeks to explain and justify a proposed or existing program of action against the Jew. It is the attempt to find reasons for what is done through prejudice and hate, to raise social ostracism, economic discrimination, and physical violence to the level of philosophy or science. It aims to supply a theology and creed for blind anger, fear, and animosity. It is the arsenal of argument and sanction, of reason and alleged fact. Its ammunition is existing social bias and popular prejudice, overcast by a veneer of apparent rationality. Since the evidence it offers and the doctrines it proposes are born of deep-seated hatred, they cannot be removed by counterargument. Its adherents are emotionally committed to its conclusions and impervious to reason or polemics.

Anti-Semitism is a theory born of the prejudices of the environment. The prejudice against the Jew has been a constant factor in the life of European peoples for close to two millennia. It erupts into violence in times of social crises. Its virulence and intensity are determined by the social and economic conditions that obtain in the land in any given time.

Opposition to the Jew grows out of a complex of causes, and assumes many guises to suit the varying circumstances which evoked it. "The Jew takes on the Protean shapes created by ever-changing panic," someone has said. Now it is the Jew as foe of the true faith who is held up to scorn; now the Jew as money-lender and exploiter; now as a member of an inferior and contaminated race; now as a political and social rebel; now as an

international banker; now as a clannish individual; now as one
who has greedily penetrated into the social and cultural life of
the country. What are the real roots of these accusations?

First is the fact of the Jew's difference. Historical circumstances have compelled the Jew to live among peoples among
whom he was from the outset set apart by appearance, language,
religion, and conduct. This difference has served as a searchlight
focusing attention upon him. He was not lost in the social mass.
The Jew was distinct, conspicuous, easily identifiable.

From earliest times intergroup relations have rarely been
amicable and just. Geographical and cultural boundaries between
nations have generally stimulated the erection of such emotional
barriers as suspicion, fear, envy, and hatred. When people differ
from us, our distrust is aroused. We find it difficult to catalogue
them since they represent an unknown quantity to us. Their
strange ways seem "unnatural," for we regard our way of living
as absolute, the sole and proper norm for all men. As such the
foreigner appears as somewhat less than human, an inferior spe-
cies. Out of our uneasiness in his presence is born fear, and out of
fear, hatred. Israel Zangwill has called this universal attitude to
the outsider "dislike of the like for the unlike." All peoples seem
to have in their language special terms freighted with contempt
and suspicion for foreign groups. Even the cultured Greeks
called their neighbors "barbarians." Hostility to the Jew is a
specific example of the usual reaction of majorities to minorities,
of one group to another which differs from it.

For the Jew was and is different. How "strange" he must
have appeared to his contemporaries in the Middle Ages! In the
midst of a society that believed in a Messiah who had already appeared, this peculiar people looked to the future for its Redeemer.
In a world that rested on the first day of the week, the Jew persisted in observing the last as his Sabbath. Among peoples who
prayed in Latin or in the vernacular, this group presumed to in-
voke its God in Hebrew. The Jew further differed in his dress
and manners, diet and language, hobbies and recreations, in code
and conduct. He lived by his own faith and followed his own
mores. To this day the Jew appears to many as an Oriental
strangely out of place in the Occident, while his religion is undoubtedly the arch variant from Christianity.

The Chestertonian paradox that "unfamiliarity breeds contempt" proved tragically true for the Jew. It was a rare soul who could hurdle the high barriers between Jew and non-Jew. Ignorance entertained by large masses made credible the most fantastic and absurd rumors and myths concerning the Jew. And as he persisted in his difference, the world persisted in misunderstanding and hating him.

In addition, other factors intruded and turned the tension between Jew and non-Jew into perhaps the most spectacular instance of intergroup friction, characterized by unusual consistency, brutality, and ubiquity. For one thing the Jew's diffusion throughout the world served to give force and plausibility to the wild charges laid at his door. A peasant from medieval Germany and a townsman from Spain chancing to meet at a great fair discovered in each other kindred prejudices in regard to the Jew. Each returned to his own country reenforced in his attitude and believing with greater certainty than ever that the Jew was his enemy. The enemy was more dangerous because he seemed to represent international power. A myth about the Jew, growing out of a local incident in one country, had export value, and could pass freely from land to land. The Jew was international, and prejudice against him was worldwide.

In addition to his difference and dispersion, Christian Europe had another score to settle with the Jew. The Church soon involved itself in the problem of the Jew in Europe. In order to remain neutral in this matter, where it did not actually support, it did not oppose the prevailing unfriendliness toward the Jew. The demeanor of many of the Church's leaders and representatives, whose activities were not repudiated by the Church, was easily taken by the faithful as a sign of approval. Thus directly and indirectly the most powerful religious institution of the West helped confer unquestioned status and respectability upon hostility to the Jew.

The Church has always regarded the Jew with special interest; indeed, Christianity is conceived of by the Church as a continuation and extension of Jewish history and experience. The Church looks upon itself as the divinely chosen successor to the chosen people of old. Christianity felt therefore that it came not to destroy but to absorb the Hebraic tradition. The Jew's

refusal to convert possessed a sting which touched the leaders of
the new religion to the quick. The Jew's incomprehensible ob-
stinacy was a silent yet eloquent denial of Christianity which the
Church felt it could not afford to overlook.

Picture the paradox. Here was a people, lineal descendants
of the group into which Jesus was born, still living by the Bible,
which it preserved in its original form, and still following that
tradition out of which Christianity sprang, refusing to recognize
its divinely destined offshoot and supplanter. A mother turning
her back on her daughter, a father rejecting his son—were not
these the perfect analogies for the Jew's perfidious behavior? If
the Church was Israel's heir, Israel's blind adherence to its own
faith constituted a counterclaim to the legacy. Clearly the Jew's
great denial was something the Church could neither easily understand nor graciously forgive.

In the capacious and retentive memory of the Church there
rankled other disturbing associations. The Jew had fought, with
that unique intolerance and fury which usually mark bitter family feuds, the early Christians, who seemed to represent not so
much a new Church as a schism in the old. It required time and
painful effort for the early Church to sever its close family ties
with the Jewish people. For a time Judaism was a serious com-
petitor with Christianity for supremacy, and in those dim early
centuries the outcome seemed by no means certain. The Church
did not soon forget its early trials. Awareness of debt to Judaism
spiced its dislike of the Jew, who loomed large and ominous to
the impassioned zealots of the Church.

The Church likewise felt that the presence of so conspicuous
a heretical group in the very midst of Christian society constituted a menace to its own unbroken rule and integrity. When the
Church was racked by sectarian revolts and theological devia-
tions, it could not help but speculate whether the existence of the
nonconforming Jewish group did not inspire such movements.
The Jew, a heretic, was always a potential breeder of heresies,
and antagonism to him and Judaism found its way into the authoritative code of the Church.

Yet the Church realized that the existence of the Jew was
not without value. That explains the attitude of more than one
eminent divine, who was not averse to suppressing the Jew yet

opposed any procedure or law which aimed at his complete extermination. They realized that what might be a normal lukewarm espousal of Christianity could become fiery and fanatic when an adversary expresses his opposition and contempt. The Church made use of the Jew as the great enemy and scorner of the true religion. The fact that Jesus was crucified in Golgotha became more conspicuous than that he was born in Bethlehem among Jews; the fact of Judas' Jewish origin was stressed above Jesus' Jewish ancestry. It was not long before the Jew was saddled with responsibility for the crucifixion in the face of all historical evidence. To this very day, the accusing phrase of "Christ-killer" can still be heard.

The Jew became the supreme culprit in the Christian drama, the archvillain of its sacred story. He was everywhere, this victim of circumstance, so that the expanding Church could everywhere point the finger at him; yet he was nowhere in the majority. He was weak and helpless. The difference of the Jew placed him under the shadow of suspicion; the Church did not have to create but merely exploit and intensify an existing antagonism and distrust.

And everywhere the Jew helped the Church appeal to the zeal of its followers. He rendered a more subtle service too: he helped endow the theology of the Church with a concreteness it may not have otherwise had. His very existence was a real and vivid substantiation of the story the Church told. The fact that the villain was real was evidence that the drama in which he participated was real. The teachings of the Church thus became touched through the presence of the Jew with an actuality and plausibility which impressionable masses could be trusted to carry over to areas of Christian doctrine less susceptible to visible proof.

The degradation which the Jew suffered was likewise a tribute to the truth of the Church's account. Having failed to accept the Saviour of Christianity, the Jews were repudiated and cast off by God. The once chosen people was now the people condemned and scorned. That many who taught and held this view believed it in all sincerity and faith does not alter the fact that the Church contributed to the subjection of the Jew. It is no accident that the treatment the Jew received in Mohammedan lands never approached in harshness and persistence the indignities he suffered in Christian countries. It was under Christian rule that the Jew was made to bear the cross through the centuries.

The effects of these attitudes to this day are to be found even in nonreligious circles. The essential deviation of the Jew from the majority and the role assigned him in the Christian scheme helped create a strong and abiding undercurrent of antipathy which became an integral element of the social environment, transmitted by the institutions which molded and nurtured Western man. It was sanctioned by persons whom he respected and to whose authority he submitted. Folklore caught it up and expressed it in a hundred myths and in a thousand quips and proverbs. "Jew" came to be a term heavily freighted with dark undertones and ominous associations. It represented hypocrisy and cruelty, niggardliness and unscrupulousness, dishonesty and Satanism. One did not have to suffer a real or imagined hurt at the hands of a Jew to become impregnated with contempt and hostility. One did not even have to meet a Jew to hate him. One "caught" the prejudice from the atmosphere: home, street, school, office, book, play, painting, popular jest—all reflected it in some form. "All Jews are moneylenders," "all Jews are avaricious," "all Jews are rich," "all Jews are Communists"—when a single Jew is a scoundrel, his individual behavior is taken as proof of the larger generalization.

To this day, a man of broad, liberal tendencies has to undergo a painstaking process before he can eradicate the unfriendliness toward the Jew which his environment and early training rooted in him. Very often his newer enlightenment does not reach down into the dark recesses where his childhood prejudices persist. Today's anti-Semitism is as potentially dangerous as that of earlier centuries since it represents the harnessing of existing animosity and fear into political and economic channels.

The basic fact about anti-Semitism, which confused Jews and sympathetic Christians often overlook, is that the Jew is not a cause but a victim of anti-Semitism. The Jew is neither better nor worse than the peoples about him. The charges that are placed at his door are themselves the effect of prejudice. Burke long ago said that you cannot indict a whole people. The numerous vicious generalizations concerning the nature of the Jew are an attempt to rationalize a previously present attitude of hostility. The roots of the social friction between the majority and a minority are not in the character of the minority but in the society created by the majority.

Anti-Semitism is undoubtedly a problem for the Jew. But it must not be regarded as exclusively a Jewish problem. Anti-Semitism is a social problem for all men, and cannot be ignored by any who are sensitive to wrong and desirous of the right. It is an outpost of that larger struggle that seeks to make the privileges of the few the rights of the many. The Jew suffers because there are elements which exploit the unfortunate tradition of hostility and will not let it die. The Jew suffers because there are masses who are compelled to lead lives of desperation and need, and whose gathered resentment and frustration seeks an easy outlet.

Anti-Semitism is thus to be regarded for precisely what it is, a symptom of social distress and injustice, a symptom which has been chronic because the disease is chronic. Even as the general weakness of a body is often reflected through pain in one organ or part, so is the persecution of the Jew, or indeed of any minority, the result of a general dislocation and maladjustment in the total social organism. Where there is want and therefore anger, where there is exploitation and therefore hatred, there the Jew is in danger. The ultimate anti-Semites are hunger of the masses, a sense of hurt carried by large numbers, unemployment and depression. The Hitlers of history only exploit these prevailing conditions. Remove this dank soil in the social life, and the weeds of dictatorship and anti-Semitism cannot spring up.

The Jew alone cannot overcome anti-Semitism. Nor should a well-meaning Gentile content himself with decrying prejudice. Nor should the liberal say, "it's not my funeral." Anti-Semitism is the spade with which the grave of freedom is dug.

Here is a common task for pacifist and laborer, for Christian and Jew, for teacher and clergyman. A common fate awaits them should the forces which create anti-Semitism gain the ascendancy. Violent and brutal attacks upon the Jew will be eliminated when ours is a society of free, secure, and equal men. So ominous a symptom is anti-Semitism that no man can feel fully free and secure till it is eliminated.

SOVIET JEWRY: YET AGAIN

*Sabbath Sivan 12 (May 23, 1964) has been set aside as a
National Day of Prayer on behalf of Soviet Jewry. The
Synagogue Council comprising the Orthodox, Conservative,
and Reform branches of Judaism has asked us to turn our
deepest thoughts to our brethren who are denied their elementary rights. I share with you on this Sabbath of Prayer
several reflections which agitate my mind.*

THE JEWISH POPULATION BEHIND the Iron Curtain is second in
number only to the Jewish community in America. Two and a
half million or more are under Soviet domination, where the
word Jew is equated once again with "traitor," "enemy of the
people," "conspirator." Once again the sole crime is Jewishness
and Jewish descent.

Nothing happens by chance in a totalitarian society; there
have been signs of an anti-Jewish policy on the part of the Kremlin before this. Several years ago the Soviet newspapers began to
refer to the "rootless cosmopolitans" in a context which made it
obvious that Jews were the object of reference. Newspapers also
began to publish the Jewish names of artists and writers though
they had heretofore been known only by their Russian pseudo-
nyms, thus calling attention to their Jewish origin. Stalin applied
the name "Talmudists" to his opponents. None of these manifestations, however, suggested the seemingly wide-ranged program
against the Jew on which the U.S.S.R. has presently embarked.

The motivations behind this most recent shocking development can only be a matter of conjecture. Do fear and insecurity
lurk behind the bold and blustering front of the men of the
Kremlin? Are there discontent and rebelliousness within the land,
and is the Jew serving once more as the scapegoat by which attention is diverted from the real cause of the people's resentment?
Have the Soviets discovered in the Jew a specific quality which
does not permit him to fit into the mold they have planned for
him?

Or do the Jews, in the opinion of the rulers of Russia, exhibit a sense of kinship with Jews outside of Russia? A totalitarian state is always a jealous mistress. It seeks a monopoly over the mind of its citizens. It is suspicious of other loyalties even when they do not conflict with the allegiance to the state. Everything must be brought under the rule of the party—music, history, science, sports. How do you control feelings that link citizens to men beyond the border?

One commentator states that the Soviets have decided that Jews constitute "a poor security risk." Since tyrants have always found Jews "poor security risks," the Communists are paying an unintended compliment to the Jew.

Or is it that the Soviets, having realistically surveyed the present world situation, have decided that anti-Semitism has political value and can help win friends and influence people who are now indifferent? Is Russia trying to forge a new internationale of anti-Semitism, bigotry, hate? The black forces that failed to rally around Marxism-Leninism-Stalinism might be attracted to an anti-Jewish program. The neo-Nazis and the unreconstructed Nazis of Germany, the Fascists in South America, the Arabs in the Middle East could be won by such a policy, and thus the unity of the West could be severed. The Soviet promise of excesses against the Jew would, it is hoped, prove more seductive than the American plea for freedom.

The Rabbis suggested long ago that a crisis which engulfs both the Jews and the world is real and deep. Such is the nature of the problem created by Russia. We, the Jews of America, have a special responsibility to help alert America. Free nations must speak out in no uncertain terms of protest and revulsion. The anti-Semites of the world must not receive the encouragement of America's silence. The hatemongers within our own borders must not be permitted to find comfort in our country's passivity. The black forces of reaction must not be strengthened by the acquiescence of inaction on our part.

No world program can bring peace to a harassed mankind which demands the surrender of Jewish group life and traditions. It is when the Jew is free to be Jewish that mankind is free to be human.

THOUGHTS ON *THE DEPUTY* *

THE APPEARANCE OF *The Deputy*, the play in which Pope Pius XII
is condemned because he did not issue a statement of protest
during the Nazi brutality against the Jews, has roused much discussion and dissension. I am neither a drama critic nor a professional student of literature nor cultural historian, and I am not
able to judge the validity of all that is said in the play. But this I
do know: that the Pope did not speak out in any formal way is
true and factual. That has been acknowledged by Catholics, by
Protestants, and by Jews who know and have studied the situation as it unfolded in the forties, twenty or more years ago. Some
say the Pope was afraid that were he to speak out it would have
enraged the Nazis even more and might have brought even
greater devastation upon their victims. Others say the Pope was
a symbol of great moral influence; his duty was to speak out, and
he committed the sin of remaining neutral when conscience
should have prompted him to speak.

Actually, *The Deputy* has nothing to do with Catholic-
Jewish relations. I resent and repudiate the statement of Cardinal
Spellman of New York that Catholic-Jewish relations are being
affected by this play. If the relations between our faiths are so
weak and frail and insubstantial that a play written by a non-Jew
can threaten that relationship, then that relationship is not a good
one. We do not want the kind of relationship where we must
pour the oil of flattery upon each other's head, where we must
constantly smile to each other, and where we haven't the right
to express differences of opinion, no matter how profound those
differences might be.

No, *The Deputy* has nothing to do with Catholic-Jewish relations. It is rather an attempt by a sensitive author to probe the
depths of a period through which we have passed. And if he is
wrong, he has the right to be wrong, and Catholics have the right
to answer and to reject his statements. But to see this as a danger
to good Catholic-Jewish relations is, I submit, a complete misunderstanding of what it means to live in a free society.

I also resent those who speak about *The Deputy* as Jewish

*Sermon, March 7, 1964.

experts. As a Jew, I have no opinion about this play. I am involved in it as a citizen, as a person concerned deeply about moral questions and as one who hopes that by probing and understanding the most abysmal period in all of our history, we may acquire sufficient humanity to avoid a tragic repetition. Any Jew, any Catholic, any Protestant has a right to express an opinion as a citizen. But we do not need experts in community relations or in Christian-Jewish relationships to speak for us.

There can be no Jewish opinion about *The Deputy* because it is not a Jewish issue. If a dramatist or an artist wishes to deal with live questions, he must concern himself with Catholics, with Protestants, with Jews. This is a legitimate area for artists. And if it were a Chief Rabbi who was condemned, I would not run to his defense as a Jew. And if there was an area in which opinion and judgment would be exercised, I would grant the dramatist a right to express the judgment that differs from mine.

As I understand *The Deputy*, it doesn't concern the Pope alone. As a matter of fact, the most attractive character is a Catholic, the Jesuit priest who appends a yellow badge to himself in order to indicate his identification with the suffering Jews who died in concentration camps. The play asks a moral question: Where were you? And where are you when hurt was and is inflicted? And it is not only about the Nazis. Where are you when thousands of black Americans are denied their rights in Mississippi and in Alabama and in places closer to home? Where are you when millions of Americans live below the rim of decent survival, and, in the midst of the greatest affluence ever seen in history, suffer poverty and need? Where are you when the concern rises as to what will happen to those who will soon be graduating from high schools and colleges only to swell the ranks of the unemployed? Where are you when segregation is imposed upon people because of the color of their skin?

This is the powerful message of *The Deputy*, which is directed to every human being—Catholic, Protestant, and Jew. One cannot practice neutrality without being blamed for complicity in the crime. The Bible said it long ago—do not stand idly by while your brother's blood is being shed, and every man is your brother. This is the challenge to all of us, the comfortable people, the dangerously complacent people, the respectable people who never before violated a law or committed a crime. Neutrality is a capital crime. There will be a judgment upon us because at a time when we should have done something, we retreated into our own comforts; at a time when we should have spoken out and added our voice to the voices of many others, we preferred to hold our tongue.

RELIGION AND PUBLIC EDUCATION*

THE AMERICAN JEWISH COMMUNITY is far from constituting a homogeneous group. It reflects the numerous diversities of social, cultural, economic, and political variations and gradations found in American life generally. Nor is it marked by a unity of approach to Jewish tradition; neither is it monolithic in its interpretation of present-day Jewish needs and programs. Even a superficial glance at the structure of American Jewish life will reveal the manifold differentiations that crisscross it at every level. When a community so diverse finds itself singularly united on one great issue, there is significance to that near unanimity, which the majority in turn ought not to regard lightly.

Such an unprecedented unity of view characterizes the approach of American Jews to the issue of religion in public education now being hotly discussed. There is evidently a point of view, an emphasis to which Jews, by virtue of their experience in the past and their position in the present, are keenly and uniquely sensitive. Three factors unite to place the Jew in a unique position in approaching this issue.

First, the Jew has had a long historic experience across many centuries with empires and governments allied to churches. He has learned from the most intimate kind of contact the dangers which inhere in this situation. He is therefore understandably alert to any proposal which moves, however guardedly, in the direction of alliance between two entities which our democratic tradition has long ago decided should remain apart and distinct. There is no minority in the land which can feel with the same

* Biennial Address, American Jewish Congress. Friday, April 13, 1956.

vividness and intensity the perils and evils to which any association between public institutions and religion can lead. The Jew's
own experience strengthens in him the conviction that the principle of separation of Church and State was not the result of expediency, a kind of practical means of avoiding the selection as
the official religion of one religious sect from among the many
that inhabit America. The Jew feels that the founding fathers of
America reached deep into human experience with governments
allied to religion as well as into their own profound sensitivity
and devotion to human freedom when they enunciated this principle. The wisdom of this collective insight which was born out
of their inspired commitment to liberty is proved not only by the
long history of the struggle for freedom in the past but likewise
by the situation in various parts of the world in our own time.

Second, the position of any self-conscious minority makes it
barometrically aware of conditions that affect the liberty of all
people. Even in a society as free as ours, the minority is at a point
in the social structure where it feels early the undesirable consequence for freedom which any proposal is likely to bring.

And third, the Jew, in the case of this specific problem, re-
acts with a particular sensitivity not shared by other faiths in our
land, even when they constitute minority groupings within the
larger frame of American life. For the Jew is the sole sizable
minority whose tradition lies outside that Christian pattern
within which about 97 percent of the American people live by
reason of identification, childhood training, and belief. Thus the
Jew in reacting to the issue under discussion helps enlarge for all
America the perspective in which this question is to be viewed.
In a country so overwhelmingly Christian, it would be natural for
many Americans to identify religion with Christianity. The Jew
invites America to look at the problem from that point of view
which recognizes a diversity greater than that which is included
within the Christian church.

As Americans and as Jews we oppose the introduction of
religion into public school instruction. We base our view upon
a number of fundamental propositions:

First, we believe that the basic American principle of the
separation of Church and State is integrally related to the whole
concept of modern democracy. Any compromise of this princi-

ple not only violates a legal tradition but also threatens that spirit which ensures religious freedom.

Second, our opposition bases itself also on a conception of religion which sees it serving its highest function and fulfilling its richest possibilities when it remains independent of entanglement with the mechanisms of government. There are areas where religion transcends politics. Religion must be free to speak out in behalf of moral values and goals which are sometimes ignored or subverted by governments serving no purpose beyond their own power. Religion must remain a free and disinterested critic of society. Political involvement, however slight, must ultimately curtail its freedom and callous its conscience. No aspect of life is in greater danger when allied to power than is religion. A study of history shows that the spirit of religion flowers best when it is disassociated from political machinery. Religions have paid for any political power they wielded with their spirituality. Union of Church and State leads not to the elevation of the political life to a higher moral level but rather to the degradation of religion to a low political estate.

Lord Bryce in his perceptive *The American Commonwealth* points out that the separation of Church and State has invigorated religion in America. "So far from suffering from the want of state support," he writes, "religion seems in the United States to stand all the firmer because standing alone, she is seen to stand by her own strength."

A close identification with government may give the Church apparent ascendency, but the deterioration of its religious sensitivity and loftiness is the almost inevitable consequence. Religion, when it has had governmental sanction and control of religious education, has not shown appreciable effectiveness in forming a more moral political life or a more spiritual citizenry. Religion functions best in the area of voluntary association and influence. The Dean of the School of Education of the University of Michigan wrote some time ago: "If I wished to undermine the importance of the church in American life, I would strongly support proposals for released time and other plans for relieving churches of their major task, which is the religious education of children and youth. It is because our churches ought to play a more significant role in American life that I oppose some of the plans which I feel menace their future."

Another characteristic of religion is too easily glossed over by those who believe that they could "contain" religious instruction, once initiated, within safe limits set up at the outset. Religion is related to some of the strongest feelings of man. It is motored by an inner dynamism which imparts to its convictions a unique emotional intensity. The universal ideals and concepts of religion are so integrally bound up with particularistic symbols, rites, and forms of expression that it is literally impossible to say where the common elements of any faith end and its sectarian components begin. Religion is meaning, evaluation, emotion, belief; and when these are suppressed or muted, it is not religion we are teaching.

It cannot be overemphasized that religion sanctifies not only ideas but also forms. Universal values are deep-dyed with the life-blood of specific associations and motivations of a particular religion. To the religionist it is not only the content but form as well which inspire loyalty and devotion. We weaken the strongest ties to a faith when we seek to liquidate its specific and characteristic manner of expressing its ideas. Indeed, we make the ideas themselves less potent to influence men. There is no great organized hostility to religion in this country. The danger to which it is exposed is that it tends to become shallow, diluted, and therefore powerless to govern the minds and actions of people. Its presence is respectfully acknowledged, its import consistently disregarded. To place religious instruction in a setting other than that of a specific faith is to rob it of its greatest strength. To hedge this instruction about with carefully designed restrictions is to attempt the impossible. Were it possible it could only result in a watered-down, wholly ineffectual faith.

Third, we are opposed to the introduction of religion into our public education because such a program would destroy the distinctive character of the public school as a unique instrument of education for citizenship in a democracy. The public school is the large unbarriered arena of education where children are trained in the common life they share with all people—a common life which takes them beyond the particularities of home, church, color, and class. If our public schools are "secular" it is in the sense not of being antireligious, but of being nonsectarian. The large common life we live as citizens of America must perforce be secular, lest it become denominational and sectarian. Engaging with fellow students of many different backgrounds in shared experiences implies religious values of no low order.

The qualities of citizenship in a free society, inculcated in public schools, involve religious values. Regard for the truth, the socializing of the individual child, the love of learning, the appreciation of beauty, the study of the complex nature of the world we live in and association with exemplary people who serve as teachers, all these have imbedded in them important religious values. Public schools, if they are to train for democratic living, cannot be neutral to moral standards and spiritual ideals. When public schools serve society well, they do impart religious values, though these are not related to a specific creed, a particular church or a definite ecclesiastic system. The "secularism" of our schools at their best does not spell irreligion. Public schools which directly teach religion must inescapably become enmeshed in sectarianism. They would then be rendered useless as the agency for the training of citizens who, united by a common identity, remain undivided by their individual differentiations.

And finally, in addition to our concern for the democratic principle of the separation of Church and State, for a religion that does not compromise its independence by involvement with the political machinery of government, and for the preservation of the public school as the great training ground for participation in our common life, another consideration adds force to our opposition to religious instruction entering our system of public education. In a democracy the narrowing of the area of voluntary association and activity on the part of its citizens tends to weaken the free character of the society as a whole. The basic theory of a democratic system is that the citizen leads an essential part of his life beyond the reaches of governmental control and power. The Bill of Rights assures the inviolability of provinces of expression and activity from political coercion or interference. The individual's life extends beyond that of the citizen. This is the chief distinction between a free society and the totalitarianisms of the right or left. The dictator claims as subject the whole man. A democracy recognizes that it does not hold sway over the total personality. The areas of conscience, faith, and thought belong to the individual.

Religion should function solely in the area of voluntary affirmation and choice. To be sure, we believe that a religious faith is indispensable to a complete and wholesome outlook upon life. The state, however, should not be permitted to assume responsibility for the whole man else the citizen, like the lean kine of Pharaoh, would absorb the entire personality of the individual. Placing religion within the sphere of governmental control means to subject what should be the voluntary and free choice of the individual and the obligation of the group or church he freely selects to the jurisdiction of the state. This reduction of the area of people's nonpolitical life as exemplified by church and home whittles away at the liberties of men.

Our views born of reflection and devotion to democracy as well as of the particular sensitivities which our history and minority position stimulate in us are weighty and significant. In presenting them we are not motivated only by concern lest the faith of a minority group be weakened but also by a desire to help America remain true to the faith embodied in its democratic heritage.

RELIGION IN A FREE SOCIETY

DEMOCRACY CHALLENGES THE RELIGIONS of the land to live with one another in a relationship neither of inferiority nor superiority, domination or subordination—but of parity. To be sure, the adherent of one faith does not, perhaps cannot, believe that all faiths are of equal truth, value, and sublimity. To believe that makes one's commitment to a particular religion a meaningless matter of whim rather than a decision involving one's destiny. Each religion believes that it is in possession of something distinctive, unduplicated—else its persistence is shorn of significance. As a Jew, I want to feel and do feel that the presence of my tradition on the American scene does not simply add to its variety or increase its diversity—but enriches the content and substance of American life. I believe that my creed has a deeper insight into cosmic realities and possesses a more authentic interpretation of them than do other creeds.

Yet there need be no conflict between such faith and the conviction that the disciples of other spiritual traditions are equal before God and have the right to enjoy the assurance that theirs too are blessed with a superior outlook and a doctrine closer to the truth. The interactions of people of differing backgrounds and beliefs must, in a free order, rest on equality. We need not revise our creeds. We must, however, in the area of our common life and the mutuality we share with others, emphasize with greater intensity than ever before the universal elements in our own faith and raise on the highest pinnacle of our affirmations the sense of human community which flows from a belief in One God. We must learn to see, as we have not done during the greater part of our history, difference not as rejection or repudiation or assault on our church—but as a valuable and necessary expression of the quality of diversity and multiple commitments which have been built into the very cornerstone of our American way of life. This is no abdication of our own faith. Indeed, it calls for greater conviction that our faith possesses vitality and sturdiness which need not cause it to tremble before every wind of differing doctrine. Diversity makes it possible to recognize and uphold more clearly the universalism of our own tradition. In leading to profound self-examination it should banish smugness and make recourse to complacency less likely.

This diversity can lead to another type of fulfillment, namely, the recognition that all religions have a common task of combating the corrosions of an amoral, materialistic, success-centered, power-mad world. The religions of democracy have likewise the supremely significant function of maintaining vital and alert those spiritual qualities, ethical sensitivities, and moral disciplines without which the forms of democracy may fall of their own inert weight. Democracy functions best when it is composed of individuals, not merely of citizens. It is in totalitarian societies that the individual contracts into the citizen and is permitted no province of expression and aspiration outside of loyalty and subservience to the state. The extragovernmental, voluntary spheres of life in a free land must be kept free and open. There are areas in a child's life which should always remain beyond the reach of the mechanisms of government and the state. Many church and synagogue leaders are equally concerned about the religious illiteracy of American youth and the adult as well—an illiteracy that is truly interfaith and transdenominational in scope. The responsibility resides with the religious community. Religion is the most important and crucial force functioning in the voluntary areas of American life through instruction, persuasion, and example.

And religions have in common the monumental obligation of serving as the moral conscience of the country. The great social and economic problems we face are deeply grounded in moral issues. Unpartisan, uninvolved in the machinery of government, speaking out of a large perspective and endowed with a tradition of love and compassion, religion can uphold the social goals to which we must direct our political and economic policies. It can and should foster uneasiness in the American people about the unfinished business of our democratic life—bigotry, segregation, political corruption, foreign policy, and international understanding.

Religion has no technical competence in the fields of politics, economy, and social need. But it does possess the qualities without which no adequate solution of the problem in these areas of our national life can ever be achieved, namely, large humane goals and a passion for justice and righteousness. There are still social obstacles that prevent men from seeing God. There is the danger of machine the instrument becoming machine the ruler. There is still the divisiveness which denies God as Father because it repudiates man as brother. There is the parochial partisanship and denominational exclusiveness which keeps us from seeing the whole man and all of mankind. There are still children deprived of the sunlight of love, the lamp of learning, the shelter of security. The thunder of greed and avarice, the race for gain and fame, the din of the conforming multitude threaten to drown out the still small voice.

Here is a task for religion, as formidable and as basic as it has ever faced. It must transcend its institutionalism by its universalism; its exclusiveness by its prophetic vision; its self-interest by its outgoing love of all men. Our society under the aspect of the Eternal must bring to bear upon the tormenting problems of our age religion's mellow wisdom, its inspired ideals, its sensitive standards—its faith in God, in life, in man.

May religion—all religion—be blessed with the generosity of spirit and the nobility of mind to fulfill the opportunities and to meet the obligations that beckon in a democracy.

MAN AND MAN

Underlying Rabbi Adler's concerns as an American and a Jew was a fundamental faith in the universal humanness of man. "A religion that starts with God but does not end with man has lost its way," he wrote in one of his "May I Have a Word with You" columns—not included here. For man is "little lower than the angels," the child of God and therefore of "highborn" stock.

This love of his fellowmen made of Rabbi Adler a great believer in "person-to-person" relationships. He always found time, even when his schedule was beyond stretching, at least to shake a hand, exchange a word of welcome or greeting. His curiosity was insatiable: faces fascinated him, and he found parables of life in every fresh encounter. "There is no human being who cannot teach us something," he used to say. "The person who sits next to us on the bus is filled with more mystery than all of Africa and possesses more depths than the deepest ocean."

In his view, man's prime duty is to love his neighbor. Since we cannot love another without first loving ourselves, this implies a clear recognition of our own worth and potential as well as that of our neighbor.

Despite his faith in humanity, Rabbi Adler was well aware of man's weakness and his propensity for evil. "Man's corruption is real and basic," he was wont to say. "He's a bundle of appetites, drives, ego-centeredness." Yet, despite all the evidence of human frailty with which his daily rounds confronted him, Rabbi Adler's belief in man's potential for self-improvement never faltered. Nonconformity, dissatisfaction with the status quo, criticism—these he saw as useful tools in man's striving toward a life of worth and dignity.

L. E.

5 • On Being American

REDISCOVERING AMERICA *

> "Thy rowers have brought thee
> Into great waters"
> (Ezekiel 27:26)

THE FACT THAT WE are at one of the great crossroads in history is writ large upon the horizon of our contemporary life. Our day confronts us with as direct and unmistakable a challenge as ever faced any previous age. If our ears were attuned to the momentous character of the era through which we are passing, we would hear an echo of the familiar Scriptural words: "See I have set before thee, this day, life and good, and death and evil." The alternatives before us are clear, stark, unavoidable. Truly destiny has brought us into great waters.

A battered and broken world alive with stalking ghosts of suspicion, hatred, and insecurity is the fearful heritage which the second global war in history has left us. The economies of many lands are in a state of collapse while their political life is a vast arena of hostile contending forces and movements. In the very heart of Europe, the mother continent of modern history, there is a great void which conflicting ideologies are seeking to invade. Needed is a quality of understanding and wisdom commensurate with the immense problems by which we are beset. We have been brought into great waters.

Our ingenuity in communication and rapid travel has brought the ends of the world together. Our amazing mobility makes of all the earth a small, compact, and intimate neighborhood. The lives of all men touch one another and unavoidably impinge one upon the other. Can we translate this physical proximity into a sense of social togetherness? Can we build our inescapable compactness into a world community? Have we the stature to reckon

---

*Radio address, Little Church of the Air. February 22, 1948.

72

the common weal as our personal concern? For we have been brought into great waters.

We are possessed in our day of a power that was inconceivable a few short years ago. A new dimension of destructive potentiality has been introduced into human society. Will our extension of power be matched by a deepening of our wisdom as to the use to which it shall be put? Or will our fate be contained in the words: "In the beginning God created, in the end man destroyed"? To survive in a world that has found the source of atomic energy it is necessary that the atomic bombs demolish more than the two doom-haunted cities, Nagasaki and Hiroshima. Our new power must demolish smugness, parochialism, racial superiority and exclusiveness, and the mad chaotic race by nations for dominion and markets. We have indeed been brought into great waters.

In the fundamental and difficult decisions that will have to be made, America is destined to play a significant if not prime role. Out of our unique economic strength, political prestige, resources, and the fact that we have emerged least impaired and depleted from the war's crucible flow unique and special responsibilities. But this day as our thoughts turn to George Washington, who was the father of our country and the representative of some of its noblest traditions, a hope piously and irresistibly rises within us. We believe that it is not primarily the external and accidental circumstances of wealth and strength that endow us with our heroic opportunity. It is rather the quality of the American dream and the essence of the American experiment that furnish us with the most significant wherewithal to meet the challenge, to undertake the task.

America, you have been brought into great waters. Only once in several centuries is a nation singled out by history to serve as a decisive factor in lifting all mankind to a new level of understanding, of policy, of act. When a nation finds itself in so severely challenging and critical a position it cannot improvise. A crisis does not create new powers. It stimulates us to evoke the deepest potencies of our latent strength. We live in a new Columbian age. It is ours to reach down into the profoundest sources of our common life and tradition to find the guidance and determination we need. We must rediscover that which is truest and best in the American dream and thus bring to the surface that which is truest and best in ourselves.

We must find again that fine sense of inclusiveness touching people of varying origins and beliefs which is at the heart of the American way of life. That inclusiveness is vividly dramatized by the presence of a rabbi on this Little Church of the Air sponsored by the Detroit Council of Churches. This American outlook grows out of the historic repudiation by our founding fathers of the old world which they fled, with its castes, conflicts, stratification, ghettos, and cruel boundaries between men. We believe in a society in which men can move vertically from level to level freely and in accordance with their ability and horizontally mingle unrestrainedly with their fellow citizens.

The American outlook is also the product of an innate generosity and hospitality toward men of different backgrounds in place of the fear and suspicion which for too long have marked group relations. We seek to prove by our American life the startling thesis that differences of religion and opinion need not be focal points of contention and struggle. They can serve as enriching stimuli to more significant living. Emerson, the American philosopher, once said, "It is the 'not-me' in my friend that charms me." Washington himself, in a letter to the Hebrew Congregation in Newport, Rhode Island, written in 1790, stated:

> The citizens of the United States of America have a right to applaud themselves for having given to mankind examples of an enlarged and liberal policy, a policy worthy of imitation. All possess alike liberty of conscience and immunities of citizenship. It is now no more that toleration is spoken of, as if it was by the indulgence of one class of people, that another enjoyed the exercise of their inherent, natural rights. For happily the Government of the United States, which gives to bigotry no sanction, to persecution no assistance, requires only that they who live under its protection demean themselves as good citizens in giving it on all occasions their effectual support.

That deep-delved characteristic of the American spirit shining forth from our land could bring light to a world lost in the dark.

And we must rediscover that profound sense of the dignity

of every individual that informs the best in American thought and tradition. The individual man is neither serf nor slave nor beast. He is endowed by his Creator with inalienable rights. The common man is the ultimate source of the state's power. His welfare should be its paramount responsibility. Jefferson wrote to an opponent, "You love the people as infants whom you are afraid to trust without nurses; and I, as adults whom I freely leave to self-government." God created man and conferred upon him a cosmic dignity. Society betrays its trust when it denies any man the full measure of a comparable social dignity which entitles him to opportunity, liberty, and equality. Will one world of peace and justice ever be fashioned that does not have a high conception of the individual as its very cornerstone?

The American dream is penetrated by a moral passion and religious conscience. The historic documents—the Declaration of Independence, the addresses of Washington, the Gettysburg Address or any of the immortal utterances of great Americans—are all motivated by more than a political philosophy or an economic program. They are rooted in the soil of a moral outlook. They spring from a deep ethical sensitivity. They are alive with the quality of a pure religious attitude toward life and man. We betray that heritage when we become the slaves of coarse materialism or gear our policy to political expediency.

Our political life must be guided by moral standards. Only as we sensitize ourselves to ethical and religious values will we attain the wisdom with which we can heal and enrich mankind.

We must rediscover the true America. A new frontier of global service beckons. May the historian of the future writing of our day not be compelled to record that ours was a lofty opportunity but a mean aspiration; a great challenge but a feeble response.

The smallest book in Scripture is that of Obadiah. It contains but one chapter. That lone chapter expresses a hope and prayer that speak to us across the centuries with miraculous aptness. The prophet hopes that his generation may possess its inheritance. The American dream is rich in the insight and wisdom that must become our own. May we, the Americans of our day, possess our inheritance and make it the possession of all mankind.

NEW CITIZENS*

As I SAT IN this court listening to the oath administered to you,
an incident out of my own childhood rose before me with remarkable clarity and vividness. The incident happened many
years ago. I was eight or nine years old. That particular weekday
morning I awoke to find an air of festivity in our home. My
father was dressed in his formal Sabbath clothes. Solemnly he
bade us farewell and left. Burning with curiosity I asked Mother
where Father was going and what was the special significance
of the day.

Mother replied, "Father will soon return. I prefer that he
answer your questions himself."

Several hours later Father came home. An unusual expression of serenity illumined his face. He seemed to walk with
greater vitality. His stooped shoulders had miraculously straight-
ened.

We surrounded Father, waiting respectfully for him to
speak. Slowly and with great emotion he said, "Children, I first
heard of America when I was about your age. I was living in a
small, remote village far across the sea. America was a word I
heard, its meaning or even location I did not know. One day a
visitor came and I listened with fascination to the stories he told
of the New World. I found a little book that told of the life of
Abraham Lincoln. I listened eagerly as my parents read letters
from fortunate relatives who had made their way to the land
of freedom. I dreamed of America where all are free, where
there are no Siberias, no pogroms, no persecution.

"This morning, dear children, I was sworn in as a citizen.
I feel as if I have finally come home. I no longer feel like an
outsider, an eternal alien, a stranger. I am part of the great
fraternity of freedom of which I have dreamed these many years.

"Here freedom is the heritage of all, not the select few.
Here all are equal, and no race or church or group is regarded as
ruler over others.

"Today we are citizens. We are now part of this land, woven

*Address delivered in the Federal Court when 105 new Americans were
sworn in as citizens, October, 1956.

into its fabric, bone of its bone and flesh of its flesh. Though we came here only a few years ago, we can sing with all Americans, 'land where my fathers died,' for in a mystic sense we are the spiritual offspring and descendants of Thomas Jefferson, George Washington, Franklin, Adams—of all who were the founders of America."

Following these words of my father, we read together a chapter of the Bible and chanted a psalm of the Hallel, which is the prayer of thanksgiving and praise recited in synagogues on the most festive occasions. Father then gave us his first blessing as a citizen.

It is in this same spirit of reverence and gratitude that I speak these words of welcome.

I know that you will bear the great gift of citizenship with pride and dignity. I know that you will recognize that, as is true of all great gifts—of love, faith, talent, indeed of life itself—responsibility is involved in your acceptance of it. You will, I am certain, live and act and think as free men, determined to preserve the great gift not alone for yourselves, but also for your neighbors and for generations yet to come. You will resist with true American courage every encroachment upon the liberty of men, and will oppose every movement that seeks to weaken or destroy our inalienable rights as children of God and as citizens of America.

May you so live and act that those who know you will think of our country not as the mightiest nation—that is not important —but as the freest; not as the wealthiest—that is not important— but as the most humane and generous; not as the leader of the world—that is not important—but as the servant of humanity and the steward of liberty for all men.

LABOR DAY

THE HOLIDAYS OF A group reflect its insights, evaluations, and yearnings. Labor Day, therefore, represents an important recognition on the part of the American people, and merits greater devotion than it has received. Unfortunately the time of the year when it occurs works against it. Coming at the end of the summer, it stimulates a last convulsive effort on the part of millions to squeeze from their vacation one more experience, adventure, or thrill. The roads are choked with millions of automobiles. Experts have already estimated the number of traffic casualties which will be exacted by this last fling of the summer. I congratulate you on being at services on this Sabbath before Labor Day. There is no safer place in the world.

Labor, toil, work are not be regarded as unworthy; this is the first word Labor Day speaks. For the Jew, Labor Day merges into an amazing harmony insights of both American and Jewish culture. No tradition has more consistently lauded the dignity of labor. The worship of the High Priest on Yom Kippur and the honest toil of a manual worker are designated in the Hebrew by the same word, *avodah*. Blessing, say the Rabbis, cannot be received either as a gift or inheritance. It comes to us most surely through the labor of our hands.

"Love the work," says Perek, using the same verb that is applied to our relation with God, "and thou shalt love the Lord thy God." He who sustains himself by the work of his hands is preferable to a devout man. Should a man say, "work is beneath me, I come from a fine family which regards labor as degrading," to him is the rebuke to be given, "fool, before thou wast born, work was instituted. God labored to create the world, as it is written 'and He rested from all the work which He had made.'"

Being a shepherd, the Rabbis point out, was not regarded as genteel work. Yet David exclaims, "The Lord is my shepherd." If Jews sometimes forgot this exaltation of work, there was always their tradition to guide and correct them.

In addition to stressing the dignity and worth of labor, Labor Day dramatizes the human needs and rights of the laborer. We tend to think of labor in the mass instead of as a group of human beings with sensibilities, affections, and frustrations. From the days of Aristotle, who called a slave an "animated tool," to my own childhood when shops advertised for "100 hands wanted," the dignity of the worker has been ignored. One felt that if employers could have engaged detached hands and feet to work on their machines they would have wished the rest of the worker to remain home. The mind, the heart, and the divine image of the "help" too often remained invisible to the "boss." The treatment of workers in the past is a story of grim exploitation, of lash, oppression, and cruelty. We fail to understand some of the things that are happening in our time if we forget how the white Western world treated its colored laborers in the colonies which its empires built in Asia and Africa. Indeed, if human history is to be pictured as being a day in duration, it is only in the last few seconds that the worker has been recognized as a human being.

To exploit labor is to mock both our religious teachings and our democratic affirmations. The test of a society is not the luxuries its privileged class enjoys but the securities and opportunities it extends to its masses. No society is higher than the level of its most neglected and humble group. The freedom of a society is imperiled when large multitudes of men are frustrated and insecure and bear the scars of wrong and injustice. The economy of a society based on mass production will inevitably collapse if masses of people, because of inadequate earnings, are deprived of the comforts and products which are turned out. Political freedom is hollow unless accompanied by economic security and dignity.

Labor is the largest group in our society. Its welfare will, in large measure, determine the state of health of the entire country. Management must appreciate the rights of labor in terms of our democratic ideals of human right and dignity, in terms of the part they play in building up and maintaining the economy of the land. America is people, and the largest proportion of people are workers. What is good for the country is that which advances both labor and industry.

Moreover, we live in an interrelated society. No group ought to be isolationist. No group can strengthen itself by weakening the rest. The welfare of labor depends on the welfare of America and the health of its economic life. A wise labor leader will ask not only "does this raise the wages of my union?" but "does this help America? Does this strengthen our economy generally? Does this add to our productive capacity as well as to the better distribution of the goods we produce?"

Labor too must realize its place in the vanguard of those

who fight for democracy. Only there can it come into its own.
Any type of totalitarianism is a threat. Hitler attacked Jews and
destroyed labor unions. Thus it has always been. The oppression
of minorities has gone hand in hand with restrictions of labor.
The union, too, must be subject to democratic rule and procedure. For a union to disregard democracy in its own affairs
is to breed contempt for democracy generally and thus to
weaken the free society in which labor alone can prosper. Labor
cannot afford to disassociate itself from the consumer, the pro-
ducer, the public. It must realize how integrally interlinked it is
with all of these.

These then are the emphases Labor Day brings to our attention: (1) the dignity of work; (2) the rights of labor; and
(3) the need of labor to see itself as part of the entire fabric of
society.

May we be alert to these insights and incorporate them in
our economy and thus strengthen our common life and our
freedom.

THE POLLING BOOTH—DEMOCRACY'S SANCTUARY

THE DETERMINATION OF THE political party and the particular
candidate to favor with our vote on Election Day is the sovereign
obligation and nontransferable duty of the citizen. It should be
his uncoerced, personal decision. There are, however, a number
of moral considerations which might well guide and control him
in exercising his franchise.

First is the imperative to vote out of a sense of earnestness.
The right itself was relatively late in coming; hence it is only in
comparatively recent times that it has become recognized as one
of the human freedoms men should enjoy. Indeed, in many parts
of the world, it has not yet been won, and decisions are made
for the people rather than by them. In an age when freedom is
under fire, for a citizen of our land not to practice this hard-won
right or to vote carelessly is to trifle with a sacred possession and
to give aid to the forces opposing our free way of life.

Second, the right to vote implies the responsibility to under-stand the issues and to know as much as can be learned about the contending parties and candidates. Through the inevitable bally-hoo and verbal extravaganzas that characterize our political cam-paigns, there comes to the discerning voter fragments of valid claims, glimpses of substantial charges, and suggestions of reliable analysis. These can be pieced together and made into the basis for intelligent choice.

Third, while the citizen has every right to identify himself with the political party of his preference, he should nevertheless attempt to transcend narrow partisanship. His decision should be made in terms of national interest. These times are too crucial for slavish, unreflective voting by habit, by label, or by rote. Parties are large massive organizations and do not always move rapidly enough to accord with changing circumstances and new needs. They must not be permitted to take the support of any segment of the population for granted or rely too much on the traditional loyalties of their sworn adherents. Only as enough citizens feel free to make their own choices are the parties stimu-lated to gear their platforms to the real problems of the day and present only such candidates as are qualified to interpret and implement their policies. An uncommitted electorate sparks the campaign with vitality and keeps the political parties on their toes.

Last, the voter should cast his ballot out of the dual aware-ness that we live in One World and that the mantle of world leadership has fallen upon America. The citizen should ask him-self: "Does my vote strengthen and fortify the solidarity and unity of mankind? Does it advance the cause of global law and peace? Does the candidate of my choice represent the kind of leadership which will aid America in fulfilling its responsibility and opportunity in international affairs?"

If a sufficient number of citizens permit themselves to be influenced by the above considerations, our campaigns will be more than sports contests and political boxing matches. They will become important instruments of our own political education and growth and will simultaneously contribute to world order and stability.

JOHN FITZGERALD KENNEDY

WHEN ONE OF THE great sages of the Talmud died, the colleague who eulogized him said: "This day is as mournful for our people as a day when the sun sets at noon." The sun set at noon for the entire world at the moment when a bullet put an end to the life of John Fitzgerald Kennedy. If he were only one of many young men, favored by fortune, superbly endowed, who was so brutally snatched, we would have grieved for the unfulfilled hopes and dreams that died with him. But John Kennedy was not one of many. He was one: one chosen by our people, vested with authority and bearing the hopes and dreams which millions of individuals entrusted to him. Our vocabulary does not yield words to suggest the enormity of the tragedy or the intensity of our shock.

The bullet was aimed at one man. Its target, however, was the human, civilized, free order under which we live. Its target was the discipline, the mutuality, and the law which through centuries of struggle and sacrifice man has built into his collective life. The demented mind that pulled the trigger represents an upsurge of the primitivism that threatens civilization, and betrays the persistence of pockets of feeling and attitude in our land not yet redeemed by American ideals and values.

Great as is our grief, we must retain an alert awareness that there are wild and savage areas in our national life. Our bereavement must not shield us from the recognition of our shared guilt. What bursts forth explosively in the case of the extremist exists in a quiescent and submerged form in the normal. What is a spot in us becomes a clot in the fanatic. When we, the respectable and law-abiding, defame another group, when we speak bigoted words, when we scorn our neighbor because of his skin, we reenforce a process which ends in someone's raising a club, shooting a gun, or burning a church or synagogue. When we give respectability to segregation, it means that a twilight mind will burn a cross on a lawn. Even as we mourn, let us be penitent.

We are diminished this day as men, as religious believers, as Americans. All who cherish freedom, who uphold the equality and dignity of all human beings and hope for world peace, are personal mourners, poignantly and intimately bereaved by the death of John F. Kennedy. The violent man who committed this crime was obsessed with hate for these purposes and slew the man who served as their symbol.

We shall not answer violence with violence, raise fist against fist or wield club against club. But we shall so reenforce our resolve, firm our determination, steel our will, that even the men of darkness and violence will recognize that their force and brutality cannot prevail against our inflexible and invincible purpose to realize fully the American promise and hope. We shall not despair nor exhaust ourselves in grief. We will walk forward, keeping bright the memory of John Fitzgerald Kennedy and striving to be worthy of it.

6 • On Being a Jew

WHAT IS A JEW?

NO OTHER GROUP IS so addicted to asking questions as are Jews. Often indeed they reply to questions with further questions. Thus when asked, "How do you feel?" a Jew is likely to answer, "How should I feel?" The most elaborate ritual of the Jewish religious year, the long Passover ceremony, is designed to stimulate the young to ask questions. Similarly, the entire Talmud, that great compendium of Jewish law and lore, opens with a question.

One of the most persistent questions is: "What is a Jew?" It recurs almost as an automatic reflex, particularly on solemn occasions. It is dealt with in sermons and lectures, at forums, at ideological conferences, and at "dialogues" between American and Israeli Jews. It is implicit and sometimes explicit in the writings of Malmud, Bellow, Roth, and Kops.

Intellectual and artistic Jews continue to confront themselves with this query, variously in tones of anguish, resentment, and scorn. Why do they keep asking? Other groups do not make a problem of their identity. Americans and Englishmen seem untroubled about their background and role in the world. They sense that they are an integral part of a corporate personality and that's that.

But it is different with the Jews. Their quest is sometimes regarded as a manifestation of a neuroticism that so often grips minorities that have been under attack. Or it is interpreted as a morbid, introspective inability to enter into completely wholesome relations with self, with others, and with life. The German-Jewish novelist Jakob Wassermann once said that when a Jew doesn't have worries, he invents them.

The Western Jew finds himself rooted in a civilization

* Copyright © 1963, by Harper's Magazine, Inc. Adapted from the article that appeared in the January, 1964, issue of *Harper's Magazine*.

which has fostered and, in many subtle, subterranean ways, still preserves an image of him as somewhat alien. The modern Jew may find fulfillment in the academic community. He may enjoy status, security and success in a profession, as an industrialist, a worker, a teacher, or public official. Although he seems undistinguishable from his non-Jewish colleagues he "receives"—so to speak—messages from his collective past. The happy present may have driven it underground, but it has not been obliterated. He is of the minority and forever bound to it. In fact, the psychic uneasiness of a minority grows rather than diminishes as its integration in the majority culture proceeds.

A minority is a breach in the wall of homogeneity, an "outsider," a deviant. The Western world is Christian, the Jew is not. Now he may not be a fervent follower of his tradition; he may even doubt its value or validity. But his birth has stamped him a Jew. Overt and palpable exclusions strengthen his sense of difference; so too do the subtle diminutions of full acceptance he is bound to encounter. Hence he is driven to ask: "What is this thing called Jewishness which makes the difference?"

Should he go to his own tradition he will not find a direct answer. Judaism has never developed an official statement as to what one must believe to be accounted a Jew. There is no Jewish equivalent of the Nicene Creed honored by Catholics, the Apostles' Creed of the Episcopalians, the Westminster Confession of the Presbyterians, or the Augsburg Confession of the Lutherans. The Jew is not taught any catechism and is not bound by an ironclad formula. The Talmud, whose interpretations, applications, and enlargements have shaped Jewish deeds and practices even more than the Bible, records the clashing views of differing schools and scholars, preserving minority opinions along with the binding majority dicta. Even the thirteen articles of faith drawn up by Maimonides in the twelfth century, which are still printed in traditional prayer books, have not gained universal acceptance.

To be sure, profound affirmations are implicit in the tradition. But these have never been formalized as an authoritative creed. It is only a slight exaggeration to say that in Judaism the deed is the reflection of one's theology. "Believe and be saved" is the Christian approach; "Do and you will believe," the Jewish.

Being the culture of a community rather than the faith of a church, Judaism never found it necessary to make uniformity of belief its central cohesion. So the modern Jew cannot easily extract a precise answer from his tradition. He must continue to live with the riddle.

The modern Jew thinks of himself as an American, a doctor, a husband, a businessman, a citizen, a father—like other Americans. Then he discovers a puzzlement in the eyes of his neighbors—and the question mark quickly moves into his own mind. So he comes home and asks: "Who after all am I?"

Thoughtfully he combs his native tongue for a descriptive term. Is he a member of a "race"? He knows enough of anthropology to realize that Jews are not a "race." Does he belong to a Jewish nation? His American loyalty and pride both rise in anger. His nationality is American, indivisibly and unqualifiedly. His political allegiance is to America alone.

An eminent Jewish thinker* tells him that Judaism is a civilization. But this definition is not satisfying either. It sounds as if he were somehow abstracted from the American scene, forming a complete civilization of his own. One does not collect civilizations like stamps or period furniture. The word "civilization" suggests both a completeness and an apartness which throws a shadow upon his full integration with America. He thinks of a hundred elements in his life as an American which he cherishes—citizenship, music, theatre, business, sports, science, education. Jewishness certainly does not contain *all* that is necessary for the complete life of the group and its members. So he rejects the "civilization" concept.

Then along come the sociologists, Jewish and non-Jewish, and tell him that he belongs to a subculture. The term irritates him. Now it is his Jewish pride that rebels. Subculture somehow suggests that, after an experience of three thousand years or more, the Jewish group is on the threshold of becoming a culture. Without going deeply into the sociologists' use of the term, he rejects it out of hand as incompatible with his Jewish dignity.

Finally, he comes to the definition that has been proclaimed with increasing frequency of late. He is told that as a Jew he is

---

*Mordecai M. Kaplan.

an adherent of the Jewish religion. He thinks of the religious denominationalism which he sees all about him. Does Judaism really exhaust itself in a church and the activities that center about it? To be sure, Judaism involves religion. Indeed, religion may be at the very heart of it. But is Judaism only a religion? He does not ask this question disparagingly. He thinks of his son at college who just wrote him at great length about his current agnostic position. He remembers one of the noblest Jewish humanitarians he ever met who quietly remarked that he had not been in a synagogue for a half-century. He thinks of Freud, Brandeis, Einstein, who did not embrace religion in their world view and yet were among the outstanding Jews of the century. Is a definition which does not include such Jews adequate?

So he feels frustrated. He still asks: "What am I?" And perhaps in the process he has provided the best answer possible at present: "A Jew is a person who is always asking 'What am I?' " Certainly this definition is as authentic and comprehensive as any other.

I CELEBRATE MY JEWISHNESS

I HEREBY CELEBRATE THE opportunities, privileges, and joys which Jewishness affords its adherents. Being born a Jew, I have not been set in the firm and unyielding mold of the fixed position of an arbitrary creed. Though the world may on occasion seek to hem me in, I enjoy in my own tradition a freedom and latitude which I greatly relish.

My birth offers me no patrimony of unruffled peace and stability. On the contrary, I must achieve for myself what a majority grants almost automatically to its members—self-assurance and status. This I can do only by a personal quest for deeper sources within myself and within the tradition. I must seek out my brethren for I cannot know them by external means of nationality, geographic proximity or racial characteristics. My identification with them stems from a long, shared group history, partnership in a destiny, common challenges and concerns. The cohesions that join us are deeper than common language, land, or pigmentation.

The discomforts which the world imposes are more than offset by the liberating knowledge that in the struggle for my equality I am involved in a fight for the equality of all men. Every step I advance toward freedom I remove a roadblock from the path of all oppressed minorities. My attempts to secure my position in society are not mere selfish strivings on my part, but are related to the large, bold, ongoing endeavor to build a free world for a free humanity.

Though society is sometimes determined to isolate me, my Jewishness takes me out in the broad places where mankind dwells. The dilemmas which inhere in human life and which all sensitive men share—dilemmas arising out of rationality, loneliness, the search for fulfillment, ambivalence, the choice of values to live by—are in my case refined and deepened as I seek to resolve them in the specific frame of my existential situation as a Jew.

My Jewishness does not permit me to skate through life on glossy surfaces. Wherever life or my tradition touch me I sense depths. History lies under my feet as I walk. I celebrate a Sabbath, and am related to the world's creation; I mark a Passover, and I am reenacting a historic saga; I recite a benediction, and a long procession of pious forebears speak through my lips; I chant a song, and the melody of ages weaves itself into my voice. I stand on the terra firma of millennia. I open my mouth to speak in Hebrew, and poets, statesmen, and orators give resonance to the words I utter. The distant thunder of prophetic exhortation, the sweet songs of psalmists yearning for God, the mellow wisdom of sages building ladders that reach to heaven inform my speech and enrich it with overtones that are intimations of eternity.

In a day of change my Jewishness blesses me with a stability that comes from rootedness in time and history. It gives me the freedom to find my place uncoerced in the large expanse of a great tradition which does not seek to drive me into a cell of dogmatic imprisonment. It enables me to join my efforts for justice with the universal struggle for human rights for all, and

it admits me into a fellowship forged out of the vital links of
common backgrounds, joint hopes, mutual concerns, and reciprocal attachments. Greatly dowered, I, the Jew, respond to the
humanizing obligation to make myself worthy of my privileges.

PRAYER FOR LIFE

MANY CENTURIES AGO THE Jew recognized the truth that the goods
of life reside within rather than outside of man. Our prayers for
life on Yom Kippur are a petition for more than the raw material
of vitality or length of days. It is man who must translate his
days and years into meaningful living. Life begins in the mind
of man.

The Jew's attitude to life enabled him to outlive his oppressors and to nullify all the instruments of persecution and
strategies of destruction marshaled against him. The history of
Israel is the supreme dramatization of the power of human determination and will over external circumstance.

The Jew survived because, paradoxically, survival was not
his chief goal. He fought not merely against disappearance and
death, but for life—life allied to purpose. The Jew survived
because every generation in fervent and ringing tones reechoed
the resolve of the Psalmist: "I shall not die but live and declare
the works of the Lord." Israel did not seek to make of his history
a monument to endurance. He did wish, however, to turn it into
an altar to God. The Jew survived because he strove to live
significantly.

How has the Jew defined significant living? What elements
render life meaningful and vital? The history of the Jew is itself
an ethical document which suggests the answers given over the
centuries.

To live meant to learn. Torah was "the elixir of life," indispensable to survival, aspiring to become life. Living in a world
of shrines, altars, temples, empires, royal courts, and sceptered
power, the Jew could state: "Torah is greater than priesthood

or royalty." Outer pressures, the bitter struggle for existence,
were not permitted to divert the Jew from study. One of the
luminous memories of my childhood is the throng of peddlers,
small storekeepers, and shopworkers who, at the end of an
exhausting day, assembled for study in the synagogue of my
father.

During eras of darkness, when a cultural blackout prevailed,
the Biblical phrase could justly be applied to the Jew, "But all
the children of Israel had light in their dwellings." Study was not
an instrument of survival or a preparation for life, or as among
some sophisticates a distraction. Study was life. Daily our people
prays: "O favor us with knowledge, understanding, and discernment." The uppermost ambition parents cherished for their
children was that they be men of learning. Eminence was ascribed
in terms of knowledge. Knowledge was life: "he who increaseth
his knowledge, increaseth life."

When Jerusalem was destroyed and the Jewish people lost
its independence, Israel survived by building a modest center of
study at Jamnia. This quest for knowledge, this restless urge to
learn is still with us as an unspent force of the past. As Albert
Einstein once put it, "The pursuit of knowledge for its own sake,
an almost fanatical love of justice and the desire for personal
independence—these are the features of the Jewish tradition
which make me thank my stars that I belong to it."

*To live meant to feel, to respond with tenderness and com-
passion to the needs and anxieties of one's fellowmen.* The Jew
has understood that we come more fully to life as our outgoing
sympathy links us with others. The Dead Sea supports no life,
for it has no outlet. Thus it is with man. A confined, self-
enclosed spirit shrivels and inevitably dies. It would have been
tragic, though perhaps understandable, if in consequence of the
harshness and cruelty meted out to him, the Jew would have
answered with bitterness and vindictiveness. Instead, himself
the victim of force, the Jew exalted gentleness and loved mercy.
The heroes whom he glorified were men of learning and kindness.
Rabbi Akiba, the greatest of post-Biblical figures, found the cen-

tral doctrine of Jewish teaching in the simple phrase, "love thy neighbor as thyself."

The tradition of the Jew is suffused at every point with a profound and enduring love of man. The calloused and insensate, say the Rabbis, may be regarded as dead, even in their lifetime. The marks of the Jew, our tradition teaches, are compassion, modesty, and kind deeds. He whose heart does not record the travail of his neighbor, whose concern does not embrace the sorrows of others, who does not in a personal way bear the scars and hurts of all mankind—he does not live at all!

To live meant to believe. The Jew was possessed of an inquiring and challenging mind, and did not fear to submit universally accepted and inherited ideas to analysis. One thinks of the prophets rebelling against practices consecrated by usage, and of Job and Ecclesiastes challenging the conventional views of their time. And these have become enshrined in the Bible, the classic book of faith.

The skepticism of Israel, however, does not end with negation. He believed that justice and right were rooted in the nature of the universe and were not an excursion into fantasy. He believed that man was clothed with cosmic dignity, and as a child of God enjoyed irrevocable rights. Therefore the Jew never accepted the misfortune of the day as final, nor did he make of the mood of the moment a permanent philosophy. Because the Jew believed, he never descended as a people into the abyss of despair. He was able to resist pressures and temptations to defeatism and pessimism.

It was an upsurge of this classic Jewish faith that led Jews in the Warsaw Ghetto to sing in their darkest hour, "Say not that this is the end of the road." A familiar phrase was turned by these martyred heroes into a triumphant hymn, as they sang unto death, *"Ani Maamin, Ani Maamin,"* "I believe, I believe."

There are questions that baffle the mind. There are sorrows that pierce the heart. There are mysteries that challenge the stoutest and most intelligent spirits. The Jew believed. And he continued to live.

CREATIVE USES OF THE PAST*

MAN'S PRESENT IS THE upward thrust of all his yesterdays. In him
and through him course forces that had their origin in a period
beyond his capacity to isolate precisely or to delineate as to
character, reenforced and altered by all that has transpired since.
Manifold impacts of man's past unite and endow him with
capacities and attributes that give him ascendency over the other
creatures in nature.

But man does not live solely in the frame of the physical
world. From the milieu of history and culture which serves as
the matrix for his life as a member of the human family, he
derives his identity as a man. "Tradition is the only way we have
of knowing who we are," Mark Van Doren says. Culture and
civilization are man's human heritage, even as his physical and
creaturely traits are the product of his animal heredity. Language, art, religion, group customs, values, and memories extend
and enrich the environment into which man the creature is born
and in which he develops and matures into man the human.

Man therefore cannot be understood without considering
the two worlds which join to form the universe in which he
moves and has his essential being. The controversy as to which
is more decisive, nature or nurture, has long waged without
resolution. Judaism did not make the mistake, common to other
religions and philosophic systems, of minimizing the one or ignoring the other. The first vague sounds which the ears of the
infant absorb, the first sights which the tiny pupils of his eyes
bring into uncertain focus, the first tender caresses to which he
responds—these are part of his human inheritance. Their inter-
penetration of the roots out of which the child's personality will
subsequently flower can never thereafter be fully exorcised. The
child has begun to accumulate the past out of which his future,
as from a womb, will emerge.

Detachment from one's fellowmen, an ancient Jewish sage
taught, spells death (human not physical) for the individual.
"Associate or perish" is an inviolable law of human life. The

*Adapted from Introduction to *Jewish Heritage Reader*, Taplinger Pub-
lishing Company, Inc., N.Y., 1965.

association is not only on the horizontal plane of fellowship with one's contemporaries but includes also the vertical relatedness to the history and culture which shaped them. Without the ample legacy granted to man almost at birth, human life would with each new generation revert to its earliest and most primitive form. We are truly "the pensioners of the past." Were the human past not accessible to us, we would, to take only the matter of speech and therefore of thought, be reduced to little more than gurgles, roars, and bleatings—the only sounds we could develop in the short span of a single life.

Culture pours the accumulated strivings, experience, advances, creations of many lifetimes, extending over many centuries, into the life stream of the individual and group presently existing. In the capacity to conserve the accretions of past centuries and to communicate them to new generations, perhaps more than in any other single factor, is to be sought the human differential which sets man apart from and above all other known creatures.

No man can escape the past. The most modern avant-garde individual cannot dispense with it, and he continues to reveal in his own acts and views its presence and influence. Men have on occasion resented and renounced the past, and have sometimes made of their negation the dominant philosophy of their life. The very force and vehemence of their revolt betrayed the hold it had upon them, since only that which deeply enters and colors one's life can excite such intensity of rejection. But there are many who recline peacefully in the maternal arms of the past and suckle contentedly at its breast. Some absorb it without the awareness that every time they speak a word, read a line, shake hands with a neighbor or cast a vote, they are paying tribute to it.

History, however, does not always move in peaceful channels or pleasant paths. There are social, political, cultural upheavals, conflicts and revolutions in history comparable to the tidal floods, earthquakes, and volcanic eruptions in nature. Discontinuities appear on the landscape of human life that have their counterpart in the chasms and canyons of the earth. Yet even in such eventualities the past preserves its hold upon men. Only the upsurge of a wild barbarism in society would attempt to erase it, and then only to return to a more distant and primitive past.

In such periods of stress and disruption, man is forced to face the past consciously, to evaluate and select from it that which appears to be precious and relevant. Such a time is now upon us. Much of the uncertainty and confusion in contemporary life is a consequence of our unwillingness or inability to face our past with adequate wisdom and insight. Uncertain of our past, we are confused about our present and are thus alienated from ourselves. The fantastic rapidity of change in our society and its continuing acceleration make the very ground under us quake with frantic movement, appearing to dissolve all the stabilities upon which we formerly built our lives. There is left for some moderns no terra firma upon which to stand.

In the absence of a tradition modern man stands denuded before the immediate. Without a past he is the captive of each solitary moment or day or year. Uprooted he sways with every impulse and fugitive whim. His existence disintegrates into episodic and disparate clots, and his life is an improvised series of unrelated variations. He is uncertain and apprehensive because the pinpoint in time which he occupies is isolated and solitary. The eminent American critic Van Wyck Brooks has observed: "No one in this country has roots anywhere; we don't live in America, we board here; we are like spiders that move over the surface of the water." Of Franz Kafka, the writer who reveals modern man in all his nakedness and dark pathos, one critic has written, "he suffered the pangs of the absent God in his life."

Contemporary man is at sea because he has lost his sense of history as well as his relatedness to it. He tends to forget that while human history may seem to take a new turn, man never really starts over. In reacting against the encrustments, irrelevancies, and follies of the past, he turns his back upon its entirety and has thus cut himself off from a vital resource of strength, continuity, and wisdom.

Modern man can find a way toward wholeness by examining the abundant bequests of the past reverently but critically and with mature independence. He can suffuse his life with its echoes without losing his own voice in the process. It cannot be either-or, either the past or the present. It must be both in behalf of the future.

The necessity for creative confrontation with the past is

perhaps most evident in the case of the modern Jew. For him
centuries of history have been telescoped into a few decades.
The transition was abrupt, sharp, and not infrequently shattering.
Several millions of Jews alive today were born in a premodern,
pretechnological, prescientific and predemocratic era. In their
own life-span they have been hurtled across a chasm of time
which took their non-Jewish peers four hundred years or more
to negotiate. Where others could walk leisurely, the Jew was
compelled to leap instantaneously. One day he lived in the
medieval world, the next in the modern West.

In the face of such upheaval, casualties were inevitable. The
holocaust which engulfed him in apocalyptic darkness stirred
apprehension and anguish. From the depths questions arose
within him, doubts, denials, resistances. It was not easy to continue to believe in the teachings of the Jewish tradition that the
cosmic order rests on justice, that the Jew has a role in the
redemption of mankind, that every individual is invested with
high and inalienable dignity.

The rise of the State of Israel helped bolster his sagging
faith. The Jew as victim began to appear as the Jew the builder,
the fighter, the pioneer. Here was a place on the world map
called Israel, built by Jews, governed by Jews, regenerated by
Jews. "Jewishness" now meant a people, a national will, a language and literature, self-respect, a calendar, a geography, a
history, a faith, an ethic, memories, hopes, a vision of redemption.
Out of this "concreteness" might come once again a word meant
for all mankind. From it too there might radiate to Jews in other
lands influences to revitalize and stimulate the will to Jewish
knowledge and the Jewish way of life.

Other powerful forces have also been at work. Today, half
the Jews of the world live in the free world, in a society which,
with increasingly minor reservations, welcomes their integration
into its economy, culture, and civic life. As fascinating interests
and opportunities outside the Jewish community invite the Jew,
his relationship to his tradition is once more at stake. Living in
the heart of the open society, like his non-Jewish peers, he too
is the object of forces that act as dissolvents of tradition, blunt
the sense of history and continuity, and assault the distinctive
and the singular.

The Jew as an individual has won equality and freedom. What will now happen to the individual as Jew? The history of the Jew in the world is that of a marginal man. Will the history of the modern Jew be that of marginal tradition? Will the larger circumference of his naturalization into the modern world obscure the smaller circle of his Jewish affiliation?

Or will the modern Jew, remaining fully rooted in his particular tradition, bring into his broader life as a member of society the liberating perspective, the passion for study, the ethical sensitivities with which that tradition is so richly seeded? Will he know now how to integrate his membership in the larger society with a Jewish identification of meaningful depth and intensity? Will he learn how to blend his historic culture as a Jew with the new learning in philosophy, science, art, and with the prevailing forms, habits, and daily preoccupations? Will he be able to communicate the faith of his fathers with such devotion and understanding that it can serve as the faith of his children born under the new dispensation of freedom and integration?

One could hardly draw up a catalogue of more perplexing problems than those with which the contemporary informed and affirmative Jew is called upon to grapple, if not to resolve. The comment of André Malraux is profoundly pertinent: "A heritage is not transmitted, it must be conquered."

The creative artist drawing from Jewish springs of inspiration can, without losing his universality, gain in fervor, depth, and vitality. The thinker and scientist, incorporating into their thought a tradition in which reason, learning, and the adventurous quest for truth are prominent, need sacrifice neither intellectual integrity nor philosophic breadth. The professional, student, businessman, or worker can within the framework of his life in the modern world enrich and invigorate his "humanity" through a positive relationship with a traditional instinct with a universal vision, a faith in the meaning and worth of life, a high estimate of man, his dignity and potentiality.

What the prophet Obadiah counseled many centuries ago—"Let the house of Jacob possess its inheritance"—applies with equal pertinence to all men who would be creative users of the past.

ON THE "CHOSEN PEOPLE"*

THE CONCEPT OF THE Chosen People, or to speak of it in more
scholarly terms, "the Election of Israel," still intrigues and dis-
turbs us. The question of its meaning, validity, and even morality
continues to be raised in print as well as at forums and institutes.
Whatever the announced theme is and however unrelated, the
idea of the Chosen People is likely to be introduced, not infrequently with marked vehemence and passion.

In light of the new type of relationships which Jews in a
free society enjoy with adherents of other faiths, a notion that
invests the Jewish group with special supremacy is likely to be
an irritant to some Jews; an important movement (Reconstruc-
tionism) in contemporary Jewish life, for instance, has eliminated
from its rationale the idea of chosenness, though it does continue to speak of the "vocation" of the Jew. This concept has
also drawn the fire of non-Jews: George Bernard Shaw and
Arnold Toynbee, as well as a host of lesser lights, have condemned it as a manifestation of national arrogance and chauvin-
ism. And it has been attacked as an expresion of ingrown and
persistent tribalism.

The basic classical passages in the Bible which exalt the
Jewish people as "chosen" are easily listed. God says of Abraham,
"For I have singled him out that he may instruct his children and
his posterity to keep the way of the Lord by doing what is just
and right in order that the Lord may bring about for Abraham
what He has promised him." In Exodus we find the statement,
"Now then, if you will obey Me faithfully and keep My covenant, you shall be My treasured possession among all the peoples.
Indeed all the earth is Mine, but you shall be to Me 'a kingdom
of priests and a holy nation.'" The term *segulah*, "treasured
possession," is repeated in Deuteronomy in one of the last dis-
courses of Moses, "For you are a people consecrated to the Lord
your God; the Lord your God chose you from among all other
peoples on earth to be His treasured people." Isaiah voices the
divine promise, "I will also give thee for a light of the nations,
that My salvation may be unto the end of the earth." The Book

*From *Congress Bi-Weekly*, October 7, 1963.

of Amos contains these words, "You only have I known of all
the families of the earth; therefore I will visit upon you all your
iniquities."

These suggestions of the preeminence of Israel occur in a
tradition in which is found "love thy neighbor as thyself" (which
Rabbi Akiba called the key sentence in Scripture) and which
repeats tens of times the admonition "and ye shall love the
stranger." Such a tradition, it should be assumed, does not seek
to demean those outside of it or to deny them that cosmic dignity
which descent from a common ancestor created by God confers
on them.

Nor is the conditional aspect generally associated with
"chosenness" sufficiently taken into account. The verse from
Deuteronomy cited above occurs in a portion of the Torah which
opens with the words, "See this day I set before you blessing
and curse; blessing if you obey the commandments of the Lord
your God which I enjoin upon you this day; and curse if you
do not obey the commandments of the Lord your God but turn
away from the path which I enjoin upon you this day and
follow other gods whom you have not experienced."

One would expect that God in addressing the people He has
chosen as His "treasure" would place only blessing before them.
Wherein is the value of being chosen if blessing is not assured
and certain? The choice set before the Jew of "blessing" and
"curse" is obviously open to all mankind. Whatever "chosen"
means, it does not mean that Israel is outside of and beyond the
moral law, enjoying immunity from the effects of its violation.
The implication that Jews, by virtue of an inherent superiority,
are incapable of committing wrong is nowhere to be found in
Jewish teaching—only the plea and hope that they prove strong
enough to spurn wrong. Chosenness is contingent upon obedience
to a moral law, and the moral law is that which obtains universally.

Nor does chosenness include a charter to exercise dominion,
enjoy unearned ease, and in general to prevail over other nations.
Were critics to read and reread the verse from Amos quoted
above, they would be compelled to moderate their criticism and
soften their rebuke. They too often tend to associate the status

of election with special opportunity for self-aggrandizement and are therefore moved to unloose their sharpest shafts of condemnation.

These critics would likewise be less exercised were they to view the concept of the Chosen People in the light of Israel's religious experience. For this idea stems with psychological inevitability from the nature of the discoveries which the Jewish spirit made about the universe and about man. Whether some of these discoveries were unique to the Jew or not is of small moment in this connection. Even if they were paralleled or duplicated elsewhere, the Jew discovered them for himself. He did not simply borrow them and insert them into his tradition. He arrived at them by dint of his own moral imaginativeness and adventuresomeness. They were the harvest of his own inner experience as he responded to life and the world.

What were these discoveries? He recognized a single supreme Deity whose unity was linked with His universality. The Jew perceived the One God to be an ethical Being, whose omnipotence and majesty were in the service of His justice. He was a God who, far from acting as a remote and unconcerned Ruler, was intimately involved in the affairs and lives of men on His earth. Moreover, He was, in a manner of speaking, represented in every human being, since He imprinted on each His divine image. His presence in history and in the individual soul was not simply a matter of exercising His jurisdiction and authority. He was prompted, as it were, by an overflowing love and compassion for His creatures whom He saw as His children.

These were obviously monumental and transforming discoveries. They changed the entire picture which the universe projected onto the screen of the human mind. The world was no longer a multiplicity, though it might appear so to the senses. It was no longer inhabited by malignancy—though evil and pain still abounded in it—for at its core there was a benign reality. And man himself was no longer an orphan, he now had a devoted cosmic Father. He was no longer a foundling abandoned by uncaring gods on the threshold of life; he was here of right, since his presence was willed by God. One cannot overestimate the

impact of these discoveries. No other complex of ideas and insights has been more crucial and far-reaching.

Moreover, these discoveries did not simply establish facts
about the nature of the world in which man lives. They were of
a different type than those discoveries which help determine the
speed of light or reveal a new star or law of nature. Scientific
discoveries do not immediately change man. They do not reach
in at once into the inner universe of man's mind and emotions.
They only refine his image of the world outside of him.

The discoveries, on the other hand, which the religious spirit
of the Jew made were not a thing apart from man's inner life.
They were more than facts upon which one stumbles or uncovers
through painstaking investigation. They simultaneously came to
him as duties, imperatives, commitments giving content and direction to his life. A God of justice meant that man must in his
dealings and thoughts conform to the demands of justice. That
man was made in the image of God meant not only that man
possesses high potentialities but that he is obligated to strive for
their realization, else he sins against his Maker and violates the
integrity of his own pattern.

These discoveries placed upon the Jew the need to reject
every idolatry and every philosophy of power and hedonism and
to walk single-mindedly the path of righteousness and peace.
These were discoveries that generated in the Jew an intense sense
of group purpose and duty. Other peoples were more artistic,
more scientific, more adept politically. The Jew, however, was
irresistibly prompted by his discoveries to see himself as one obligated to embody in himself and to bear aloft, so that others may
follow, the values, attitudes, and qualities which such discoveries
contain within themselves.

This is the deepest meaning and essence of the concept of
Chosen People. It represents imperatives, not privileges; a call to
live on the heights, not a disdain for others; a consciousness of
purpose, not an open sesame to ease. This concept of chosenness
paradoxically does not deny chosenness to others. Israel saw itself
as the instrument for the dissemination of these discoveries to
mankind.

In a recent article in *Harper's Magazine* entitled "The Hard

Kind of Patriotism," Adlai Stevenson wrote that America is unlike other nations. We are, he says, a land "dedicated to a propo-
sition." Here is the nub of the idea of the Election of Israel. As
long as the Jewish tradition communicates the passion and excitement of its discoveries, Jews must be moved by a compelling
sense of *noblesse oblige* to live by its light and to bring that light
to all mankind.

THOUGHTS AT THE *B'RITH* OF A NEWBORN INFANT

JUST BORN AND ALREADY he enjoys the longest genealogical record
in the Western world. Was he not admitted to the "Covenant of
Abraham"? So-called blue bloods and their *Social Register* are
upstarts and parvenues alongside this little fellow. And the list
of his ancestors is studded with the prominent names of creative
spirits who enriched the life of all mankind. He seems a little frail
to bear so great a patrimony.

Yet what possibilities he represents. He is without fanatic
loyalty or assimilationist tendencies. He has a capacity for such
attachment to Jewish traditions as to enhance his life and to acquire a sense of deep companionship with Jews everywhere. He
can be a good American imbued with profound democratic sensitivities and a fine awareness of the interdependence of all men.
He is qualified to join in beautiful synthesis the two currents of
influence in his life, the Judaic and the American. The past and
present can unite to prepare him to work for a desirable and
realizable future.

The symbols of Judaism can add beauty to his daily life, and
its culture can enrich his ethical and intellectual background. He
can enter American life proudly and with dignity unbent by the
centuries of Jewish deprivation, and unhurt by the underground
streams of misconception and bigotry that still run beneath the
surface of rhetoric and profession of freedom, equality, and
brotherhood. He can feel kinship with the great Jewish communities of the past without ignoring the fact that the American

Jewish settlement must respect the logic of its particular climate
and background. He can hold strongly to convictions without
defaming those who differ.

He can live by a system of high values without surrendering,
in the name of modernity, to the vulgarities and errors from
which no society is totally free. He can be versed in the Bible
and help reinstate the Jew as a "people of the Book." He can be
a faithful Jew without being parochial, a loyal American without
being the less Jewish.

ON BEING A *MENTSH*

THE MOST RELIGIOUS STATEMENT about the nature of man is found neither in the Bible, Talmud, nor any of the classical texts. Nor does it come from the mind or pen of outstanding religious thinkers and writers. Indeed, its authorship is anonymous and probably multiple. It was frequently on the lips of simple untutored men and women. It is part of that wonderful folklore created in the Yiddish language by Jews in Eastern Europe.

I am talking about being a *mentsh*, the connotation given in that culture, now tragically destroyed, to the term "human being." A mother would express the hope that her son would grow up to be a *mentsh*. The individual who was slipping was spurred and admonished to try to make a *mentsh* of himself. The highest praise given a person was that he was truly a *mentsh*.

One of the most significant convictions of religious belief is the high valuation it places upon man. Man is viewed as being stamped with the divine image, the object of God's love and concern. This doctrine is a corollary of religion's conception of God and the nature of the universe. It might even be said to possess an importance in the structure of belief not far below that attributed to faith in God.

Hence the apology or attempted exculpation as is contained in the oft-heard explanation—"After all I am only human"—is a denial of religion: indeed, the single small word "only" is a masterpiece of both heresy and blasphemy. Being "human" represents a goal and an achievement. Being a *mentsh* means calling upon capacities which are sometimes permitted to lie fallow. Man is never to be defined exclusively in terms of his present stature and attainments. There is more to him than what he is at any given moment. Within him are possibilities unrevealed by his current posture; if he wills, he can move upward from level to level. He

never arrives—and this applies to the greatest geniuses—at the full
realization of all of his powers.

Man need not be a prisoner of his physical nature nor the
victim of external pressures and circumstances. There is a dimension of *mentshlichkeit* which is not encompassed by a physiologi-
cal and sociological study of him. To realize this dimension is
man's greatest goal and adventure, to approach its fulfillment his
greatest accomplishment.

MAN'S GOALS

WHAT DO MEN WANT? What are the ambitions that have pro-
pelled human beings throughout all ages? In the words of Rabbi
ben Zomah, "Who is wise? Who is rich? Who is powerful? Who
is honored?"

The sage answers that there are four things every human
being wants: knowledge, man's curiosity to understand his environment; wealth; the power to rule over others; and the respect
of others.

These are good ambitions, says Rabbi ben Zomah; yet their
fulfillment does not always bring happiness. In our day, we know
learned men who are uneasy, neurotic, ridden by frustration.
Men of wealth do not always find joy, pleasure, or relaxation.
Some men who sit in high places and cast long shadows over their
times suffer inner uncertainty and fear. And there are persons of
great fame and prestige who are unhappy.

The tragedy is that we have not always understood the right
meanings of these goals. That is why Ben Zomah asks the question and probes for answers.

Who is wise? The man who has many diplomas? The man who
arrogantly boasts of his great knowledge? No, the truly wise man
is the one who is always learning. It is not how much one knows
that gives zest to living, but eagerness and curiosity. The wise
man is he who learns from *Aram* or "every man," says Ben
Zomah. There is no human being who cannot teach us something:

the woman who comes in to sweep our house, our neighbor, our subordinates, and even our superiors. The person who sits next to us on the bus is filled with more mystery than all of Africa, and possesses more depths than the deepest ocean. Education beckons every time we encounter a person anywhere. Every event, experience, and circumstance say something we should be able to hear. Life is a constant school, and we are eternal students.

The Rabbis say, "The truly learned have no rest." They also say that scholars do not have peace even in the world-to-come because if they were at rest and nothing troubled them, it would not be heaven and they would not be scholars. Restlessness, the knowledge that one never knows adequately, the constant reaching out—these make the learned man happy.

What is wealth? The accumulation of many possessions? No, true wealth is the knowledge when to be satisfied. We know when to run, when to be aggressive, when to promote. But we do not always know when to stop, when to let go. "Therefore shall a man leave his father and mother and cleave unto his wife" (Genesis 2:24). To know when to leave and when to cleave—this is a great human wisdom which escapes many.

There must come a time when we are satisfied with what we possess and accumulate. A man says, "Look, I'm easy to please. All I want is two hundred thousand dollars. As soon as I get that I quit." And he gets two hundred thousand dollars, and moves into a new circle of people who have five hundred thousand. Once again he is low man on the totem pole, and his wife is pushing him. When he gets five hundred thousand dollars, he joins a fancy country club. Since most of its members already have a million, the poor man is never appointed to an important committee. He does not even play golf as well as the others, and he can never match their gifts.

The wisdom of wealth is that there must come a time when we are not victims of our work and when we take the time to enjoy what we have. He who has all the wealth in the world but cannot limit his need is the victim of his own lust for possession. He is not wealthy; he is an alcoholic of acquisitiveness.

Who is powerful? The man who rules others? Alexander,

Napoleon, and all the Caesars of history? No, the truly powerful
man is one who possesses mastery over himself. The greatest of
all power is the ability to rule our life by our judgment.

In one town in Norway, there is today a monument to the
brave persons who resisted the Nazis. It bears the single word:
"NO." It takes courage to say no to conformity and to our own
appetites and weaknesses, and to permit our reason and judgment
to make decisions.

Who is honored? The guest of honor at a testimonial dinner?
We often elevate persons who are not worthy of being examples
for our community. If we honor the man who has nothing to
commend him except his bankroll, we are corrupting all ethical
values and lowering all communal standards.

No, the really honored man is he who honors others, who
recognizes the dignity of all persons with whom he comes into
contact whether they be his subordinates, equals, or superiors.
That man is honored whose heart can respond to the sorrow and
dilemma of another, who writes upon the tablets of his own
heart the anguish of another, who never violates the self-respect
of others.

Says Rabbi ben Zomah: By all means, let us seek wisdom,
wealth, power, and honor, but let us be sure that we understand
their true meaning. Correctly defined, these goals can lead us to
serenity and stability even in a world of flux. They can bring
fulfillment and illumine our lives.

IN FLIGHT FROM OURSELVES

A MAN WHO LEADS an extensive social life came to see me some
time ago. He appears at every important public occasion in our
community; is a frequent attendant at concerts and the theatre,
goes to many private parties and functions, and is widely traveled.
He frankly revealed himself to me as he explored in my presence
the situation which disturbed him. As he spoke, I made a sudden

and startling discovery. This man was not as gregarious as he appeared. His social life was not pursued in fulfillment of his own needs and temperament but rather as a means of escape. It was not that he enjoyed the company of others, but that he feared to be alone. He was not running *to* the many gatherings which crowded his calendar; he was running *from* a solitude of which he was pathologically afraid. Here was the true reason for his overactive social life.

Do we have a clue in this for the surprisingly great number of parties, functions, dances, programs, meetings, which go on nightly among us? Is it not less the pursuit of pleasure and relaxation that drives us to surround ourselves with others than the disinclination to face ourselves in privacy?

The dilemma of modern man is that at the core of him there is a void, an emptiness which he dare not confront. We have lost faith in the meaning and dignity of life and therefore in our own significance. To remain sane we must constantly keep running. We think we are going to business, on a trip or vacation, to a function, but in reality we are running away from ourselves, hoping that in the company of others and in activity we may somehow leave ourselves behind.

John Kenneth Galbraith, in a recent book, has advanced the theory that though affluent privately we are miserly in the arena of our public life. This may or may not be true from a sociological point of view. The spiritual truth seems to be the reverse—our public visible affluence is accompanied by personal insolvency.

We move and we run, we leap and frolic, we fly and jump, but we cannot stand still with dignity. The emptiness within does not permit us to balance ourselves in an upright posture and in a stationary position. We cannot worship, we only go through the motions of prayer. Since prayer involves looking at ourselves sharply, perceptively, and fearlessly while in the presence of God, we dare not risk such an exposure to ourselves.

We are swept along by a world in which we cannot find anything firm to which to hold. If everything is tentative, experimental, transitional, how can we be sure of our own worth? We strive for success, riches, for power, yet all the while there is a gnawing consciousness deep within us that these are not ultimates. Comfort and ease which once beckoned to us as from a peak are now commonplace and do not yield the satisfaction they promised before we attained them. Wealth, though we are reluctant to concede it, is more exciting in anticipation than in realization.

We must, however, continue in the race since to stop means to view ourselves in our frightening nakedness. Perhaps a future student will truly describe us by saying that this was an age of anxiety, an age when man was in flight from himself.

T'SHUVAH

IT IS CURIOUS AND paradoxical that *t'shuvah* is numbered among the 613 *mitzvot* set down according to tradition by the Torah. Repentance, as *t'shuvah* is commonly rendered, is thus the obligation even of him who fulfills with exemplary devotion and in scrupulous detail the other 612 Biblical prescriptions. *T'shuvah* speaks to all men—to the respectable and righteous as well as to the "enemy of society," the outcast, the criminal, the renegade—and it speaks in all seasons.

T'shuvah is always available to us. Because man is sin-prone, his fallibility and frailty expose him to temptation and error, and he can never relax in the assurance that his virtue is so fully and definitely rooted that it cannot be dislodged. Indeed, this very sense of the security of his righteousness may itself be the thrust of the sin of haughtiness. With virtue as with humility, self-consciousness is fatal. Albert Schweitzer once remarked, "A good conscience is the invention of the devil."

T'shuvah, as Judaism understands it, indicates that man may never lay down his arms in his struggle with sin. The price of righteousness, like that of liberty, is eternal vigilance. The records contain many instances of people who through the years gained a deserved reputation for honor and integrity, and indeed were held up as exemplars of the good life, but who succumbed to an overwhelming temptation, reflecting a weakness that they had never before betrayed. In an instant of surrender they destroyed that which had taken a lifetime to establish.

Who knows where his Achilles' heel is located and when the

circumstance will arise which will cause him to expose it? The story is told of a high public official who was approached by a man and offered a bribe. The official laughed in his face. The man doubled his offer. The official continued to laugh scornfully. Then the man mentioned a huge sum, far in excess of his previous offers. The face of the public official became instantly clouded, and with unrestrained anger he took hold of the man and shook him vigorously and shouted, "Get out. If I ever see you again I will have you arrested. Go now before I strike you." The would-be-briber had come dangerously near the price that might have tempted him.

The virtue of each of us has its limits. If we have been fortunate enough not to have been tested at its breaking point, let us not relax into the smug assurance of our utter incorruptibility. None is immune where sin is concerned.

The Rabbis spoke of the *yetzer hara*, the evil inclination which resides in every human being. It may be dormant for a while, suppressed through many years, yet is never fully crushed. Indeed, as the selfsame Rabbis point out, were it crushed, not only would it rob virtue of its glory, but it would deprive human life of rich resources of energy and power. Who would marry, they ask, or engage in business, or be stirred by the ambition that often results in social progress and advancement were our motives entirely unstained by the urges, the egotism, and desire for power that derive from the evil inclination? The larger one's capacity, talent, leadership quality, and creative force, the stronger the evil inclination, the greater the need for vigilance.

All men have propensities for sinfulness, and he who has strayed need not feel that he has read himself out of the race by reason of an abnormality. It is his human-ness that leads him to sin. The Hebrew tongue has no equivalent for the concept "lost soul," for no man can move outside the orbit of God's concern and forgiveness. On the other hand, no man of virtue has the right to feel that he is out of danger since his victory over temptation from without and weakness from within is neither decisive nor enduring. Every man is at every moment in mortal danger of his soul. Let none fall asleep for he is in the midst of war. The battle is never won once for all time. It must be waged all though one's lifetime.

But if the battle is never won, says Judaism, the war need not be lost. A profound rabbinic teaching has it that "man is higher than his sin and sin is not higher than man." A universe of faith and optimism is contained in this apparently simple assertion. It sets Judaism up as a life-affirming and man-affirming faith in contrast to those philosophies, ancient as well as contemporary, that see corruption and evil as the most characteristic and deepest truth about man. In such an outlook man is always in the grip of his own sinful nature, and can never move beyond the rim of darkness in which he is enveloped.

No sin, says Judaism, involves all of man. He possesses virtues and resources for goodness which, unelicited, remain independent of the sinfulness which he expressed through his wrong and evil deeds. He need not go down into the pit which his sin seeks to dig for him. There is more to him than the evil which is so frequently displayed by him.

If man is not all virtue, he is similarly not all sin. If his life is a battleground between the polarities within him, the victor is by no means predetermined by the inescapable mold and nature of his own being.

If the saint is not without sin, the sinner is not without saintliness, or at least the potentialities for a degree of saintliness. Sin cannot annihilate, although it can wound grievously and bring a man low. Hence, *t'shuvah* says to each of us, burdened by memories of wrongdoing and oppressed by many guilts, "Do not despair. You are bigger than any of your sins and than all of them. Rise, for though you have suffered setback and hurt, you are not defeated. You possess the resources for triumph. God does not despair of you. You need not despair of yourself."

SINS OF THE TONGUE

EIGHT TIMES DURING Yom Kippur we recite the confession (*Al Het*) which is couched in the plural and forms an integral part of the day's liturgy. No repentance can be effected, nor forgiveness hoped for, in the absence of a clear awareness of the gravity and extent of one's sins of deed and of neglect. The sins enumerated are listed in alphabetical sequence. Since each letter of the Hebrew alphabet is employed twice, forty-four culpable acts are cited in all.

Of these forty-four, ten refer to speech: a man's tongue is a major offender in causing him to sin. Not all the trespasses mentioned are, to be sure, of equal seriousness, yet all could be avoided by exercising greater care and self-control.

I offer herewith my own plea for caution in utilizing the lethal weapons at our verbal command:

The hasty judgment we passed upon another which sober deliberation revealed to be based on a single impression, an unproved rumor, or an unreasonable prejudice.

The quip we failed to repress which brought laughter to most but offense and hurt to one in our hearing.

The promise lightly given, which in our heart we never seriously meant to fulfill.

The calumny of another we heard uttered and knew to be untrue, and yet allowed to go unrebuked and unchallenged.

The gathered irritation and resentment born of unpleasantness elsewhere, which we brought home to darken and embitter the words we spoke to those nearest us.

The story we repeated presumably only for its humorous content, but which derided a whole class or race of people.

The time we spoke idly when we might have listened profitably.

The untruths we masqueraded under a plenitude of words.

The opinions we advanced with a certainty out of all proportion to the authority of the few facts we possessed.

The innumerable words we spoke which were born of envy, dipped in venom, or prompted by unjustified resentment.

The occasions when we failed to say the word of encouragement and friendliness though it was sorely needed.

The evasive statement, the ambiguous declaration, the misleading pronouncement in place of a forthright, clear, and honest expression of our views.

Who among us cannot extend the list?

ON BEING CONTAGIOUS

EACH OF US IS inevitably a center of contagion. Whether we are aware of it or not, something passes from us into the life of every person we encounter. Though there is no instrument capable of measuring our effect upon another, yet we have altered his life to such a degree that he will never be the same. We may have met an individual as a customer or a salesman, as an elevator operator or taxi driver. However brief and transient the meeting, the effect is lasting.

What is it that passes from us into the memories and personalities of others? With what do we enrich or infect them? Does our relationship stir in them a kindness which otherwise might never have been evoked or do we fortify them in their cynicism? Do we help them to open a somewhat wider aperture upon life or do we force them to shrink into an ever narrower shell? Do we enkindle their minds or do we justify them in their prejudices? Do we touch off a chain reaction of sympathy and humaneness or do we explode in them new hostility and greater resentment?

Do we encourage faith or stifle hope? Do we invite the handshake or compel the fist? Do we foster their relapse into self-centeredness or do we bid them move forward into a wider circle of association and interest? Do we open their eyes to larger frontiers or do we make them even more cognizant of boundaries that are closing in upon them? Do we help them raise their eyes to the mountains or do we drag them down into the valleys of futility and stagnation?

Do we humiliate them or do we call them to greatness? Do we help release pent-up goodness and sensitivity or do we incarcerate them into prisons of malice and pettiness? Do we illumine with friendship or darken with suspicion? Do we lead them out of loneliness or drive them farther back into their own cell?

Do we instruct them in integrity or victimize them with deception? Do we uphold their dignity or tear down their self-respect? Do we impart a brighter awareness of life's friendliness or do we down them with our bitterness and despair? Do we awaken their mind or lull it into a sleep of death? Do we arouse them to an appreciation of beauty or do we impress upon them

the ugly untrustworthiness of the universe? Do we humanize or
do we brutalize those who come near?

The answers to these questions are of crucial importance not
only to the others in our life but also to ourselves. It is within
ourselves that the illness we spread by contagion is most virulent,
the health most vitalizing.

THE NEAR AND THE FAR

THE SEVERAL ASTRONAUTS, American and Russian, who have
orbited around our planet, enjoyed a larger, more encompassing
view of the earth than any previous individuals in history. They
saw more of the globe at one time than anyone before them, and
in broader perspective. In a second they flew over cities; in an
instant they passed a continent. Their never-before-attained alti-
tude allowed their glance to embrace the widest areas upon which
human eyes had ever looked. They, more than all others, can
recognize that from a certain stance all that man has wrought is
a pinpoint on a large cosmic canvas.

Yet there is so much that the astronauts did not and could not
see. They did not see a farmer in Japan at work in his rice paddy;
a mother in Singapore singing her child to sleep; a boy in Aus-
tralia studying his lessons; a young couple in London approaching
the marriage altar; an artist in Paris laboring to suggest by means
of his brush the feverish imagining of his mind; a congregation in
Holland united in prayer; a funeral procession in Algiers; a starv-
ing man on the streets of Hong Kong; a beggar in Delhi; a wall
in Berlin; a jungle in Vietnam; a Negro child barred from school
in Georgia; a dying patient in a hospital in Belgium.

A man walking on foot in the country sees many sights to
which the astronaut is of necessity blind: the full-branched tree,
the bird on wing, the greenness of the grass, the stream slowly
flowing, the ruts in the country road, the corn ripening. The man
on the ground has eyes for the individual and specific; the man in
space only for the general and vast.

Living in an age when our minds are directed to the limitless and challenging magnitude of the universe, we allow the particular, the local, the individual to be blotted out. We think of China as a vast country representing a threatening potential of power and do not see its millions of men, women, and children; Vietnam, the Congo, and the Middle East are seen as political factors and not as places teeming with human beings, hungry, aspiring, apprehensive, and invested with the rights and dignity we claim for ourselves. We frequently cite the statistics of destruction which a nuclear war will bring about, but our ears are deaf to the death rattles that issue from the throats of the individuals doomed to be its casualties.

Our range is global, but it does not embrace the neighbor who disappears in the haze of the immensity upon which we focus. We utter grand phrases on the indivisible destiny of mankind and its unsunderable unity, but we do not feel at one with a Chinese peasant, a Korean student, a Congolese houseboy.

The Bible opens with the majestic account of the creation of the world which it climaxes with the story of man. We, on the other hand, by ignoring and reducing man may be engaged in an adventure whose apex will be the destruction of that world which God created.

MAN AND THE SABBATH

THE OPENING PORTION OF the Torah depicts on the largest canvas possible a picture of the universe emerging out of chaos and void. There are two climaxes to this cosmic epic: the creation of man who crowns all of nature and who in a sense is the noblest expression of God's creativity; and the Sabbath, which marks the culmination and fulfillment of God's activity in fashioning the universe. These two are integrally intertwined one with the other. They parallel, complement, and fulfill each other.

The Sabbath, as the Rabbis point out, was made for man, for it is compatible with his specific character and needs. It points to the truth that while man is part of nature, he transcends it. Man is not bound, as are all other creatures, to the cycles and seasons of nature. Every other being is attuned by native endowments to the rhythms and processes of nature and has no existence apart from it. Though man's drives and instincts link him inexorably to the physical universe, he can step outside the rigid limits of his inherited natural creatureliness.

The Sabbath, which is not indicated in nature and which does not emerge from the processes, cycles, and inevitabilities of the natural environment, can have no meaning for animal life. The Sabbath is something added to the universe that meets our senses and reflects horizons far beyond those envisioned by forms lower than man. Man is bidden by the Sabbath to rest, to desist from the drudgeries of habit and routine. Into his week freedom enters, and his life is made complete by this interval of liberation and detachment.

Sabbath leads man to a frontier beyond mere existence, to an area in which his humanity asserts itself over his earthiness. Sabbath represents one of the most revolutionary doctrines of all time: life is more than work, and man more than a being of natural hungers and drives. This is true of all men, unbounded by social and economic class lines. The Torah commands that freedom be given on the Sabbath day not only to citizens but to slaves, the handmaiden and bondswoman and the stranger "within thy gates." To be human means to possess rights that override all man-made authority, convention, and classification.

Sabbath also expresses the distinctively human motif in that it bids man turn his thoughts to the purposes of life. Man descends from his human level when he lives exclusively in terms of the instrumentalities and mechanisms of life. The food placed before an animal is an end-goal; its impulse of hunger does not go beyond it. But man looks farther; he does not find complete contentment in control over his environment and in his mastery of the means of production, domination, and acquisition. He asks himself a question with which, as far as we know, no animal has ever confronted itself—"What is the purpose of my life? To what does all my activity lead? What is it that is worthy of my effort and striving as a man?"

In Hebrew the word *hayim*, life, has a qualitative undertone. More than a biological term, it represents an achievement, a goal for which man is questing, a form of existence which corresponds to the human in him. On Sabbath, therefore, man withdraws from the vortex of pressures, involvements, and harassments in which he is daily entrapped, and seeks to recapture and reemphasize that sense of purpose which may have become obscured in his normal and customary endeavors and struggles.

The Sabbath is more than an escape from the week of toil and entanglement; a refuge from his exertions; therapy for his weariness. It is the fulfillment toward which all his labor reaches out. The Sabbath brings detachment from the immediacies of life that man may achieve attachment to the great purposes of life. Neither the state or business or success are the farthermost limits of man's loyalty or the loftiest goals of his striving. To serve God, which in human terms means the realization of his own most characteristic potentialities, is man's final and most authentic purpose. Any government, social system, or doctrine that intervenes and stays man from pursuing that goal is destructive and dehumanizing. The Sabbath upholds with a constancy and emphasis, equaled by no other institution, the right, indeed the obligation, of man to make the fulfillment of his humanity under God the greatest goal and ultimate purpose of his endeavors, to discover for himself the meaning of re-creation.

Sabbath dramatizes the fact that every human being is invested with a creative potential. There is something of the artist in each of us, even if we have never painted on canvas, sculptured, or joined words together in poetic harmony. Getting and spending we lay waste our creative powers. We often nip our most human capacities in the bud. We doom to sterility fruitful possibilities. Tenderness, love, vision, appreciation are stifled amid the hurry and tumult of our habitual lives.

Sabbath is the time for renewal and regeneration, a time to stop and wonder, pause, and reflect. The most important things in life cannot be achieved by a direct assault. The human being must place distance between himself and the impinging environment. The creative impulse needs peace and freedom in order to flow freely and rise to the threshold of consciousness. We visit others as a matter of social obligation. How long has it been since we have visited with ourselves? Are we dooming to atrophy elements within our constitution which could be artistically molded into a harmonious and creative personality?

This then is the Sabbath, climax of creation even as man is its climax, the day on which man can become fully human.

Blessed is he who opens his life to it and frees himself of the encrustments of routine, the dictatorship of the contingent, the authority of the impulsive, and the enthronement of the trivial. Both man and Sabbath are the climax of creation. Man fully becomes man when he has the Sabbath in his life.

HAYIM GREENBERG: THE WHOLE MAN *

THE MONASTIC IDEAL NEVER loomed large in Jewish tradition, and monastic discipline as a means of attaining a life of holiness was not stressed by Judaism. On the contrary, a Talmudic dictum goes so far as to declare that he who vows abstinence only from wine is to be regarded as sinful. Yet temporary or provisional withdrawal from life was practiced from time to time by individuals who were firmly rooted in the tradition. One thinks of the *Matmid* immortalized by Bialik in this connection. There are found in *Hasidic* lore moving stories of noted Rabbis who set aside intervals for solitary meditation, and who left their communities and followers to spend days in reflection and prayer in the woods. The motivation, to be sure, was not a spurning of the world or a flight from life but a desire and need for a detachment conducive to spiritual renewal and reinvigoration. They hoped to effect by such a brief removal from the immediacies and impingements of daily life what might be called "an ingathering of the self," a reunion of the scattered and broken fragments in which man tends to be segmented. "Dispersal of the self" is to be guarded against. Hence the prayer, "unify our hearts," which is recited daily.

I, who am a *Mitnagid* by descent, tradition, and temperament, have recently emulated the example of *Hasidic* masters and have sequestered myself with the writings of Hayim Greenberg and in solitude have lived with memories and thoughts of him.

Jewish Frontier, May, 1963.

He seemed to speak out of a profound inner privacy, and inspired in his readers the wish for the type of experience and reflection associated with solitude. He spoke to us at large meetings and yet evoked in us a mood for contemplation and self-confrontation, a need for silent meditation in private. He stirred us to a devoutness which linked us to him as disciples rather than students, reacting with a religious responsiveness compounded of piety and reverence.

The impact he made had a mystic dimension. It would not occur to us, at the close of even his most effective addresses, to comment: "how beautifully he speaks"; "how well-reasoned his presentation"; "how masterly his style." We reacted not to an eloquent discourse or brilliant argument but to a personality, a presence. Hayim Greenberg's influence upon us derived from his total being rather than from the fraction of him communicated to us through speech or essay.

All who knew Greenberg recognized the presence of a pervasive paradox. Here was a Zionist whose basic philosophy was universalist in scope and interest, whose essential rootage was in *k'lal Yisroel.* Here too was an outstanding orator whose deepest message is to be found in unspoken and hidden undertones and silences, a leading figure who in his most public moments gave us a presentment of an inwardness. Formally a "secularist" (though he would have objected to such a characterization) few spoke in deeper religious accents. An aristocrat marked by elegance and delicacy, he was at ease with *amcho,* the masses of his people. Thrown almost constantly into the midst of political situations, his main concern revolved about ethical principles and moral issues. Though his mind turned frequently to broad philosophical questions and spiritual concepts, he had to meet a weekly deadline as editor. Immersed through many years in public activity and controversy, he preserved an air of immaculateness, purity, and moral chasteness. He was a liberal with an enthusiasm for tradition. Widely heralded as a great public speaker, his noblest and most memorable words were spoken in private conversation over a cup of tea. (I remember an evening at my home which stretched till four A.M. when he related reminiscences and interesting encounters which I have not been able to find in his published writings.) He was one of the few Jewish leaders of his time who had never attended a yeshiva, yet his references to traditional sources and his quotations from rabbinic literature reflect an unerring mastery of the authentic and quintessential in the classic Jewish outlook.

Yet the term "paradox" does not reflect the dominant quality of Greenberg's mind and spirit. He did not represent in his outlook or personality a juncture of contrasts, a multichotomy (if the word is permissible) of inconsistencies. There was a seamless wholeness about him. He was a *tamim* in the full sense of that term, possessing integrity, completeness, and unity. He was the whole man. He suggested a man in quest, eager to probe more fully, to sense more exquisitely.

His was a broad-based, wide-ranging view from which he did not have to exclude the one to include the other. He achieved a calming, effulgent wholeness which comprehends without necessarily resolving the polarities of life and the dilemmas of the human situation. His was a world outlook which did not aim at alleviating the restlessness within by eliminating one or another of the elements in apparent opposition. All were needed to mirror the multidimensional character of life and to satisfy the amplitude and exuberance of his temperament. Universalism and nationalism had their place in his philosophy: both were aspects of the totality of the human spirit. So was it with faith and reason; liberalism and traditionalism; ethics and politics; Israel and the Diaspora. Greenberg's outlook was the confluence of many streams that flowed into a single sea.

Whence this completeness and unity? Hayim Greenberg, a modern of moderns, European, American, Jew, literate in a dozen languages, naturalized in several cultures, attained a consummation denied to so many of his generation.

Though Greenberg constantly grew through reflection, experience, and inner creative questing, it might nonetheless be said that he did not grow out of any stage in the process of his development. There were no breaks in the line of his personal evolution. No fossils of outlived eras were to be found in him. The earlier level was swept upward to the new phase of his thought or feeling, retaining its vitality without impeding the advancement of the whole personality. He accumulated and preserved not simply the memories of previous ideas, reactions, and events, but

the poignancy and fullness of their initial impact and the drama
and color of the original confrontation.

His was not a total recall, but a kind of total viability. He
gave immortality to the moment. Ideas matured and ripened in
his mind, feelings deepened and mellowed, perspectives became
extended. Yet his personal past continued to function in his consciousness, unblurred and unrevoked by the present. To hear
Greenberg tell of an early encounter or relate a childhood epi-
sode was to be present when he was, as it were, actually living
through it. He could animate the past and project it so fully into
his narration because he did not have to reach into the recesses of
memory for the experience he was describing. He did not have to
dig up old springs. His past was coincidental with his present and
remained part of the living stream of his consciousness. This explains both the vividness with which his account was informed
and the rich detail in which it was unfolded to us.

His inner life was not segmented into steps and stages. It was
like the menorah in the ancient Tabernacle of which the Bible
says, "You shall make a menorah of pure gold; the menorah shall
be made of hammered work; its base and its shaft, its cups,
calyxes and petals shall be one piece" (Exodus 25:31).

There was something in Greenberg, to broaden the meaning
of Robert Frost's phrase, "that doesn't love a wall." His intellectual vigor, the outreaching of his sympathy and concern, the
alertness of his moral sensibilities tolerated no barriers. His was a
largeness of view that refused to be stopped by the boundary of
tradition, convention, party program, or contemporary usage.
His was not the fury or delight of the breaker of idols. Even
when he differed, he did so with dignified calm. His was a temperament which was at home only in the widest circumference in
which an idea, a concern, a loyalty could be set.

The frame of reference against which he measured events
and ideas was universal and moral, and this ideational background
illumined the entire foreground, imparting to it something of its
grandeur and scope. His world view did not stop short at the
visible limits of reality, and his moral concern took him beyond
Western civilization into the heart of the East. This was not a
bohemian sortie into the esoteric.

As always, Greenberg was reaching to the farthest attainable beyondness. This characteristic helped give a sense of expansiveness and unity to his personality and thought. This spaciousness of outlook and interest enabled Greenberg to admit the diversities and polarities, the near and the far, the universal and the particular into the ken of his *Weltanschauung*. Though he never organized a systematic philosophy, he recognized, with the intuition of a poet and the insight of a religiously oriented thinker, the protean nature of life as well as its fundamental unity. He rejected every monastic interpretation—whether economic, political, or cultural—which reduced the multicolored tapestry of reality to a single strand. His own many-faceted personality and the many-sidedness of his background admirably fitted him to experience the universe and life in its variety and multiplicity. There was thus an artistic symmetry between the man and his philosophy, which further reenforced the sense of wholeness and unity which he conveyed to us.

His personality is not fully captured in his work. His written and spoken words opened only a small aperture upon the opulence which he truly possessed. He loomed larger than his writings, addresses, and public activity but under different circumstances. Hence he always suggested to us depths beyond the depths he uncovered. An allusion, a parenthetical comment, an aside, often served to make us aware of an expansiveness beyond the words he spoke or the idea he enunciated.

Religion in its deepest and most universal form was a magnificent obsession of Hayim Greenberg. It is explicit or implicit in everything he wrote. It was not for him a subject to treat, a theme that lends itself to an address or essay. It was a dominant motif in his own search. Greenberg saw religion not simply as a private matter for the individual but as the content which can give direction and spirit to the life of society. He felt that one does not fully probe a human problem—be it personal or social—until he penetrates to its religious substratum.

Greenberg never gave architectural form to his religious philosophy of life. The nearest he came to it is ironically enough not in any essay devoted to the subject but in a list of apparently unrelated words which might at first glance seem to have been chosen at random. This list is found in his memorable address before the World Zionist Congress in August, 1951. Greenberg was pointing out the inadequacy of a Hebrew that was limited to functional and daily needs, unrooted in Jewish history and culture. He called this a kind of "pidgin Hebrew." Hebrew is the harp which releases the "music" of the Jewish spirit.

It was then that he enumerated key words which must be mastered by those who wish to play "a part in the choir that gives voice, consciously or not, to which I have called 'the Jewish melody.' " Were one to attempt to formulate Greenberg's view of life, I would suggest that he seclude himself with these words, analyze their meaning, investigate their interrelationship, and weave them together into the coherence which they possessed for Greenberg. The words are *mitzvah*, *averah*, *geulah*, *tikkun*, *tum'ah*, *yirah*, *ahavah*, *zedakah*, *hesed*, *mesirut nefesh*, *kiddush ha-Shem*, *dvekut*, *t'shuvah*.*

The spiritual biography of Hayim Greenberg is to be found in these words. All else is commentary.

---

*Though most of these words defy translation, and have far broader meanings than can be indicated, their literal meanings, respectively, are as follows: command, observance, good deed; transgression, sin; redemption; restoration of harmony; defilement; fear; love; charity; loving kindness; dedication of the soul; sanctification of God's name; cleaving (to God); repentance.

~ PART III ~

MAN AND GOD

Though himself a Mitnagid, *of what he called "dour" and rational Lithuanian stock, Rabbi Adler frequently turned to the more mystical* Hasidim *for illustrative tales. This he did in presenting the tension-paradox in which man finds himself: fashioned by God, yet set like a pinpoint in a vast universe in which "the mountains dwarf him, the seas declare his feebleness, and the firmament proclaims his transitoriness." Said a certain* Hasidic rebbe: *"Each man should have two pockets. In one he should keep the reminder that, as the Rabbis say, 'the world was created for me.' In the other, the verse, 'I am but dust and ashes.' "*

This saying sums up Rabbi Adler's approach to religion as a kind of counterpoint-synthesis between man and God. "The truly religious man," he once wrote, "is one who is constantly in the presence of the King of the Universe since all the earth is His royal court." Man sees before him all the wonders that God constantly performs. And these wonders, for Rabbi Adler, are in the world of man as well as in the world of nature. To him the smile of a child, the possibility of love between man and woman, laughter, tears, "the word in whose womb an idea lives" are as awesome as are the rising sun, the mysteries of sea and sky.

Such awareness—which for Rabbi Adler is the heart and core of religious faith—means that man knows his place in God's universe. He knows too that the Angel of Death hovers in the wings, and that his life on earth, all too short for the tasks he alone can do, must therefore be purposeful. He also comes to understand through prayer and study—which are of equal importance in Judaism—*what his responsibilities are as God's copartner in building a better world.*

L. E.

8 • *What Religion Is*

ON BEING RELIGIOUS

IT HAS OFTEN BEEN POINTED out that when one becomes aware of one's humility one no longer possesses it. The man who knows he is humble betrays pride. Similarly the individual who proclaims by word or bearing "I am religious" thereby indicates an absence of the spirit and attributes of the truly religious life.

For what is implicit in the claim that we are religious?

We are saying that we are not only different from, but better than others not so fervently disposed. We are suggesting that we are invested with special virtue. Above all, we are exhibiting a self-righteousness and self-complacency that are the very antithesis of genuine religious feeling.

To be religious means to live with an ever-present disquietude about the adequacy of our attainments. It is to refrain from judging another with the severity and rancor that can only spring from pride and hostility. It is to fulfill obligations to God and man without the faintest consciousness that we are doing more than our share. It is to sense an intensity of kinship with all men. It is to be restless in questing for the fuller life, the deeper understanding, the greater service. It is to be impressed with our own limitations and mindful of the fact that the best among us may easily suffer a lapse of virtue. "Do not believe in thyself until the day of thy death," the Rabbis warned.

To be religious is to remain alert to duties unfulfilled rather than to feel smug about duties done. It is to know that he who serves God best is he who comes before Him with a contrite heart. It is to be severe with ourselves and gentle with others. It is never to demand special rights or to feel that we have earned special commendation. It is to live out of a great humility and love before God and our fellowmen.

DUAL CHARACTER OF RELIGION *

RELIGION HAS ONCE AGAIN, after a lapse of some decades, become one of the frequently discussed subjects of our day. Yet I doubt if there is another field of human aspiration and human endeavor about which so many misconceptions cluster. For religion is often misunderstood both by its opponents and its adherents, the former caricaturing it, the latter distorting it. Some regard it as a panacea —the automatic assurance and guarantee that all will be well. Others regard it as a projection of man's inner desires—an illusory and highly idealized picture of the world and life. The Communists have banned it because it is an opiate, while the Nazis have fought it because it makes people restless and unreceptive to the order which they wish to impose.

Nowhere does the Bible, the great taproot of religion, offer a concise, comprehensive definition of all the manifestations of the religious life. The religious experience of its great personalities was too intense, too tempestuous to be poured into neat little systems. The early great spirits of Israel were too much occupied with living the religious life, fighting for it, experiencing it to pause and compile a coherent philosophy. A theologian was once said to be so busy seeking arguments to prove the existence of God that he had no time to say his prayers. The prophets and seers of the Bible, on the other hand, were so absorbed in experiencing God and in communing with Him that they had no time left to define Him.

What we do find in the Bible are two types of references to God. One speaks of the Lord as "my shepherd," the other describes Him as a man of war. The one proclaims: "the Lord is my strength and song," the other calls God He "who traineth my hands for war so that mine arms do bend a row of brass." In the words of one, "The Lord is my light and my salvation," "the Lord is the stronghold of my life" (Psalm 27). In another, God is addressed: "For Thine arrows are gone deep into me and Thine hand is come down upon me" (Psalm 38). God is described as "my high tower, the God of my mercy"; He also "will bring

---

*Radio address, Church of the Air, April 19, 1942.

a sword upon you" (Leviticus 26); "the Lord doth roar from on high" (Jeremiah 25:29).

These metaphors indicate the dual character possessed by the religious experience. Religion is song and refuge; it is also sword and spear. It is defense, but also offense; it is exaltation, but also compulsion; it is salvation, but also, in Whitehead's phrase, "a program of discontent."

At its broadest, religion is a triumphant affirmation about the universe. The world is man's dwelling place in which he should feel at home. A scientist once said that if he were granted one question to ask of the Sphinx, he would inquire: "Is the universe friendly?" The single most important question in life is: "Is there something out there to correspond to man's inner needs and aspirations?" The answer of religion is clear and unambiguous. The strange, baffling, complex, mysterious, often threatening universe is basically friendly. Man's hopes and aspirations are related to the reality about him—for at the core of things there is a moral purpose. We are not the dupes of our dreams. Justice, peace, and righteousness may be for a time refugees, yet they are native in the universe. That is the profoundest song of triumph that can burst forth from man's lips.

Life has meaning. Ideals are everlastingly real and therefore ultimately victorious. Over all of life and man's destiny a benevolent and protecting God rules, giving it a significance and purpose "which binds in one book the scattered leaves of all the universe." Ancient peoples looked out upon the universe and saw it inhabited with demons and evil spirits, alive and teeming with a thousand terrors and malignancies. While modern sophisticates look out upon a gnawing void, upon a bottomless futility, religion proclaims: "The Lord is my shepherd." Loving care and tenderness are meant for me; a Guardian is above and beyond, eternally watching, protecting, caring. Religion is a song.

Religion is also a refuge. It is a refuge against that cynicism which sees life as a "tale told by an idiot, full of sound and fury, signifying nothing." The Psalmist describes those for whom "death shall be their shepherd" as they who see the ultimate goals of life as annihilation and desolation. Religion is a refuge from loneliness, an awareness of a reality to which we can relate ourselves in an intimate, personal way. It is a refuge against inferiority. Devious and perverse are the ways in which man seeks to bolster his sense of self-importance. He climbs mountains, he forms secret societies, he propounds race theories, he oppresses his fellows, he divides the world into "my people" and outsiders. The most basic sense of importance, however, can only derive from belonging in a universe in which God is Father. Religion enables man to say, in the words of David's psalm, "He brought me forth also in a large place; He delivered me because He delighted in me." There is no basis in history, psychology, biology, or sociology for so high a conception of man. It is basically a religious doctrine.

Religion provides that large frame of reference which, in the upper reaches of life, releases one from the narrowing and imprisoning limits of state, class, race, or social group. Because religion has been rejected by many, they have found it possible to place at the center of their life the state, the class, the race.

Religion is thus a song of affirmation and triumph, the conviction of ultimate victory, the refuge from hopelessness and despair, the cheering and uplifting message.

For many religion ends here. It becomes a soft pillow on which to recline. Man can sleep peacefully because God is on guard. Such a religion often serves as an invitation to complacency, to passivity, to submission. There are, it is true, religious teachers who cater to this conception of religion, who appeal to their people to relax, to submit, to resign, for "God's in His heaven and all's right with the world."

But this passive, easygoing, nondemanding type of experience is a caricature of religion. There is a Negro spiritual which is far nearer to the essential mood and spirit of religion when it proclaims, "You can't go to heaven sitting down." The Lord is our shepherd, true. But He is also a man of war. Religion also has for its objective so to sensitize our conscience that we shall be everlastingly disturbed in the presence of injustice and iniquity.

Perhaps none but the truly religious person can measure by his own life and ideals the infinite distance between our highest aspirations and the social realities about us. None can feel as wrought up, distressed, gloriously angry and discontented in the presence of this contrast, for religion is not a retreat from life but an offensive upon it, upon its Pharaohs and Sodoms, upon its Egypts, upon its inequality and injustice.

In this realm religion is grimly realistic. It knows full well the power and desolation of sin. It knows full well the abysmal depths of depravity which still lurk within man as a heritage from his primeval past. And there are moments of disillusion even in the life of the religious person, though he does not make of his transient mood a philosophy.

Elijah laments: "I, even I only, am left." Jeremiah cries out to God: "Wilt thou indeed be unto me as a deceitful brook, as waters that fail?" And another prophet asks: "How long, O Lord, shall I cry and Thou shalt not hear?" None is truly religious who has not scaled the heights of its ideals and has not likewise gone down to the valley of life's miseries. He who has not known pain has not truly prayed. He who has not been bruised and scarred and distressed in the war on evil has not truly seen God. He who has not gone up like Isaac to Moriah, prepared to sacrifice himself, has never been granted a true vision of God. It is in this area that we have failed. We have not been desperate enough in our struggle with evil.

To be sure, religion is a refuge; but it is also a sword. It is salvation but likewise sacrifice. It is promise and compulsion together. Which are the most disturbing books in the world—books that tear and rage and upset? Are they not the prophetic books, written by artists of religion who mounted the highest peaks of religious experience? Religion is eternally uneasy in the presence of wrong, and out of this uneasiness comes challenge. It is not God who has failed man, but man who has failed God. The question in this dark hour is not—Where is God? but Where is man? They who are ready to give up God in periods of travail and sorrow never really had a hold on Him. Their religion was fragmentary.

We must embrace in our view these dual traits of religion, and draw from them both relaxation and restlessness, song and strength. Perhaps never before has our country so required both aspects of the religious experience as in our day. What is needed is not simply a morale that is the frenzied foam of oratory or parade. True morale can only grow out of a great and deep faith in the inevitable triumph of truth. But to that conviction and faith we must respond with determination to take up the challenge that will not give us rest until the world shall be rebuilt.

Metternich once said of Napoleon, "Peace with Napoleon is not peace. A state of calm and quiet must be renounced as long as Napoleon lives." The religious man will renounce smugness, comfort, and ease as long as evil rules and injustice prevails.

To that kind of faith America must dedicate itself in this hour so big with destiny—a faith that leads to salvation, but simultaneously a faith that compels, demands, and commands.

THEY HAVE EARS, BUT LISTEN NOT

"To Church where a sorry dull parson"
—Diary of Samuel Pepys

I HAVE FREQUENTLY FOUND myself thinking about my unknown colleague whose dullness won him anonymous immortality. Did he arise on that distant Sunday in the assurance that he was prepared to preach a memorable sermon that would certainly hold the interest of his congregation and evoke much favorable comment? Perhaps on Saturday night he had read several excerpts of his manuscript to his lady, calling her attention to some of the more felicitous phrases and telling illustrations. Did she, long-suffering veteran, dutifully fortify his feeling that this was a sermon that would leave its mark upon its auditors? Buoyed up by his wife's commendation, he probably went back to his study to polish some of the phrases more brightly and add a thought which had but now occurred to him.

But he had miscalculated. He discovered, as alas so many of his craft do, that his judgment and the congregation's did not coincide. The problem which he had thought so germane and immediate was obviously of little interest to the people in the pews, and his effort fell flat on their ears.

Though we can feel sorry that Mr. Pepys's visit to church that Sunday was marred by the poor sermon, we must, however, reserve the greater part of our sympathy for the preacher who tried nobly only to fail ingloriously. While his failure is by no means unique, his was the supreme misfortune of having his homiletical miscarriage recorded in a book destined to be read by posterity.

Perhaps there is a grain of comfort in all this. Despite Pepys's harsh judgment upon and curt dismissal of the discourse, it is obvious that he listened and thus paid the preacher the tribute of his attention. Many are the preachers who would be gladdened by even an expression of disfavor—at least it reveals that they were heard. More than one colleague has pathetically commented that one speaks week after week into a vast indifference, and that one's words fall muted into an abyss of oblivion. The people sit before them in full observance of the proprieties of religious decorum. Indeed, some have learned through many years of practice to affix upon their apparently devout faces a simulated expression of transfigured absorption, though their minds had left the sanctuary much earlier. (Is it possible that they forgot to bring them?) Where neglect and indifference are always an offense, refutation and condemnation are in a certain sense a tribute.

For while the circle that Samuel Pepys represented was occasionally critical of the pulpit utterances, they did not stop their ears so that none of the preacher's words would gain entry into their consciousness. Our generation makes the proper obeisance to religion. Indeed religion today is on the crest of a wave of unprecedented popularity. The membership rolls of our religious institutions are at an all-time high. Our radio and television media give a respectable allotment of time to religious programs and presentations. New houses of worship add grandeur to suburbia. People courting political success make every effort to foster an image of religious devotion. At no time in recent centuries has our society evidenced, by so many diverse indications, its apparent interest in religion.

Yet appearances notwithstanding, the realities are something else. There is no wholesale rejection, to be sure, of religion and its doctrines. The warfare between science and theology has long since subsided, and even the cold war between these doughty antagonists has been called off. In some quarters one encounters an amiable reconciliation; in others a more distant relationship prevails.

But, in every case, the weapons have been laid down, and even verbal argument is rare. The refutation of religion in our times is insidious and hence more dangerous and effective. Religion is respected but ignored, listened to but not heard, assented to but banished from the centers of influence and authority of the personal lives of its adherents, proclaimed but disenfranchised.

ROLE OF RITUAL

MANY PEOPLE RECOGNIZE THE validity and value of religion but seem to feel that ritual is an artificial appendage perverting and reducing its basic purity and loftiness. But in truth the rites and symbols of religion are neither embellishments nor accidental accretions. They grow out of both the nature of man and of religion. We must stop looking at ritual as something that was "put over" by a clever self-serving priestcraft.

Ritual and symbol play a part in every phase of life. The flag, the Statue of Liberty, the Lincoln Memorial, the salute, the handshake are all part of a dramatization of attitudes and values which Americans share. Many who oppose ritual in religion are the first to incorporate a great deal of ritual in other phases of life. Their marriage rings, the clothes they wear, the pictures of loved ones they assemble, the dinners at which they preside, the manner of greeting old friends and of introducing new ones are all rituals and symbols, serving as the visible and physical style in which contemporary life garbs itself.

Ritual is the language of religion. To question its right is to question the right of literature to convey its meanings, however universal, through the medium of a particular religion.

Ritual brings into our daily life with a vividness to which reflection alone can never attain the invisible world of the spirit and the unseen presence of God. The lighting of the candles on Friday night suggests the supreme meanings and induces the inspired mood of the Sabbath in a way that no treatise could.

Ritual renews and fortifies our sense of linkage with a tradition and our continuity with a community spanning centuries. Ritual sanctifies life and transposes the mundane act to a higher key of meaning. It seeks to involve our emotions in the service of our ideals. In the words of William James, it is "a daily down payment" on our convictions and aspirations. The concept of freedom and the dignity of man penetrate into our muscle and bloodstream through the annual reenactment, by means of symbols, of the drama of liberation at our Passover tables, as it could never do by intellectual exposition alone.

Ritual should not become, as our prophets and sages never tired of reminding us, a substitute for morality or an escape from principle. Mere observance is not religion. It is, however, an invaluable instrument for preserving morality and principle. In an ennobling religion ritual reenforces ideal, disciplines and refines man, binds him more closely to God and to humanity. Woven into the daily texture of his life, ritual is a constant reminder to man as to who he is and what his supreme goals and duties are.

AMERICA'S FOURTH RELIGION

WILL HERBERG HAS SUGGESTED* that the true diversity of America is to be found in the religious rather than in the cultural or ethnic area. This idea has commended itself to other students of our national scene. C. Bezalel Sherman† has pointed out that no ethnic group in American life, save the Jewish, has perpetuated itself and preserved its corporate integrity beyond the third generation. Gerhard Lenski ‡ made religious affiliation the base for

---

*In *Protestant Catholic Jew, An Essay in American Religion Sociology.*
†In *The Jew Within American Society.*
‡In *The Religious Factor.*

his study of the differing social, political, and economic views of
a large sampling of the Detroit population. There is widespread
agreement among sociologists that we should think of America
as a land of three faiths—Catholic, Protestant, Jewish.

The student who is more interested in religion as an effective
and significant force rather than as a sociological datum, however, must conclude that the religions of America are not
exhausted by the enumeration of the three creeds generally
named. Indeed the most popular is not included in this list: the
"Fourth Faith"—faith in faith—which has the largest number of
communicants. Without benefit of clergy or organized structure,
it is the country's most powerful religion.

If one were to ignore the formal adherence of people and
their professions of belief and determine their religion solely by
the lives they lead, we would find that most Americans live not
by a specific creed but respond rather to a faith in faith. They
believe that religion (without spelling out any definite duties or
articles of belief) is a precious thing and that it promotes
morality and the social good. A person not identified with religion is suspect: he is a heretic who denies a widely held American conviction—that of the value and necessity of religion.

The religion of America is therefore a vagueness, a fine
general sentiment, a large abstract feeling that neither makes
immediate demands nor imposes definite obligations. The empty
pews in the land's churches and synagogues do not represent
denial or rejection of religion. They are eloquent expressions of
the prevailing conception that religion does not require imple-
mentation, since for each of the unoccupied seats in our country's
sanctuaries there is a member of the rolls duly affiliated and
recorded. This explains too why people who belong to organized
religious groups do not sense the sharp conflict that exists between the teachings of their faith and their own practices in
business or in race relations. Religion is poetry; religion is sentiment; religion is the honor we pay forefathers; religion is the
foundation of national life; religion is character. But life is life,
business is business, and, after all, we have to be realistic.

Americans with remarkable ingenuity are thus able to in-
herit the best of all possible worlds. They are citizens of the

kingdom of heaven: do they not affirm, uphold, and exalt religion? This citizenship, however, does not interfere with their
full exploitation and enjoyment of life on earth.

Such a general and indeterminate religion cuts across all
denominational lines and unites devotees of various specific faiths
into a populous church of the general, the vague, the abstract.

THE FREEDOM IN FAITH

O Lord I am indeed Thy servant. I am Thy servant, the son
of Thy handmaid. Thou hast loosed my bonds.
                                        (Psalm 116—Hallel)

THESE WORDS WERE SAID by an ancient Psalmist. He was no
stranger to fear, no alien to sorrow, loneliness, or hostility. As
he finds himself enmeshed in the coils of trouble and grief,
heart-rending words escape him: "The cords of death have en-
circled me, and the straits of the netherworld had overtaken me;
I was in anguish and sorrow." Enemies hounded him, and pur-
suers gave him no peace. Only when he turned to God did he
know release from anxiety and trouble. Thus he proclaims in
gratitude: "Thou has loosed my bonds." In faith in God, he is
saying, I have found freedom. My religion has brought emancipation.

Ourselves not unversed in anxiety, we can understand the
Psalmist's inner turmoil. But his description of religion as liberation is likely to baffle many of us, who see it as a system of
disciplines, a code seeking to check the unhampered rein of
human thought, a hedge about conduct, a fence around the
mind, a chain on the impulses. Do we not call one who repudiates religion a "freethinker"? Does not a man who prides himself on his liberation from dogma and ritual speak of his religious
phase as a time when he was hampered and limited by the "thou
shalt not's"?

What is the element of emancipation that religion embraces?
What freedom can faith bring? What experiences of liberation
did the Psalmist and others find in their creeds?

Religion brings freedom from fear. The Psalmist elsewhere says, "Though a host should encamp against me, my heart shall not fear," and "The Lord is my light and my salvation, whom shall I fear? The Lord is the stronghold of my life, of whom shall I be afraid?" (Psalm 27). We are so puny, each of us, alongside the vast universe in which we are set. The world dwarfs us and the contrast staggers us. There is an impenetrable area of aloneness in each of us, out of which comes fear. The future is a huge question mark, especially in our time, alive with ominous possibilities.

Religion pictures a universe in which we can feel a great measure of at-homeness. It is law-abiding, dependable, governed by a Power dedicated to justice. To be sure, there are mystery and uncertainty too. That mystery, however, is the result of our limited comprehension. It does not overthrow the basic pattern of regularity which religion perceives behind all the variety and appearances. No sudden spirit of evil will spring from a bush upon us. No malignancy inheres in the nature of things, nor is it an ineradicable part of reality. This is a world in which man will often grieve, frequently recoil in pain, and on occasion meet with frustration. Deeper than all these, however, is the fundamental character of a life governed by a God who cares for man. Fear is banished when such a Power allows us to relate ourselves to Him in love and reverence. Faith frees man from fear.

Faith also liberates from an overhanging sense of futility. Man is so constituted that he cannot achieve stability except as he feels he is serving a significant purpose. One of the characters in Dostoyevsky's *The Brothers Karamazov* exclaims that he seeks neither wealth nor position; he wants only to know where we are bound and whether there is any meaning to life. In our day, the bottom of meaning has dropped out from many lives. History seems a series of unrelated episodes, with no underlying motif or purpose.

Religion affirms that while here too the entire pattern of human life does not easily reveal itself, a pattern does exist. Man's collective experience is a drama, marked by coherence and ultimate purpose. To be sure, it does not move onward in a straight line to its denouement. There are setbacks, detours, hesitations, and defeats. There is, however, a direction to human affairs. Man is not an accident. He is a player in a meaningful drama, and this belief frees him from despair and futility.

Faith can also free man from failure. We live in a competitive world in which appraisals of success are made by contrast. The greater wealth which a few have amassed throws a shadow upon those of us whose efforts in a commercial society have not yielded so rich a reward. The higher rungs which some have reached on the ladder of fame and public esteem stigmatize our lower position on that ladder and betray our failure. All through our society lines of demarcation divide men into successes and failures; the "right" people and the others.

Religion offers freedom from this throttling and humiliating feeling. The true goods of life are not distributed on a competitive basis. The success of one does not determine the failure of another, nor does it depend on circumstances outside of himself. No man has failed who in the sphere of his life, however modest, has fulfilled the prophetic prescription of doing justly, loving mercy, and walking humbly with God. The honorable life is the successful life. The man of integrity need never feel subordinate. He who has built a home, has extended affection to his children, and has stimulated in them an attachment to right values, need never be burdened by the frustration of failure. Life is not a race in which the largest number is inevitably doomed to failure. All can be numbered among life's successful.

Thus does religion loose the bonds. It liberates from fear, futility, and failure, and enables us to enjoy the dignity and self-assurance of free men.

9 • *To Believe, to Pray*

UNIVERSE OF WONDER

SAMUEL JOHNSON ONCE REMARKED that "the two most engaging powers of an author are to make new things familiar and familiar things new." His statement points up the two varying (though complementary) functions of science and religion. The first seeks to confer the assurance and satisfaction that knowledge of the world about us yields. We are uneasy in the presence of the strange and the unpredictable. They spell mystery and to some degree danger. The unknown intrigues our curiosity and inspires restlessness within us.

One of the finest attributes of the human mind is its insatiable hunger to know and understand the world. Our feeling of at-homeness in the physical universe grows with our increasing grasp of the forces and laws that operate within it. Thus science brings the hitherto uncomprehended into the ken of our knowledge. It makes the world a "familiar" place, and thus enables us to live in greater peace and security within it.

Religion's task is the converse. It aims to have us live with an unfailing sense of wonderment and excitement. Every sight which our eyes behold, every breath we draw, and every encounter we experience are charged with mystery and depth. The laws that operate in the universe—are they not marvels of infinite wonder? The sun rising every morning is a tribute to an order beyond the ability of the human mind fully to fathom. The stars in their courses sing hymns of praise to the Cosmic Poet in whose mind they first arose as thoughts, even as "the heavens declare the glory of God and the firmament shows His handiwork."

Our growing knowledge should augment our awareness of the wonders about us. The man of faith seeing the hand of God in all that transpires is constantly agitated by the unending procession of divine manifestations everywhere he turns. The mind within us that thinks, the heart that feels—are they less wondrous than the mountains on earth or the constellations in heaven? There is a universe of wonder within us. The passing days and moving years are themselves enchanting fragments of an eternity beyond human reckoning.

Nothing is commonplace in a world over which the spirit of God hovers. A universe which renews itself daily has no room in it for the dull and commonplace. The Psalmist prays, "Open Thou mine eyes that I may behold wondrous things. . . ." Only he whose eyes are closed and whose heart has hardened will fail to recognize that he is participant in and spectator of a cavalcade of daily wonders. For in the world of faith everything is new and wonders never cease.

THOUGHTS AT SEA

THE SEA BRINGS TO a landlocked viewer a refreshing sense of liberation from the "four ells" of his usual preoccupations. The person who prides himself on his wide-roaming interests and pursuits feels humbled in the presence of the sea.

For the sea speaks of far-ranging, unexplored dimensions of reality which reach far beyond the limits of our habitual movements and concerns. The sea suggests depths in the universe alongside of which we appear to tread surfaces and live in the shallows. It reminds us that the world is not exhausted by the activities which dominate our lives—our doing, getting, spending, loving, laughing. Even our thoughts, however far we extend them, project themselves forward only to the nearest edge of the limitlessness of the sea.

The cities in which we live speak of man's power, and the machines and work of his hands reveal his dominion. But here at sea one senses an energy which makes all the manifestations of human strength and ingenuity appear as the work of a child playing in the sand. Both Rabbi Akiba and Sir Isaac Newton, separated by centuries, and living in vastly differing cultures, invoked this selfsame figure to express their continuing perception of the unrecorded mystery and vastness of the cosmic background against which human life and thought are enacted. We have succeeded in climbing mountains, in spanning continents, in annihilating space. The sea alone suggests something of the awe and wonder, the mystery and power of a world we are prone to think of as having been completely subdued to our purposes.

In our modern day, for the first time in history, we live in an almost exclusively man-made environment. Space is orbited by satellites thrust there by man. Even the heavens seem as frontiers that beckon rather than boundaries that exclude. Yet modern man seems hemmed in by his own works, and his view too often ends at the ramparts he himself has built. His philosophy too often betrays a self-assurance growing out of his sense of power over the areas he controls instead of revealing a humility arising from an awareness of the infinite expanses of his ignorance. Perhaps that is why neither great poetry nor significant theology is fashioned in our day.

Man has never needed so much the eloquent testimony which the sea offers of worlds beyond the world he occupies, of time beyond his time, of meanings and mysteries beyond those encompassed by his facile mind.

WHAT PRAYER IS

PRAYER IS THE DOOR that takes us out of the imprisoning moment into the time that flows from uncounted yesterdays to unborn tomorrows. Prayer builds a bridge from the silences of our loneliness into the heart of another. Prayer is the step on which we rise from the self we are to the self we wish to be. Prayer affirms the hope that no reality can crush, the aspiration that can never acknowledge defeat. Prayer is the ladder on which, in rising Godward, we can see that large timeless movement of life of which we are but a point. Prayer is the assertion of all that makes us human over the creatureliness that would stifle it. Prayer opens the eyes to that invisible universe in which justice, beauty, truth, and goodness are the most solid facts. Prayer reveals truths about ourselves and the world that neither scalpel nor microscope can uncover.

But to be a vital and transforming force in our life, prayer cannot be an occasional mood, a moment's thought, a passing response, or a fugitive insight. It must be given permanence in our normal outlook and habitual behavior. Its rewards are great, for it rings us about with large horizons and evokes from us the greatness to live in their presence. Wherever we go, we carry a sanctuary with us.

Such rewards are not easily achieved. We cannot gulp a prayer down. We cannot run into a house of worship and quickly arm ourselves with its spirit. We cannot forsake its cultivation and then in a dark moment of need expect it to yield instant comfort, strength, and healing. We cannot lead a life that is a daily refutation of all that worship means and expect occasional prayers to compensate for our failure. The words of our prayers have no life apart from the work of our hands.

One of the most moving prayers in the Torah reads, "Look forth from Thy holy habitation, from heaven, and bless Thy people Israel and the land which Thou hast given us as Thou didst swear unto our fathers, a land flowing with milk and honey." When did the Israelites of old speak these words? Only when, as pilgrims, they brought their tithes to the Levite, stranger, fatherless, and widowed, and could each testify, "I have hearkened to the voice of the Lord, my God; I have done according to all that Thou hast commanded me."

Prayer is no escape from duty, no substitute for deed. Prayer seeks the power to do wisely, to act generously, to live helpfully. It helps to reenforce the act rather than replace it. When Sanballat and his associates threatened Jerusalem, how did the Hebrews respond to the peril? "We prayed unto the Lord, our God, and set watch against them day and night, because of them." They prayed and kept guard; men of faith, they prayed even as they acted. Prayer does not mean casting our burden upon God, but drawing upon faith for the resolve to bear our own burden. When Pharaoh and his hosts pursued the Israelites at the Red Sea, Moses began to pray. God rebuked Moses: "Speak unto the children of Israel, that they may go forward." Deeds were what was needed.

To pray means to believe in ourselves because we believe in God. To pray means that a divine image stirs within and seeks to be heard. To pray means to be humble, for we pray out of need for and dependence upon Another.

Said the Rabbis of old: "Do His will as if it were thy will; let thy will give way before His will." Not what "I want" but what "right demands"; not what "I desire" but what "love commands"; not what "I like," but what 'God requires" should be the mainspring of what we wish to do. Prayer takes us beyond the self and its narrowing surface wishes. Joining our little self to the selfhood of humanity, it gives our wishes the freedom to grow large and broad and inclusive. Our prayers are answered not when we are given what we ask but when we are challenged to be what we can be.

LIFE'S MANY BLESSINGS

AN ANCIENT TEACHER, Rabbi Meir, suggested that a man should in gratitude recite at least a hundred benedictions daily. Even on the most ordinary and uneventful of days there are many occasions for the expression of gratitude to the Great Provider.

Charles Lamb once lamented that religion had not ordained grace for books, "those spiritual repasts—a grace before Milton—a grace before Shakespeare—a devotional exercise proper to be said before reading the *Faerie Queen*." A benediction over a book might open our eyes to the recognition that the reading of a good book is a miracle inviting us to adventure and high companionship.

Should not friendship be sanctified with a benediction? At the core of each of us is an impregnable island of loneliness and apartness. The world so often appears impersonal, unconcerned. Along comes a true friend, and warms the heart within and the climate without. Should not he who brings blessing be greeted with blessing?

And does not a letter merit benediction? Overcoming distance, it punctuates absence with a cordial and friendly encounter. We are connected with a near one who happens to be far by a message from his mind and heart. The characteristic turn of a phrase, the subject of the correspondence, the warmth of the style, do they not give body to the absent and bring near the distant? Do we not recite benedictions over lesser miracles?

The sight of a child is another fitting occasion for thankful prayer. He symbolizes a beauty, an innocence, and virtue beyond the power of our senses to penetrate. A seedbed of infinite possibilities, he carries within him potential riches unduplicated in the greatest treasury or the largest laboratory. Into a world of grime and guile, evil and intrigue, he wafts breezes of cleanliness and goodness. Surely a child calls us to prayer.

Literally thousands of other gifts deserve to be crowned with blessing—the magic of a melody that captures the heart, an idea that exalts the mind, tree, bird, falling snow, refreshing rain, home, congenial conversation, the freedoms to which we awake every morning, twilight and dawn, autumn leaves, rebirth in the spring.

Someone has said that life is most truly measured by the depth and scope of one's awareness. Is it less true to say that the quality of our life is reflected by the nature of things that move us to pronounce a blessing?

THE CANTOR

THE WORSHIP OF THE Jew is inconceivable without song. Indeed, say the Rabbis, he who studies Torah without melody fails to penetrate to its essence. We may not ourselves be blessed with the gift of song, yet if we worship with earnestness and devoutness, our prayer creates its own song. Moses is described in the Torah as being "slow of speech and of a slow tongue," but it is he who leads the people of Israel in a song of incomparable ecstasy and power.

The truly dedicated and sensitive *hazzan* or cantor gives voice both to the articulated and the soundless songs of the congregation. Like every artist, he must first express the deep feelings, visions, and experiences of his own soul. But he is more than an artist working in isolation, struggling only to bring forth his own yearnings, love and anguish, seeking only to communicate the unique and individual universe whose solitary inhabitant he is. He is the *Sheliah Tzibbur*, the "emissary of the community."

Hence the cantor must also gather into his song the wide-ranging melodies of many hearts. He must awaken the mute and lethargic. He must give nobility of expression to those who can only inadequately sing their own song. They must recognize their song in his life as he stirs and evokes unfulfilled and unsuspected depths of the melody imprisoned within their own spirits.

But the community whose song he captures, interprets, and releases is not only of the now and here. It has its roots in history. It has lived long with time, and the present generation is only the most recent of a rich procession of generations who yearned and worshipped and sang. The cantor's melody must embrace the song of the centuries. For though "a generation goeth and a generation cometh," their prayers remain and become a part of the ever-expanding and ever-deepening tradition. The song that does not speak to the contemporary ear will not be heard, but the song that does not have the overtones and echoes of the many who have prayed across the expanse of time will not redeem and sanctify.

Thus the *hazzan* must weave the hopes, sorrows, joys of his generation into the noble religious tapestry of many generations, and thus liberate the prayers of our day from their restricting immediacies and narrowing presentness.

The true *hazzan* leads us more deeply into our soul and more richly into the faith of our people as our prayer fuses with his on a plane beyond our own power to attain.

THE NEW SHAAREY ZEDEK *

Laying the Cornerstone

THERE ARE RARE and unduplicated moments into which all of the
tenses seem to be compressed. Such moments are multidimensional and overleap the limitations of their own time to fuse
with all of time. This is such a moment. The past, present, and
future live within it with extraordinary vitality and vividness.
At a significant pass in the early history of Israel, Moses addressed
these words to the assemblage, "Not with you alone do I make
this covenant and this oath; but with him that standeth here with
us this day before the Lord our God and also with him that is
not here with us this day. . . ." Thus do we feel that on this day
of consecration and festivity we are at the center of a throng
who have come out of the near and distant past to join us, as
well as of generations of unborn successors who will one day
stand where we stand today.

In their presence and with a profound awareness of their
nearness on this bright Sunday morning in June, we lay a cornerstone of our new sanctuary, to be dedicated soon, as were its
predecessors, to the worship of God and the service of man.
If you will look at the box which we shall soon place into the
cornerstone you will see an oblong bronze receptacle in which
will be deposited various records and mementos of this occasion.
But we ask you to look at it through the eyes of the imagination
so that your view may exalt the heart and excite the mind. The
cornerstone of this great edifice contains much more and much
else than the physical articles to which I have alluded and which
time and the elements can destroy.

This sanctuary rests upon a cornerstone of affirmation—
values and beliefs immune to the corrosions to which the material and earthy are subject. May there rise from the cornerstone to pervade the entire structure the undying spirit which
has ever inspired the Jew to be a builder of shrines and altars.

Embedded in the cornerstone is a firm and unweakening

---

*Address at the Laying of the Cornerstone Ceremony, June 17, 1962.

hope for the future. We are building not for ourselves alone but for those who will follow. We build not simply in the faith that there will be a future but also out of the conviction that the future will be congenial to the ideals and values we cherish. It is not easy in our day to look forward with assurance to a future beyond our time. The entire inhabited globe is darkened by a sombre cloud of apprehension and foreboding. Despair has taken up residence in millions of human hearts, and fear enslaves multitudes. There are even young people among us whose eyes are anxiety-haunted as they raise them toward the horizons of their future.

We here affirm and carve into the very cornerstone of our faith our belief in the capacity of man to move forward from the gloom and confusion of today to a morrow bright with healing and peace. It is out of our profound and unalterable commitment as Jews to the idea that history under God has direction and purpose that we proclaim that there will be a future. History was not meant to end in dissolution, in a gasp, a sigh, and death. Man is a principal in a history that is going somewhere, and his collective life, though often tortuous and perverse, is not without a destination. Within our own hearts we here reenforce our faith that there will be morrows for humanity during which the striving for peace, justice, understanding will beat high, and that man's intelligence in the service of his ideals will bring about their greater realization.

Even as our eyes look forward to our unborn successors, we are mindful of those whom we have succeeded. We are born of a great ancestry whose bequest enduringly lives on within us. Mankind grows not by leaps and bounds but by steady and persistent accumulation. Culture and civilization embody the gathered wisdom, insights, talents, and creativity of generations. To turn our back upon the past is to skate precariously on the thin surface of a single lifetime. We live in a community of time. Our roots go back centuries in the experience of mankind. To isolate ourselves from our forebears is to imprison ourselves in the confines of the transitory moment. To scrap the past is to pauperize the present. Only as we see ourselves as the inhabitants of the frontier of a vast historic background that stretches behind us can we rise to the larger view and achieve the greater perspective. Only then can we focus upon the persisting problems of human life, not the flyspeck of a single generation's restricted experience but the funded wisdom of many generations. We affirm today with gratitude and humility our reverence for the past, our indebtedness to it for guidance and stimulation, our deep sense of continuity with its noblest aspirations and profoundest cognitions.

United with our faith in the future and our linkage with the past is also our vital response to the present in which we live and function. As we look at posterity and ancestry, we also encompass ourselves in the total view. We recognize anew that the great cohesions that weld us into a Jewish community are not incidental or accidental. They are not born out of the circumstances of sorrow which have overwhelmed us in recent decades and to relieve which so much of our effort and substance have properly been expended.

What unites us is not the misunderstanding of which the Jew has historically been the object and victim. We have frequently banded together to repel our detractors and to stay the hand of those hate-perverted segments that would do us hurt. But we are not primarily or essentially a fraternity of the aggrieved, a society for defense, an agency of relief. We are a community sharing a history, a faith, a hope. The foundation of our common life is our Torah with its ethical principles and prophetic spirit. Heirs of a tradition saturated with a passion for justice, peace, and truth, we bear within us the imprint of its moral impulse and power. This structure itself is merely frame and habitation. Its significance and sanctity derive from the word and the doctrine that will form the curriculum of its life and the goal of its endeavors.

May there go forth from this place to all the community that undying hope which will impel us never to desist in building the future that will embody our cherished ideals; that mellowing reverence which will lead us to fortify ourselves with the strength and substance that only a noble past can afford us; and that view of ourselves and our community which will stir our deepest potentialities as Jews to fulfillment so that we and our fellowmen may know life at its richest and most sacred.

May He who inspired us to build this sanctuary and whose

Name will ever dwell in it cause love and devotion, friendship and understanding to dwell among us.

First Service

IT IS WITH AWE, gratitude, and solemn anticipation that we assemble to worship for the first time in this, our new sanctuary. Its majesty, the beauty of its appearance, and the grandeur of its design awaken in us a warm and trembling responsiveness. This is henceforth to be our spiritual home and that of our children after us. The real importance of the structure is, however, not to be found in its spaciousness, its attractiveness, the boldness of the plan which it embodies. Its basic significance is to be sought in what it symbolizes. What do its walls, its stained-glass windows, its chapels, its library and classrooms say to us? What are the affirmations that have been, so to speak, built into this physical structure?

We affirm here a belief in a God of justice and love, whose existence underwrites all our hopes for peace, understanding, and human cooperation. This affirmation is not abstract doctrine, a theological principle to be professed on occasion, but that solid base upon which we rear our systems of beliefs and values. Over all the myriad appearances of the world, its clashes and strayings, its perplexities and perversities, a Presence hovers who represents both a way of life and a judgment.

We affirm here a reverence for and an acceptance of a past. As Jews we are not foundlings abandoned on the threshold of modern life. We are the rich products of a long and civilizing history. We are the heirs of a large experience which gives scope to our otherwise pathetically restricted individual lives, and provides us with wisdom, compassion, and insight. We invite the prophet, the sage, the saint, the poet, the philosopher, the artist of all the yesteryears to dwell here in our midst so that our perspective may be enlarged and our understanding deepened. Here the rush of daily life is subdued, its raucousness mellowed, its impulsiveness checked as it encounters the maturity of history. We here are dedicated to keep open and clear the many channels through which the Jewish past may communicate with us.

We affirm here a faith in the future. Clouds darken a great part of the globe in our day, and a black and ominous question mark sits astride the entire horizon. Our generation has mastered the technology of death, and its newly discovered skill is a constant threat. Though some are ready to write an epitaph for a mankind whose destructive powers outpaces its wisdom, we here speak in accents of hope, a hope grounded in determination, dedication, and discipline.

We here affirm the enduring dignity of the human being and the invincible potentialities of the human mind. In an age of massive corporateness, global pressures, and impersonal forces, we insist that the basic reality in human society is the individual and his freedom, his integrity and dignity. We likewise proclaim our faith in human reason as an indispensable factor in advancing the world. To all theories that belittle the mind and express their scorn of the intellect, we say nay. Passion unillumined by reason, faith unguided by the mind can lead society into the darkest corners of peril and perversity.

This inanimate structure will come to life and rise to sanctity only as we imbue it with the great objectives, the reverent worship, the selfless devotion which our tradition teaches us.

WHAT THOU GIVEST

Shall I cry out in anger, O God
  Because Thy gifts are mine but for a while?
Shall I forget the blessing of health
  The moment it gives way to illness and pain?
Shall I be ungrateful for the moments of laughter
  The season of joy, the days of gladness and festivity,
  When tears cloud my eyes and darken the world
    And my heart is heavy within me?
Shall I blot from mind the love
  I have known and in which I have rejoiced
  When a fate beyond my understanding takes from me
  Friends and kin whom I have cherished, and leaves me
  Bereft of shining presences that have lit my way
  Through years of companionship and affection?
Shall I in days of adversity fail to recall
  The hours of joy and glory Thou once hast granted me?
Shall I in turmoil of need and anxiety
  Cease blessing Thee for the peace of former days?
Shall the time of darkness put out forever
  The glow of the light in which I once walked?
Give me the vision, O God, to see and feel
  That imbedded deep in each of Thy gifts
  Is a core of eternity, undiminished and bright,
  An eternity that survives the dread hours of
    affliction and misery.
Those I have loved, though now beyond my view,
  Have given form and quality to my being.
  They have led me into the wide universe
  I continue to inhabit, and their presence
  Is more vital to me than their absence.

What Thou givest, O Lord,
  Thou takest not away.
  And bounties once granted
  Shed their radiance evermore.

BORN UNTO TROUBLE

"MAN IS BORN UNTO TROUBLE, even as the sparks fly upward."
In these words in the Book of Job, the Hebrew term for "man"
is *adam*, the most comprehensive of all designations embracing
the entire human race. Being human means to resolve the conflict between judgment and appetite, reason and drive, self and
society, right and caprice, mutuality and egotism, hostility and
kindness. To live without problems is to descend to a subhuman
amoral level of apathy and attrition.

"Man is born unto trouble." That is both his lot and his
opportunity. His lot since he is often caught in a vortex of
pressures and tensions that banish ease and peace. His opportunity, because in wrestling with the challenges and difficulties
that assail him he has the possibility of winning a redemptive
and humanizing victory.

"Man is born unto trouble." The real trouble, however, is
that men permit themselves to be tormented by problems unworthy of them: that vex but do not uplift, oppress but do not
purify and enlighten. "Why does another have more than I do?
Why was I not invited? Why cannot I join an exclusive club?"
Such problems spring not from high idealism, curiosity, yearning
for beauty, but from envy, hostility, greed.

"Man is born unto trouble." He will never know complete
ease who in his devotion to justice is pained by every manifestation of evil, cruelty, and inequity. He will never relax into
serenity who cannot accept the tawdriness and shabbiness that
prevail in so many places. He who is devoted to freedom will
know unhappiness and frustration as he views the oppression
under which many still live and the arbitrary denial of people's
rights which is still practiced. The heart full of compassion will

not withdraw into a shelter of calm and placidity as long as there are people who suffer anguish and grief. The true worshipper of God cannot retreat to quiet and remote meditation in a world in which men continue to bend the knee to idols of gold and vanity, and burn incense on altars dedicated to power and dominion.

"Man is born unto trouble." Out of his trouble man fashions his keenest insights, his most delicate sensitivities, and his loftiest aspirations. To be troubled by great problems is to be most human.

PAIN

PAIN IS A MANY-FACETED and multidimensional phenomenon. It cannot be easily defined nor summarily treated. Though pain may sometimes seem to be concentrated in a specific area, it is really never local, since it serves as an expression of a total personality. Whatever its origin, there are inevitably mental, emotional, and spiritual undertones, involvements, and impacts that embrace the entire being of the sufferer. The intimate interrelationship of body, mind, and soul makes it impossible for an individual to experience severe or sustained hurt in any one part without waves of reaction coursing through the whole system. Pain thus affects, even as it reflects, the personality in its fullness and intricacy. To deal with the problem of pain with any degree of adequacy, one would have to bring together several disciplines that have man as the object of their specialized study. Physician, psychologist, psychiatrist, sociologist, religious counsellor—all have a particular interest in this field, and each has a specific contribution to make toward our understanding of the problem of pain.

The intensity and character of pain felt by a person bear a relationship not only to his bodily condition, but perhaps primarily to his background, temperament, experience, and outlook

---

* Lead article in the *Bulletin*, Sinai Hospital of Detroit, spring, 1960.

upon life. This fact suggests divergent approaches to its treatment in different individuals. Pain varies with individuals, and indeed will often vary in the same individual at different moments and at successive stages of his life. A man's response to pain-inducing situations will rest more largely on subjective elements than on objective causes. Cultures likewise vary in the attitudes to pain which they impart and induce, and these cultural attitudes become incorporated in the individual reactions of those who have lived within the province of the cultures. The stoicism and apparent impassivity which we associate with the Oriental response to suffering and grief represent such a cultural influence. One culture, someone has pointed out, may stimulate its members to regard pain as one regards bad weather, something impersonal over which one has no control, and which will pass in the course of time; another society may instill a concept of pain as an attacking marauder, to be met with the hostility and resentment proper to the assault of an intruder, and never to be accepted with equanimity or resignation.

The person undergoing severe pain is often overwhelmed by a humiliating loss of dignity arising from the feeling that he is no longer master of himself. From within one's own body, or from some external source, there comes a force which in asserting its power over the individual reduces him to helplessness and dependence. In our particular cultural setting no virtue or achievement has been more emphatically extolled or more consistently upheld than "independence," the ability of a man to stand on his own feet, to be self-determining, self-sustaining, self-supporting. Our supreme national holiday is "Independence Day." One of the most famed of American writings is Emerson's essay significantly titled "Self-Reliance." Our national life began with a "Declaration of Independence." Hence pain that results in the loss of this most admired attribute induces in Americans intense frustration and hurt.

The deprivation of his independence and the necessity of reliance on others become aspects of the patient's reaction, complicating and deepening his pain. If the patient is rooted in a religious background and outlook, much can be done to ease the humiliation he feels in consequence of his reduced status of dependence. It can first be shown that independence properly understood does not exclude dependence. Dependence, far from being shameful, is related to that interdependence from which human progress and achievement directly flow. That "no man is an island unto himself" is a fact to be celebrated rather than lamented, since it enables us to engage in enriching interrelationships with others, with contemporary society and the past. Dependence in and of itself is neither a sign of failure nor an occasion for pity.

Religious teaching goes further. It stresses not only man's supreme dignity but also his sublime dependence. Indeed, there have been students and thinkers who have defined religion largely in terms of man's awareness of dependence. The doctor and the hospital are visible symbols of man's dependence upon the healing forces in the universe, which are one of the manifestations of God's presence in human affairs. Religious literature is filled with references to man's dependence. There is nothing debasing about a state of dependence in which one is the object of God's love and concern. One aspect of man's dignity is precisely his subordination to and reliance upon his cosmic Father. A man's innate worth is not at the mercy of circumstance.

Pain often isolates one from others by giving rise to the conviction that one is being visited by an unduplicated experience which another cannot possibly comprehend or estimate. Some of the well-meaning sentiments of visiting friends are mentally dismissed by the patient, for he feels that since they are unaware of the extent or poignancy of his suffering, their words must perforce be shallow, formal, and unrelated to his true condition. This attitude is widely indicated by the words of the Biblical elegy, "Behold and see, if there be any pain like unto my pain which is done unto me; wherewith the Lord had afflicted me in the day of His fierce anger?" (Lamentations 1). One concludes that one has been singled out for a fate of particular grimness, and its severity is incommunicable by reason of its uniqueness. A complex of aloneness and isolation joined to resentment is formed.

A religiously oriented patient may slowly and gently be reawakened, even in his despondency and rebellion, to an awareness of God's benign nearness and of His unsunderable kinship with His children. There is a cosmic heart which feels the pain of every human. The Divine Father understands and is indeed sym-

pathetic to the mood which underlies the exclamation of the
Psalmist, "Why standest Thou afar off, O Lord? Why hidest
Thou Thyself in times of trouble" (Psalm 10) and "My God, My
God why hast Thou forsaken me, and art far from my help at
the words of my cry? O My God, I call by day but Thou an-
swerest not, and at night and there is no surcease for me" (Psalm
22). Jeremiah sadly asks:

> Why is my pain perpetual,
>   And my wound incurable, so that
>   it refuseth to be healed?
> Wilt Thou indeed be unto me as a
>   deceitful brook,
>   As waters that fail?
>   (Jeremiah 15:18)

Through counseling the sufferer may be brought to the recognition that his pain, far from being unparalleled, has been the
lot of others. He has not been chosen for special punishment.
Sorrow and pain are constant companions of life, and rare indeed
is he who is unacquainted with them. "No man is free from pain,"
say the Rabbis. Even in our extremity we are not alone, not only
because others have known pain equal to our own, but also because God is near. The religious counselor will strive to relieve
the patient's sense of guilt stimulated by his rebellious and resent-
ful thoughts. Quotations from the Bible will indicate that God's
compassion extends particularly to those in distress. "The Lord is
nigh unto them that are of a broken heart and saveth such as are
of a contrite spirit" (Psalms 34:19). His divine compassion is
compounded of love and understanding, and He recognizes that
suffering can bring a man to anger and irritation. With this understanding comes forgiveness.

It is also helpful to indicate that religion does not paint life
as eternally unclouded and man as being always at ease. Faith is
not a naïve and romantic conception promising uninterrupted
serenity. It is rather a triumphant affirmation, in the full knowledge of the pathos and tragedy with which life abounds, that pain
and sorrow neither constitute the ultimate fact nor reveal the
deepest reality of human existence. Faith demands realism,
strength, resolve, not softness, tender-mindedness, and complacency. While there is no complete or final answer to the mystery

of human sorrow and suffering, one must not see one's pain as proof of life's injustice. A patient who has been brought up in a religious home may be led to a resurgence of confidence and a renewal of hope by a mature interpretation of the religious outlook.

It seems to be God's plan, we know not why, that man struggle upward through pain, frustration, and grief to heights of spiritual insight. There is a wisdom and a humaneness which can be achieved only as we have endured the discipline of pain. Every person, the Rabbis tell us, is tested of God. Our response to pain reveals authentic dimensions that abide far beneath the surfaces of our being and that are not evoked by the routine of our daily life. The man who goes down into the valley of anguish may often through his familiarity with sorrow ascend to the peak of sensitivity and spiritual vision. Whether we suffer or not is not determined by us. But we can decide whether our sufferings crush or purify us, chain our spirit or open new vistas of understanding.

Man's ability to transmute pain into growth and thus triumph over adversity is of itself eloquent testimony to and evidence of the existence of a benign Creator. In sorrow man can enlarge his compassion and patience, elevate his mental and moral sights, and emerge more human and more mature.

> For Thou hast seen mine affliction,
> Thou has taken cognizance of the
>   troubles of my soul . . .
> Thou hast set my feet in a broad place.
>   (Psalms 31:8,9)

This is the victory man can win. Without minimizing the sorrows of life or dismissing pain as being of little consequence, the religious man will regard his affliction as a challenge. It is a test of his spirit. It is a trial which by the proper response man can turn into a triumph.

NOBLE MEN LIVE MANY LIVES

NOT ONLY COWARDS DIE many deaths. From the Jewish viewpoint, death may intervene in life many times, and interrupt the living of many different types of people. For life in the Hebraic sense is not a biological phenomenon, a physical fact, or a social condition. It is a human achievement. One lives when one realizes one's human potential and capacity; one dies when one stifles or perverts one's human faculties.

Life begins at the point where our similarities with the animal kingdom end and where our human differential begins. Life is thus a qualitative matter, not a quantitative or physical one. This is the meaning of the phrase "A Torah of Life" and the verse "It is a tree of life unto them that grasp it."

Hence we die when we regress into unreasoning hostility which springs from the primeval inheritance we share with all creatures. We die when we tar an entire people with the thick brush of our prejudice, and indiscriminately stigmatize an entire race or group, when we abdicate our powers of judgment and allow passion and hate to rule us.

We die when we allow our own good fortune of social, economic, or political status to breed in us a spirit of superiority and exclusiveness. We die when we shut our hearts to the cries of those in need, hoping to find in insulation escape from sadness and responsibility. We die when we do not share the common life, and fail to bear with dignity and willingness our share of its burdens.

We die when we hurry through life, denying ourselves moments for calm reflection, spiritual renewal, and the viewing of the beauty of nature and the drama of its seasons. We die when we permit ourselves to become so earthbound as never to see the heavens.

We live more fully when we open our hearts in love to another. We live when we allow our mind to receive a new idea and slowly and reverently explore its meaning. We live when we play, however humbly, a part in the unending struggle for freedom and justice. We live when from us there flows even the smallest trickle of wholesomeness and health into our community. We live when through a book, a painting, or a song, we commune with a noble and creative soul.

We live when in the midst of fellow worshippers we respond to a quickening sense of the presence in us of a great and rich tradition. We live when we recognize a sacred place, and humbly and prayerfully enter it. We live when beneath the swirl and rush of the life about us we find a central calm and meaning. We live when we become aware of our dependence upon others, and glory in the benefactions received from home, culture, tradition, and friends. We live when we cease seeking mastery over others, and attain self-rule in terms of high humane values. We live when we joyously pledge to serve the welfare of others, the advancement of great purposes, the enrichment of society.

How fortunate are we who can live many lives, and need die but once!

WHAT THE MATURE YEARS OFFER *

THE WIDESPREAD DISCUSSION about senior citizens, the aging, and the organization of golden age groups in many agencies indicates a great awareness of a problem that has achieved special prominence in our time. In a sense the problem is a tribute to our advance in the realm of medicine and our success in conquering ailments that heretofore claimed great numbers. The life expectancy of the average man and woman has been greatly prolonged with the consequent result that a greater proportion of the population now belongs to the older group. Whereas in 1850, 2.6 percent of the population consisted of people sixty-five years of age or over, a century later there are close to 8 percent in that category. It has been estimated that in 1990 more than 13 percent of our citizens will be in the seventh decade of their life. We are, therefore, confronted by the need to make definite provisions for people who have retired from work, and yet have before them, thanks to medicine, a stretch of years to live.

The fact that our population has also become increasingly urbanized in the last century aggravates this problem. In 1850, 16 percent of the people lived in communities of 2,500 and over. Today more than 60 percent live in urban areas, while less than

*Presented at the Annual Conference of the American Physical Therapy Association, Detroit, June, 1957; and printed in *The Physical Therapy Review*, Volume 37, No. 12, December, 1957.

18 percent have chosen to remain on the farm. A farm is more hospitable to the aged than the metropolis. In rural areas man continues to live in close association with family and neighbor. The impersonality of life does not strike as forcibly, and though burdened by many years, one does not feel as detached and as alone. The senior citizen in a city finds time hanging heavily upon his hands, and is also in danger of succumbing to a feeling of uselessness. Though the doctors will not let us die, the problem of continuing an effective life still remains.

Another factor that adds difficulty to the situation is that ours is a youthful civilization, placing a high premium on youth. There are people who are offended when told they look their age, though one finds it puzzling why this should be so. People are highly flattered when told that they have not changed in twenty years, despite the fact that the entire world about them has undergone profound transformation. It is regarded as a compliment that one has stood still while all the world has moved. Whole industries have been built up that promise to keep their clients looking young. Indeed, many people are wearing themselves out and aging themselves unnecessarily in the desperate attempt to keep youthful. The older person feels that he has been placed on the shelf in a world which belongs exclusively to the young.

This was not always so. In the Bible the aged are spoken of with great respect. We are commanded to rise in reverence before the hoary head. Of the old man it is said that with him are wisdom, counsel, and understanding. One of the books of the Apocrypha states, "As the lamp that shineth upon the holy candlestick, so is the beauty of the face in ripe age." Since, however, our civilization rests more on activity than on reflection, more on practical achievement than wisdom, the aged have been pushed into the background and must adjust themselves to a situation in which they are neither honored nor useful. Our economic structure has been largely unprepared for the great achievement of our time in providing longer life. The senior citizen finds himself displaced, unwanted, regarded as incapable of pulling his weight in society.

To this must be added the fact that most people are unprepared for the situation which longer life creates. We put off thinking about our later years. We feel as if we will remain eternally young. We prefer not to think of what has become an unpleasant fact—age. We do not, therefore, set in motion early enough a process of preparation for our life in those years when we shall not be able to engage in our present activity, and when we shall not have to make allowances for the concomitant effects of the aging experience.

There are accomplishments and qualities that one cannot have without age. Only he who has lived long can have the greater experience and greater wisdom. Time helps to provide experience and enables us to acquire wisdom. Age permits a detachment from the turmoil and rush of life and helps us to secure freedom from the pressures and drives of ambition that characterize youth. It is the time of life when we need not be consumed any more by a gnawing impetuosity and compulsion to seek a higher position for ourselves. Undisturbed by stormy ambitions, we can settle down to a more peaceful existence.

Age brings with it a new series of experiences and offers new opportunities. We can launch upon a second career which, unlike our first, can bring us rest and calm. Our ship of life, not yet entering its harbor, can remain afloat in more placid and pleasant waters.

Christopher Morley once said that "man is a folder of unfinished business." This folder has been gathering dust as pressure after pressure caused it to be buried deeper and deeper under a rising mountain of urgencies. Within this folder may be memoranda about books we had wanted to read but never did, reflections that had come in a moment's insight which we did not seize before, the possibility of renewing friendships which we had permitted to fall into disrepair, the time and freedom to visit museums and libraries which we had for too long ignored.

Doctor E. J. Stieglitz, in his book on geriatric medicine, states, "The increased longevity of men may be made an incalculably valuable advance . . . the reward may be the dawning of a new era of intellectual conquest, man may then live long enough to think." The older citizen need not be simply a yearner after a past. He can be a pioneer of the future. Bernard Berenson, perhaps the world's greatest student of art, at eighty-eight expressed the wish that he could stand at a corner with hat in hand and beg people to throw him their wasted hours.

It is an undeniably scientific fact that the older person can learn and perhaps learn with a unique intensity, since he brings to bear upon the new knowledge the experience of a lifetime. In our personal philosophy of life we shall have to discard some of the false values that see in vigor and wealth the sole goods of life. True success in human living lies elsewhere.

The Bible points out that we grow not by what we get but by what we give. Indeed, living is giving, and growth is a product of service. Our society needs volunteers who can aid in the various fields of communal endeavor by coming as selfless volunteers interested not in personal advancement but in serving their fellowmen. Such lives can never be without meaning or excitement. People who live this way will never be overwhelmed by a sense of uselessness or futility. The real invalids and discards of our time are the self-centered, the socially unaware, the prisoners of selfishness who live in a world of low ceilings.

All of us are moving toward the setting sun. The path of life leads to the western horizon. There is beauty and radiance in the sky colored by the setting sun. Let us walk forward with the glow of that light upon our face.

TRUE IMMORTALITY

ONE OF THE MOST TENDER and poignant scenes in Biblical history is that of the last moments of Moses. He ascended Mount Nebo and viewed the Land of Promise concerning which he had spoken so often to the children of Israel and which he was himself not destined to enter.

What thoughts passed through the mind of the immortal Lawgiver as he looked out across the Jordan? He had devoted a lifetime to his people, bringing them out of Egypt and painstakingly guiding them through the wilderness. He had striven to wean them away from false gods and pagan practices. He had patiently borne their burdens and bickerings and had tried to elevate them to higher standards and sensitivities.

And now that they were about to move forward to a great

fulfillment, to end their wanderings and begin life as a settled people, he was not permitted to accompany them. Moses would have been more than human had he not reflected that his efforts and sacrifices might soon belong to a forgotten past. And what of his teachings, doctrines, and ideals? Would they endure? Perhaps Moses surrendered to the feeling that he had lived and labored in vain.

Yet the subsequent history of Israel is dominated by his towering figure. The sense of commitment and the memory of the covenant were constantly being recalled to the people centuries later by the prophets and other leaders who continued to walk in the footsteps of Moses. Though he did not enter the promised land, his spirit continued to guide and direct the people whom he had served in his lifetime.

Here is a touching parable of the immortality exercised by those who have deeply touched our lives and enriched us with their love. A dear and cherished one is taken from us. The Jordan symbol of the boundary between life and death intervenes between us. Yet as we move onward, the enduring spirit of the love we have known and the life we have shared continues to shape and inspire us. The yesterdays are beyond the reach of death as our love transforms them into current and living influences. We continue to live by a light that defies time and death.

YIZKOR

The earth has covered only that which was mortal
   Of those to whom we have said our farewell.
We shall not see again
   The familiar glowing face, the warm, illuminated eye,
   Nor hear the beloved voice.
We shall not sit face to face,
   Across the family table, or side by side
   In the home of a friend or in worship.
We shall not feel the kiss
   That once evoked our deepest response.

Yet death has failed and must surrender.
For the beloved who is gone
  Lives and will always live through the years
  Not in some distant corner of our being,
  To be uncovered only in a rare moment
  Or by a sudden surge of recall.
The beloved has become a presence—indwelling and inseparable,
  Rooted so deep that life cannot
  Carry us far from the cherished
  Now hallowed center of memory and love.
Your hand, O Death, has been stayed.
  You can no longer inflict oblivion,
  Or doom to full disappearance
  Those who were life of our life.
They live and move within us,
  In spheres beyond your dominion.
We thank Thee, O God of life and love,
  For the resurrecting gift of memory
  Which endows Thy children fashioned in Thy image
    With the Godlike sovereign power
  To give immortality through love.
Blessed be Thou, O God,
  Who enablest Thy children to remember.

11 • *To Know and to Do*

TORAH

THE WORD *Torah* is a key term of Judaism. It is the attempt of a people covenanted with God to fulfill its obligation. It is the quest of the mind for understanding and of the spirit for fulfillment. Torah is the ladder by which the Jew seeks to ascend to God. It is the bridge he builds between himself and humanity.

Torah is the worship of God by means of study. It is the prayer of the mind. It is the science which seeks to discover the laws of the moral universe, and thus it deals with the realities that lie above and beyond the world of visible nature. It is man's pilgrimage through life in search of himself. Torah is the shrine which the Jew builds of thought and feeling and aspiration. "It is a tree of life to them that grasp it, and of them that uphold it," and in its shade alone can the Jew find completeness. "Its ways are ways of pleasantness and all its paths are peace."

To the Jew who affirms his readiness to accept Torah, there comes a unique and precious privilege. His life becomes linked to a larger background, and he steps beyond the confining limits of the point in time he happens to occupy. His personal life is not dwarfed by the large process of which it becomes part, but, on the contrary, is invested with a depth and a dignity it could not otherwise attain. Lower creatures live solely in the physical environment into which they are born. Man, through his capacity to create culture, to preserve and transmit it, lives in history. Of the cultural riches accessible to the modern Jew, none is more humane, more devoted to higher values, more elevated in its striving than the culture and history into which Torah can introduce him.

JEWISH VIEW OF EDUCATION *

THE ACHIEVEMENT OF RUSSIA in putting a satellite into space has precipitated a widespread discussion of American education—its lacks, its needs, its goals. The problem of education has suddenly captured the front pages of our press and has become a major problem occupying the public mind. It took a dramatic show of power by the Soviets to awaken the land to the fact that national safety and security are tied up with education. A recognition has now gained ground that the defenses of the country rest not on its industrial plants and armaments, but on its colleges and training programs. The school, at long last, is now seen as the ultimate arsenal of our free way of life.

The Jew has not needed the lessons of an international emergency to arrive at these conclusions. Such insights about education have long been part of his wisdom. Jewish literature and thought can accurately be described as a continuing discussion about education—its purposes, its content, its need. Of the very first of the faith, Abraham, God said, "For I have known him, to the end that he may command his children and his household after him, that they may keep the way of the Lord, to do righteousness and justice." At the very outset of Jewish history there is concern for the proper upbringing of the child and the effective transmission of the growing heritage to each succeeeding generation: "And ye shall observe this thing for an ordinance to thee and thy sons for ever." The paragraph of Scripture singled out for an emphasis second only to the Shema itself, upon which it follows, contains the command which became an abiding part of the consciousness of the Jew: "And thou shalt teach them diligently unto thy children and shalt speak of them when thou sittest in thy house, when thou walkest by the way and when thou liest down and when thou risest up."

Isaiah looks forward to the day when "all thy children shall be taught of the Lord" and when "the earth shall be full of the knowledge of the Lord, as the waters cover the sea." The prophet Hosea exclaims, "My people are destroyed for lack of knowledge;

* *Congress Weekly*, January 20, 1958.

because thou has rejected knowledge, I will also reject thee." The longest psalm, Psalm 119, containing 176 verses, is an extended hymn of praise to the Torah and its study. An entire section of Biblical and post-Biblical literature is designated Wisdom Literature and speaks throughout with enthusiasm of the pursuit of wisdom as man's most significant endeavor. Wisdom is man's greatest need, his most beautiful ornament, the source of his security, his support in adversity, his protection against evil and its blandishments, his guide to righteousness, and his noblest assurance of grace and glory. "The beginning of wisdom is, 'Get wisdom,' " admonishes the author of Proverbs.

This stress on education and the acquisition of wisdom looms equally large in the teachings of the Rabbis. Empires fall because they do not give priority to learning. Jerusalem itself fell before the enemy because its children were not receiving instruction. The learned man takes precedence over the High Priest and indeed over the prophet too. The untutored cannot be truly pious. He who has knowledge has all; he who has no knowledge, what has he? "Wisdom and understanding," says one of the sages, "is like the sand that surrounds the sea and makes a fence and is as a rampart and wall, keeping the sea from inundating the land." Thus does discernment preserve man from the evil of his own nature and from the evil forces about him. Without knowledge there can be no true discrimination between right and wrong, the important and the trifling, the holy and the profane.

The effectiveness of the rabbinic emphasis on study and the exaltation of education is perhaps best evidenced by the fact that the hero-patterns of the Jewish group are teachers and men of the book. The figures that entered most deeply into the consciousness of this history-minded people are those of scholars and sages. Leadership for many centuries was entrusted to the learned men of the community. A history of the great landmarks in the Jew's experience is simultaneously a history of his literature. The Bible, the Talmud, the works of Saadia, Maimonides, Rashi, Judah Halevi, Rabbi Joseph Caro—these open new periods and place their stamp upon their own epoch and also upon succeeding ages.

The object of such learning is not merely to amass voluminous knowledge. The Rabbis scornfully refer to a man whose memory is crowded with facts as "an ass laden with books." Nor was the purpose to gain a diploma and achieve professional status. For centuries Judaism fought against the professionalization of scholarship. It sought to have its great teachers remain "amateurs," in the fine, original sense of the term, namely "enthusiasts" and "lovers" of learning. Subtle corruptions invade, and unseemly pride insinuates itself into a class of men who make a profession of their learning. Scholarship is not to be used as a spade with which to dig, or as a crown with which to adorn oneself, say the Rabbis. The goals of learning were therefore neither status nor title nor increased earning power.

What then was the purpose of study? Implicit in the Jewish conception are the following goals which learning was to advance. To study was to do God's bidding. It was an act by which man glorified the Torah and Him who gave it. In our modern phraseology we may say that through study man fulfills his "noblest capacity" which mirrors the divine image in which he was created. The development and use of his intellectual powers are an indispensable condition for expressing his greatest potentiality. To allow the mind to lie fallow and uncultivated is to doom to atrophy man's most glorious asset. There are problems that lie beyond the range of the human mind and which the intellectual process cannot solve unaided. But the Rabbis would say of thought and mental effort, as one of their number said of study generally: "Thine is not to complete the task nor art thou free to desist from it."

The Jewish view recognizes that the intellect is not a sovereign and independent resource, functioning in detachment for its own needs. The mind that centers on learning will imbibe a definite morality as a consequence. Love of truth, precision, the humility that comes from an awareness of the infinite scope of knowledge, respect for the minds of others—these are qualities that the devotee of study will develop. To be sure, now and then, as the Rabbis were fully aware, a scholar of undoubted learning exhibits petulance and arrogance. Two answers may be given. The first is that these undesirable traits might have appeared in an even more aggravated form had this individual remained uneducated. The second is that his approach to learning was faulty at the outset. The need is for more study, not less. When our public education system is accused of being "secular," meaning that it is indifferent to moral values, the important influences of the educational process are ignored. Education can induce responsibility, respect and reverence for truth, but these qualities are not instilled by a special course in morals or morality. They are the results of the learning process when it is properly guided.

The Jewish view asserts that instruction in spiritual realities and ethical goals is an important part of the curriculum both of education and life. Torah is neither abstract knowledge nor intellectual exercise for its own sake. It is a spiritual and ethical literature and is directed toward the socialization and spiritualization of man and the shaping of a more moral society. The corollary for modern education is clear. Technical training should not displace those humanistic studies which help cultivate the esthetic, social, and moral sensibilities. Those who prepare for specialized pursuits should receive their training for their lifework within a larger context of knowledge so that they have access to the idealism and ethical values which are to be found in the thought and world view of significant moral teachers.

In a free society, however, the education of the whole man should not be entrusted to the government or any of its institutions. The individual, in a democratic order, encompasses more than the citizen, and the state should not be permitted to absorb or dominate the whole of man's life, belief, and thought. That is the reason why voluntary association of like-minded persons, banded for common purposes and united by common convictions —political, social, religious—are indispensable to American life. That is also why the deep insight of the founding fathers, alert to the ever-present danger of an overreaching government and conscious of the restraints states have historically wished to impose upon the freedom of thought and belief of their citizens, evolved the doctrine of separation of church and state. That is the deepest significance of this policy, which has the sanction of American tradition and law. It was no mere expedient to avoid the rivalry of competing creeds, each of which would have wished to become the "Established Church" of the land. It was a profound intuitive realization by men who recognized the nature of democracy that led to the formulation of the fundamental principle that religion was to be free of entanglement with the machinery and processes of government.

Americans must learn that public education is only part of
the total education which they and their children need. Churches
and synagogues should bear the full responsibility for the religious
training of their adherents. This is the most important function
which religious institutions are called upon to fulfill in our democracy. The prevalence of religious illiteracy and the failure of
so many people to live in terms of a religious orientation should
be taken as a challenge by organized religion and not as a pretext
for placing a great share of their burden upon public education.
That would endanger both democracy and religion. Religion
functions best when free of political involvement. Democracy
that dictates to men's consciences ceases to be democracy.

The Jewish education of both Jewish children and adults is
thus not training in specialized skills or facts relating to a single
ethnic segment of the American people. It is rather a necessary
completion of and adjunct to the education Jews receive in the
public institutions of learning. It enables them to function as individuals who are citizens and not as citizens who are subjects. It
provides that spiritual base for those attributes of mind, heart, and
spirit that free men need in order to live in freedom and dignity.

THE SHEMA: JUDAISM'S CENTRAL AFFIRMATION *

THE RABBIS BOLDLY CROWNED a single verse out of the 5,845 in
the Torah with a significance shared by no other. Though it is
not set apart in any way within the text, the Rabbis presumed to
suggest that in this one verse was concentrated the essence of the
whole, almost as though it were the divine will to condense the
entire tradition to a single affirmation without diminishing its
spiritual intensity and comprehensiveness.

This verse found its way into the prayer book—that most
widespread and most frequently invoked volume in Jewish literature—and was likewise accepted almost spontaneously as the key
sentence of the tradition by all subsequent generations. The
prayer book appears in a diversity of versions, Ashkenazi, Sephardi,

*From *Jewish Heritage Reader*, pp. 38–43.

Italian, Yemenite, Moroccan; in more recent times it has undergone revision, sometimes drastic, to conform to changing conceptions and interpretations. But no group or individual editor has
deleted or modified this sentence.

The reference can be to no other verse than "Hear O Israel:
the Lord our God, the Lord is One." The Shema (six words in
Hebrew) was usually the first line of the tradition a child was
taught even before he had mastered fully the power of speech;
they were the words on the lips of martyrs led to their death.
Who can estimate their impact upon the consciousness and spirit
of a people?

The Shema also symbolized the unity of that people in its
far-flung dispersion as well as the kinship of the various elements
that united in a single community. Spanish and German; East
European and Oriental; poor and rich; learned and untutored;
young and old; proud and humble—all were as one in the devout
and deeply emotional response which the Shema elicited.

In addition, the Shema suggested the basic content of Jewish
belief, to which all else is commentary. It has often been pointed
out that Judaism avoided a dogmatic formulation of its creed. No
single statement of belief is binding upon all. Leo Baeck describes
this aspect of Judaism as follows:

> The dominant form of Judaism always remained that of a
> religious philosophy of inquiry, a philosophy which pro-
> duced method rather than system. . . . There was always
> tolerance and even indifference toward modes of expres-
> sion; it was the idea which was held to be central. Judaism,
> and the Jew as well, retained an unorthodox air; they neither
> would nor could rest in the easy comfort of dogma. . . .
> Jewish religious philosophy had as its purpose the constant
> renewal of the content of religion by means of which it was
> best preserved and protected from the deadening rigidity of
> formula. It was a religion which constantly imposed upon
> its adherents new labors of thought.

The absence of dogmas, however, must not be regarded as a
lack of specificity and conviction. Judaism is no amorphous or
characterless tradition. It developed around a cluster of ideas
which were open to interpretation, to be sure, but which could
not be stretched to limits that would dissolve the core pattern.

Judaism has an inner integrity which sets bounds upon flexibility. This inner integrity—which in another context might be called its theology, though Hebrew thought and language possess neither the term nor the idea—is concisely and powerfully expressed in the Shema.

Though it embodies the main theme of Judaism, the Shema is not presented as the grand climax of a subtle intellectual process of speculation and thought. For the Jew did not reach his belief in God and his conception of the nature of God as the result of a painstaking rational investigation, moving step by step from observation to conclusion to conviction. Intuitively and with surging moral imaginativeness, the Hebrews first conceived of God as a Reality and Presence and only subsequently refined and organized that overwhelming initial insight by the use of reason. In the words of the non-Jewish scholar, A. B. Davidson: "The Hebrew thinker came down from his thoughts of God upon the world rather than rose from the world up to his thoughts of God." Thus, the Shema is not a theological formula involving only the mind but an impassioned declaration claiming total commitment.

The Shema is the leitmotif of the Jewish faith, its dominant and central theme. In order to prepare the worshipper for the great affirmation, the Rabbis, wise and creative teachers that they were, introduced two benedictions to precede the Shema (*B'rakhot* 1:4). In the first benediction, known as the *Yotzer* prayer, God is Creator of the world, Source of the universe, its immensities and power, its galaxies and intricacies, its design and order. This theme recurs in many forms throughout the Bible.*

Creation is not a completed event, permitting God to withdraw into a cosmic vastness outside of it. Creation is a dynamic, ongoing process. The *Yotzer* benediction includes one of the most profoundly religious ideas: "Who daily in His goodness reneweth continually the work of creation."

The modern Jewish philosopher Hermann Cohen suggests the richness of this concept:

> Thus this idea of the continuousness of renewal was made
> into a cardinal doctrine whereas the older doctrine of crea-

*See Psalm 19, Psalm 104 (which is read in the synagogue on Sabbath afternoons during winter), and Job 38.

tion at the beginning receded in importance. Every day is
a new beginning. The mystery of the initial creation is
assimilated into the daily miracle of renewal and conse-
quently into that of the maintenance of the world. The
Creator becomes the Maintainer. The uniqueness of God
fulfills itself in divine Providence.

The second benediction introducing the Shema, known as
the *Ahavah Rabbah*, opens with the words: "With abounding
love has Thou loved us, O Lord our God, with exceeding compassion has Thou revealed Thy mercy unto us." Israel Abrahams
has described it as "one of the most beautiful in the liturgies of
the world." God is not only the omnipotent Creator, the just
Ruler; He is also the loving Father who reveals Himself through
his Torah to His children. He instructs His children in the "law
of life." He is near and ever-present. In this prayer God's compassion and mercy are invoked, not through a plea that His children be granted material gifts and personal safety but that they
be imbued "with the will to understand, to discern, to hearken
and to learn, to teach and to obey, to practice and to fulfill in
love all the teachings of Thy Torah." We ask for the spirit that
will lead men to obey His commandments and to serve Him with
an undivided heart. The concept of God as the Teacher and
Father of mankind is celebrated more fully and more fervently
than that of God as Creator.

Once our awareness of God as the mighty Ruler and the
loving Teacher has been renewed and deepened, we are prepared
to recite the Shema with a better understanding of its meaning.

"Hear O Israel: the Lord our God, the Lord is One" (Deuteronomy 6:4). (The newest translation of the Torah by Jews
offers the rendering "Hear, O Israel, the Lord our God, the Lord
alone.") Both the Oneness and Uniqueness of God are projected,
opposing every type of polytheism, dualism, pantheism. God is
Creator but is apart from His creation; God is One not in an
arithmetical sense alone but primarily in His unduplicated singu-
larity. He is above and beyond and yet in His providence near
and accessible. With this declaration, say the Rabbis, we accept
the kingship of God and subject ourselves to His rule.

The Shema, "the watchword of Israel's faith," is followed

immediately both in the Torah and in our prayer book by the paragraph:

> And thou shalt love the Lord thy God with all thy heart and with all thy soul and with all thy might. And these words which I command thee this day, shall be upon thy heart; and thou shalt teach them diligently unto thy children, and shalt talk of them when thou sittest in thy house, and when thou walkest by the way and when thou liest down and when thou risest up. And thou shalt bind them for a sign upon thy hand and they shall be for frontlets between thine eyes. And thou shalt write them upon the door posts of thy house and upon thy gates.

These words are directed to all the people. Upon each devolves the duty of fulfilling the law of God; to each is given the privilege of relating himself in love to God. Man, created in the image of God, is endowed with an innate capacity to respond to God with his total being. Man's faith in and love of God are to be reflected in every aspect of his life, to govern and inspirit every relationship and activity.

Religion is an attitude and a quality which should permeate the whole of life. To love God and obey His words has implications for man's conduct within his family circle; his relationship to neighbors; his responsibility to the community; his practices in his business and at his leisure; in the daytime and at night. Incumbent upon the man of faith too are his own study and the training of his children. Thus human existence, even in its most mundane and physical aspects, becomes transposed to a higher key of sensibility and spirituality, mirroring the reality of a God who loves us and expressing the love we have for Him. Man is not and cannot become pure spirit. His body and physical needs have their place and are not to be suppressed. "The Torah," say the Rabbis, "was not given to ministering angels." It was given to men. Its purpose is to release all the potentialities for being human that flow from man's kinship with God.

The second section of the Shema (Deuteronomy 11:13-21) voices the Jewish belief in the dependability of the moral order of the universe. To be sure, virtue is not always rewarded in immediate sequence. The large plan of God's universe is fulfilled through obedience to God's will. Wickedness and evil are a re-

bellion against the moral character of the cosmos and will ultimately reap the whirlwind of punishment. One cannot contravene
the laws of nature with impunity; health is the fruit of conformity to them. In the moral realm, one who breaks the basic principles will be broken by his own misdeeds.

While the rewards enumerated in this section employ a
terminology suited to an agricultural society, the principle that
they establish remains valid. Man's vision may be too limited to
see the operation of this law of reward and punishment, and his
life-span too brief to recognize its unfolding—"For a thousand
years in Thy sight are but as a day that is past and as a watch in
the night" (Psalm 90)—yet the law is as certain and as inexorable
as any natural law discovered by science.

But reward and punishment are not to be taken as the motivation for man's conduct. They are included to suggest the view
of the universe that derives from the belief in a God of justice.
Early in the Mishnah of the *Ethics of the Fathers* we are told,
"Be not like servants who serve their master without thought of
reward" (1:3). Ben Azzai said, "The reward of mitzvah is mitzvah
(since one good deed paves the way for another) and the reward
of sin is sin" (4:2). In a moral world man cannot escape this
ironclad consequence; he stoops to wrongdoing and diminishes
himself; he rises to virtue and fulfills himself.

The third paragraph that forms part of the *Kriat Shema*
(Numbers 15:37-41) deals with one specific Jewish practice,
namely the wearing of *tzitzit* or fringes. The law of God which
we accept as part of His divine sovereignity is supported by the
cosmic order which He created and is evidenced by the life of
personal holiness which each individual is to lead. Man, frail,
mortal, exposed to temptation from without and to the pressure
of impulses and drives from within, is asked to follow disciplines
(symbolized by the *tzitzit*) which will keep him from following
the dictates of a rebellious heart and from straying in obedience
to his senses—"that ye may remember and do all My commandments. Be ye holy unto God." The last sentence in this section
makes reference to the fact that God brought Israel out of Egypt
in order that He might "be your God. I am the Lord your God."
Thus liberated, man is free to live on the highest level of his
potentialities.

The Shema is concluded with a benediction known as the *Geullah* prayer. He who has guided His children in the past and has brought them forth from bondage into freedom is the promise of that redemption of Israel and all mankind which will climax man's history. The last syllable of recorded time is not futility; the last accent of human history is not destruction. Redemption of man from his own and the world's evil will not spring into being as a sudden and unrelated culmination. It will reveal, so that all may see, the deep divine design which underlies all of life as it ushers in the day "when all the earth will be filled with knowledge even as the waters cover the sea" and "the Lord shall be King over all the earth; in that day shall the Lord be One and His name One."

TRIBUTE TO A TEACHER

In memory of Theodore H. Baruch

HE WAS A TEACHER—this was the first and most vivid impression he gave. He was one whose personality did not contract into his profession, but on the contrary his calling, for it was more than an occupational pursuit, broadened and streamed into his entire being.

He was a teacher, and therefore his was a poetic sensitivity to growth, to enlargement. Only a poet hears the grass grow, witnesses the flowers in their actual blossoming, beholds the ripening in process in field and meadow. And only a teacher actually sees the seedlings of the youthful mind reaching out for the light, germinating and sprouting under the loving touch of an inspired gardener.

He was a teacher and therefore a creative artist working in the most precious and intricate of all media—the human complex of mind and heart and conscience. To mold and to evoke, to guide and to ignite, and yet not to trespass upon the inner integrity and individuality of the child—this was the incredibly difficult and significant task upon which he was set.

He was a teacher and therefore one who is forever bent on

the greatest adventure of all, the exploration of another's mind, the delving into another spirit to mine, uncover, and bring forth into the light the possibilities that lie hidden in the deeps. No diver descended into the sea in search of treasure, no explorer journeyed to unknown continents with greater anticipation and higher excitement.

He was a teacher, and therefore he loved his fellowman. Neither his skill nor his diligence were substituted for the love which led him to devote himself to the instruction of his neighbor and his neighbor's child.

He was a teacher and therefore one who revered the word, honored ideas, exalted thought, and fostered the great dream. He was a teacher and knew with conviction that the hope of men lies not in their machines or in their power or in their uncultivated ego but in the refinement, mutuality, and sensitivity which the thinker, poet, saint, and dreamer awaken in them. He sought to redeem men, not by enlarging their mastery over the outer world but by cultivating their inner universe.

He was a teacher and therefore a man of abiding faith. Whose path is strewn with greater obstacles? A harsh and competitive society denies by its daily realities the gentle and chaste truths the teacher seeks to impart. A torrent of vulgar and shallow matter from the mass media is destructive of the reflection and discrimination which the teacher begins slowly to nurture within his charges. Social climate, home, and the recalcitrance of the unwilling student are so often arrayed against him. He persevered undaunted because he could draw upon a faith that conquered every passing mood of weariness or disillusionment.

Unrecognized and often unthanked, the master teacher continued to build, in the deeps of the present, the mansion which houses our future.

GRIM MEN OF DOCTRINE

THEY FRIGHTEN ME, the grim men of inflexible doctrine. They speak with a certainty that banishes discussion and with a self-righteousness that rules out reappraisal. In a world of flux and change, they stand on a Gibraltar-like bedrock of sure and final knowledge. Those who are outside the magic circle of their ultimate truth are either ignorant or heretics meriting ostracism, contempt, opposition.

The world and all that is in it they sieve through the doctrine they uphold. Theirs is a simple and direct approach to the problems and dilemmas of our day. Upon a multiplicity of issue they press the rigid mold of their doctrine, emerging with definitive answers. Without any compassion for people, they divide men into good and bad, adherents and antagonists, friend and foe. They blur the subtle and coarsen the delicate, for they have eyes only for two colors—black and white. They inhabit a monolithic universe of thought which has no room for alternatives or difference. They are ready to crush their uncertain or questioning neighbor upon the block of their absolute judgment.

They have no sympathy for the eager and searching mind that is not prepared to come to rest for all time upon a definite and terminal point of thought. They are uneasy in the presence of a probing mind. They would through surgery excise from man his unpredictable, irreverent, and insubordinate faculty to inquire, examine, and ponder.

These rigid men are "perhapsless." No quiver of uncertainty is ever felt by them, no undercurrent of doubt. They seek only to overwhelm with their massive certainty.

For all their appearance of strength and assurance, one has the feeling that beneath the militant surface, there are depths of doubt, hesitation, and perplexity. They raise their voices and hammer their points not so much to convince an adversary as to overshout and down the questions that from time to time gnaw at their own certainties.

INADEQUACY OF FACTS

ONE OF THE TENDENCIES of our times is to overstress the part facts play in our life. The development of science through the slow, painstaking accumulation of tested knowledge and the transformation which the application of this knowledge has worked in our lives has won increased respect for the hard, proven, irrefutable, stubborn fact.

It has been a long time since I attended a meeting which did not call upon us to be practical and face facts. We challenge our adversaries in discussion: "Are you sure of your facts? Can you prove them?" A fatal criticism of a proposed idea is to call it "mere theory." Not so long ago many liberal people projected a program of teaching the young "the facts of life" in the belief that such knowledge would save many future marriages from dissolution. Even now there are those who agitate for more and more education of American citizens in facts about their government and its political life. The scientist, the physician, the businessman are honored in our society for they represent pursuits devoted to facts, discernible realities.

No one in his right mind would wish to minimize the supreme importance of "the fact" in human life. Mastery over our environment, the development of the comforts and luxuries now available to us, the lifting of many burdens that formerly rested on man, the conquest of numerous diseases that once threatened him may be attributed to human persistence in ferreting out facts, assembling, testing, and finally using them for the advancement of human welfare.

But not by facts alone does man live, nor can he achieve his goals only through the increase of his proved knowledge. Many of the facts we now know resulted from a theory which man imaginatively projected beyond the facts known in his time. Yesterday's hypothesis became today's certainty. Behind the discovery of every great fact was a man of vision with an adventuring mind. We cannot live by surrendering to unhappy and visible facts and allowing them to have the final word.

Slums are facts, and war is a fact; bigotry is a fact, and so is segregation; cancer is a fact, and so is heart disease. Beyond them are higher facts by which we can control, redeem, or even erase these undesirable facts. The man who prides himself on his adherence to facts tends to become their captive. Earthbound, he fears getting off the ground to the level where higher facts may be found. Ultimately it is human values which determine how facts shall influence our life.

Perhaps Chesterton went too far when he said that "the center of every man's existence is a dream." Yet who can deny the far-reaching effects of man's inner life, his attitudes, aspirations, sensibilities, evaluations. The scientist must be motivated by a love of truth before he can find important facts. The stateman must have large vision and deep compassion if he is to utilize the facts of international politics to advance justice and peace. What is needed is the vision of a better day in order to create the fact of a better world.

DYING OF COMPLACENCY

IN PAYING TRIBUTE to Supreme Court Justice Hugo L. Black, on his seventy-fifth birthday, a government lawyer is quoted as saying: "The test of his impact on the Supreme Court is to try to envisage it without him. Despite the great issues that have come before the Court, without him these would have been years of complacency."

This description is high praise indeed. They serve us best who bring with them disquietude and challenge. The problems of life, even in an apparently stable era, are mightier than our attempted solutions. The human mind functions best not when it is at rest, but when it is troubled, beset by concerns, agitated by perplexities.

In a world constantly in movement there are no final solutions to the large issues which rise out of the restless tide of life. However judicious and appropriate any answer, there is always a beyondness which it does not encompass. A residue of questions remains unresolved in the case of every solution offered or attempted.

This should not be a cause for lament or cynism. On the contrary, it affords society and the individual a sense of both motion and adventure.

The item "unfinished business" has a permanent place on man's agenda. Responsive and reflective individuals do not therefore live with their backs to boundaries but rather with their faces to frontiers. The great questions of society, as of life, cannot be trapped in neat formulae or closed systems once and for all time. They will insistently reappear and enjoy a thousand resurrections. Justice, love, and human dignity are eternally true as goals of social and individual endeavor. But we must not become sanguine that our definitions and applications of these lofty, perennial purposes are always as enduring and inclusive as the purposes themselves.

In the human situation complacency is fatal and may well be the most formidable of all obstacles to progress. The undisturbed mind is soon out of touch with reality and begins to live in a world of imagination. Even more pathetic than its irrelevant solutions is its inability to recognize the questions which the ever-changing, mobile world emphasizes with sharp and startling urgency or creates anew. King Canute was no more foolish than the economist or statesman who believes that his program, if it claims finality, can stay the waves of movement and change and prevent new problems and challenges from breaking upon the coast of contemporary life. Alertness is the measure of human vitality. In a world where swift torrents of events rush onward with increasing power and speed, a great measure of uneasiness and intellectual ferment are the very conditions of survival.

COURAGE OF DOUBT

ARCHIBALD MACLEISH, in paying a memorial tribute to the late Adlai Stevenson, praised him for having "the courage of his doubts." What appeared to some as hesitancy, reservation, and indecisiveness was the result of a great and rare virtue.

In public life it may indeed be easier to have the courage of one's convictions than of one's uncertainty. People turn to their leaders for finality, unequivocal judgment, and definite assurance with no undercurrents of doubt and no stammerings of indecision.

Yet the problems we face are complex and labyrinthine, the situations unprecedented. No single person has adequate knowledge of all the facts, and none is infallible enough to presume to know the complete answer.

To be sure, decisions have to be made, and action has to be undertaken. All the more important to possess the saving and humanizing grace of doubt, which makes for greater tolerance for opposing views and allows a degree of vital flexibility in adjusting conclusions to the ever-changing scene of life in our day.

Dogmatism and cocksureness threaten man no less than ignorance. To ascribe absolute truth to a teaching and to say with triumphant certainty what should be said with qualification and restraint are to impede the search for greater refinement and precision in our knowledge and belief. Man must spend much effort, sacrifice, and time in combatting the entrenched dogmatism of earlier days as well as that of contemporary apostles of finality. When individuals or institutions take fixed and categoric positions that are unwarranted, they betray an uncertainty which they try to mask beneath overconfident and doctrinaire assertions. Or they fall into what John Stuart Mill once called "the deep slumber of a decided opinion."

I see only good in teaching that there are important areas in religious thought which cannot be entirely established as irrefutable axioms. To be sure, there are values and principles which religion upholds that have stood the test of time and are powerfully supported by insight, experience, and the genius of many great spirits. But there is also a vast circumference of teaching that can only be honestly viewed as the reflection of religion's present evolutionary state or of previous historical situations, and which should not be closed off from further development through continuing analysis and thought.

Nor will religion be weakened by such a tempered exposition of its outlook. On the contrary, it will gain the respect of some gifted people who presently react against what they feel is its consistent and all-embracing dogmatism. An expression of humility in this sphere might well dramatize the contrast religion has traditionally pointed out between the infinite mystery of the universe and the limitations of human comprehension.

CONFORMITY TO WHAT?

THE QUESTION A PERSON in a free society has to decide is not "to conform or not to conform." The true question is: "What shall I conform to?" or "Conformity, yes, but to what?"

Unless a person's life is entirely aimless and responds only to reflex action (even then it conforms to one's impulses) one must guide oneself in accordance with some principal, pattern, or code. There are some who make of nonconformity with popular or conventional forms their particular brand of conformity. They are conformists no less than those from whom they seek to diverge in so conscious and dramatic a way. "Beatniks" stand convention on its head and conform to a system of denials and negations.

There are those who glory in the claim that in their rejection of a traditional faith and discipline they have achieved independence of any code or creed. They so often turn their program of dissent into an orthodoxy of their own, as they uphold a rigid creed of noncompliance. There is not rarely an air of bravado about their denials, which might reveal to a psychologically oriented observer a degree of sentimental attachment to the code they apparently delight in discarding, as well as a measure of guilt.

Conformity to a great tradition need not be the easy and complacent thing which the heretic pictures it to be. To conform to justice means to oppose instances of injustice though they be popularly condoned and socially approved. To conform to truth means not only to denounce error and falsehood but to pursue truth with undeviating single-mindedness. To conform to mutual responsibility means to be alert to the needs of others and to seek that program which will afford a base of security for all men. To conform to religion means to capture in every relationship and in every act something of the awe, aspiration, and consecration which the religious experience at its best embodies.

There are people who, when you meet them, make you aware at once of their repudiations and denials. It is, however, often hard to learn from them what they espouse and affirm. There are others who are apparent conformists, but their conformity is so fragile and shallow that their professions of assent do not become the true basis of their manner of living. They deny with their lives what they affirm with their lips.

The test of a man is to be found in the validity and value of that to which he conforms and the sincerity with which he lives by the principles he approves.

HUMANIZING POWER

CIVILIZATION HAS GROWN GREATLY through the extension of man's power over his environment. Man's increased control over nature not alone releases energies and affords time for the cultivation of specifically human and humane interests and pursuits, but also stimulates self-assurance which is necessary for his most creative endeavors.

But power, being amoral, has within it the seeds of its own misuse and corruption and can be a curse as well as a blessing. It may breed not self-assurance but arrogance, even self-deification. It may stimulate such an insatiable lust for more power that vast destruction and wanton killing may result. The potentiality of power for peril grows at a geometric pace with its own arithmetical growth.

What then is the remedy? Shall man forego the benefits which expanded power enables him to enjoy in order to avoid its dangers? Shall we call a halt to those studies and investigations which promise even greater control over the forces of nature? Such a policy is as undesirable as it is impractical. History will not be turned back; it moves irreversibly onward. The theories of a Thoreau in our country or of a Gandhi in India may awaken in us a nostalgia for the uncomplicated life we have long since left behind. The success we have already enjoyed has unloosed a dynamic force for the growth and extension of power that will not be inhibited. Man will not voluntarily surrender the advantages which his mastery over the environment have already brought him.

The one and only means of curbing the perils that reside in power—all power—is to match every enlargement by an enlargement of the moral sense. As mutuality among men deepens, the likelihood of using power to destroy others diminishes. As man's devotion to the right becomes more intense, the probability of making power the instrument of evil purposes becomes more dim. Science alone does not possess the instruments or criteria for determining the right uses to which its discoveries shall be put. Far from making religion unnecessary, as some of the early rationalists thought in their naïveté, science makes moral responsibility more essential than ever before.

BUILDING A BETTER WORLD

As ONE READS THE PASSAGES in which our sages refer to the concept of *olam haba*, "the world yet to come," one begins to understand what was in the mind of those who expounded this idea long ago. They were saying that each man should live in two worlds simultaneously: the one which he actually inhabits, and the one which wisdom and goodness can build. It is not enough to live within the confines of one's day; one should also live in the presence of tomorrows yet to be. Beyond the world in which physically we have our being is the world of the future, free of inequity, ugliness, and conflict. Through the concept of *olam haba*, the Rabbis are saying that each man ought to have something else as an alternative to the shoddy and imperfect world in which we now perforce must live.

Both the realism and faith of Judaism are reflected in this concept. Our tradition, unlike others, does not bid us turn our back on our world, to flee it and seek shelter from its corruptions and evils in a remote and isolated fastness. It does not condemn the world as being completely and unredeemedly foul. It does not see it as the enemy of man's spirit bent upon destroying all that is good and lofty. It knows of the temptations to wrong and sin to which man is often exposed.

But Judaism also knows of the development which has taken man in his collective life from the lowest rung of primitive superstition and savagery to his present station. Much evil persists, and much wrong remains. But man will not achieve in isolation what mankind cannot achieve in cooperation. The world which is the habitation of evil is also the center of hope.

Hence we should not desert the present world; but as we live and move in it we should hold high and firm before us the vision of the more righteous, the more humane, the more beautiful world that man has it in his power to build. *Olam haba,* as it unfolds in the tradition, not only affirms that the better world can be but also that it *will* be. It need be no mirage, if men bring to bear upon the world that is the sensitivities and values which characterize the world that is yet to be.

To abandon this world is to render ourselves ineffective in our solitariness. To give up the world-yet-to-be is to surrender hope and acquiesce to wrong. Living in the here and now, let us live by the higher sights of *olam haba.*

~ PART IV ~

PURELY PERSONAL

In June, 1960, Rabbi Adler received an honorary LL.D. degree from Wayne State University. He responded with the Talmudic tale of the two sages who, arriving at a strange city, asked to meet "the guardians of the city." First the police officials were presented, then the political leaders. But the sages refused to accept them. Only when the teachers were ushered in were they satisfied. "These are the guardians of the city," they affirmed.

Morris Adler was himself "a guardian of the city," a teacher in Israel. His "city" included not only the 1,500 families in his Detroit congregation but the larger community as well.

Like the young lady in the song who enjoyed being a girl, Morris Adler loved being a rabbi—at least part of the time. He poured into his chosen profession the rich endowments of his total personality: patience, kindliness, warmth, erudition, wit, and imagination, backed up by a strong physique that enabled him to take on more burdens and tasks than seemed humanly possible.

The synagogue was for him a second home, a holy place where past met present and where life's most important situations from birth to death could be sanctified. He plunged with zest into every phase of Jewish life, frequently traveling to distant communities to deliver speeches or participate in conferences. He made several visits to Israel—the last in early 1965—which took on for him the aura of religious pilgrimages.

Despite the great success he enjoyed, however, Rabbi Adler frequently questioned his calling. Moody and sensitive, he often recoiled from the vulgarity and shallowness of Jewish communal life. He was troubled by the difficulty of reaching modern Jews, particularly the more intellectually oriented.

Then, too, he was pained by the many frustrations of the rabbinate, which he summed up in "The Rabbi: 1966," written less than a week before his fatal accident. Much of his published work as well as a vast amount of unpublished material record his feeling that the rabbi is trapped is in "a condition of pathos." Always in a race with time, he resented the hours wasted on useless

185

meetings and hollow public functions. A rabbi could, he once humorously observed, spend his entire career at banquet tables eating "one long chicken dinner." "Eating for God's sake" was too often the order of his day. He sometimes found it easier to communicate with secularists and nonreligionists than with his own colleagues. He hungered for intellectual challenge from which his position of authority too frequently isolated him. In his own words, "the deepest aspects of his life remained private and lonely."

And yet, there was no other profession he would rather have followed. The many lives which the rabbinate enabled him to lead were, in the final analysis, Morris Adler's triumph over his mortality.

L. E.

THE CHANGING AMERICAN SCENE *

I AM OLD ENOUGH to remember a time when informed, intelligent Jews in America were seriously concerned about Jewish survival. That earlier generation saw many signs of threatening doom for the vital tradition they had brought from Europe.

Jews had heretofore survived every type of persecution, and their history corroborated the prophet's promise that "no weapon fashioned against them would prosper." The question was whether a people which had learned to live under adverse and oppressive circumstances would know how to live in freedom. Or was Jewish life as a historic entity to decline and perhaps disappear at the very moment that Jews as individuals were coming into their own?

Fears of such a cruel paradox were fed by the fact that the generation growing up knew little if anything of the Jewish heritage. There was either a widespread attempt to flee from Judaism, a revolt against it, or indifference, the most humiliating reaction of all.

Knowing observers voiced their anxiety and pessimism. Historian Salo Baron spoke of "inverted Marranos"; unlike persons of the past who had appeared in public as non-Jews but in the secrecy of their homes practiced Judaism, these present-day "Marranos" were outwardly Jews who in their private and personal lives showed no signs of Jewishness.

Horace Kallen, the distinguished educator, warned against "amateur Gentiles" emulating the surface aspects and traits of Gentiles and feeling most praised when told they did not "look Jewish."

Mordecai Kaplan described "euthanasian Jews," prompted

---

* *Jewish Heritage*, winter, 1962–63.

by a persistent death-wish as Jews, who in their subconscious
would like nothing more than to awake one morning and find
that Jewishness and Judaism had disappeared. In his book *Germany's Stepchildren,* Sol Liptzin brought to life a glittering procession of brilliant men and women of talent, erudition, and social
passion, differing in their ways of life and interests, but united by
the common tragedy that they were Jews. They could not accept
their Jewishness, yet found it impossible to reject. Victims of an
inevitability, many were led to suicide.

Although there were very few such extremes in America, we
did produce people who hovered on the periphery of Jewish life.
Some left the Jewish fold entirely; others sought to find a way of
life in which Jewishness would be muted.

There was much Hamlet-like self-questioning: "to be or not
to be" a Jew. Having ended its useful course in history, Judaism
should have the grace to bow out rather than continue its lifeless
way. Even the sociologists denied Jews a future as they pointed
out with irrefutable statistics that the Jewish family and its rate
of reproduction were becoming increasingly smaller.

Today the situation is completely reversed. We no longer
hear these voices of doom. On the contrary, Jews in America
seem to have entered upon the greatest period of affluence they
have ever known, not only in the economic but in the social, cultural, and organizational senses as well.

The apprehensions of the past have been silenced by a resurgence of identification. The synagogue was never so prosperous,
and never were so many persons enrolled under the banner of
organized Jewish life. Schoolrooms are filled, and membership
rosters bulge.

Clearly, Jewish life is here to stay. We have indicated our determination to remain Jews, and, fortunately, the history and
character of American life, based on diversity, give us a rightful
place on the American scene.

We need no justification for our existence. It is no longer
necessary to prove that Jews ought to be permitted to live because
they make or have made a great contribution. They exist by moral
right.

The problem has now been transported to a new key. Are
we ourselves content simply to survive? Or do we want something

more fundamental and valuable than mere existence? Do we not wish to feel that our community pours something of quality as well as variety into the mainstream of American culture?

In his book *America and the Image of Europe*, Daniel Burstein indicates certain insights and sensitivities which the Jew derives from his unique historic experience. But to possess these insights the Jew must be rooted in that experience and make the history of his people part of his own biography.

The question is no longer "to survive or not to survive." It is: "what kind of survival?" What will emanate and radiate from the fact that five million Jews in America have declared themselves to be Jews, and have expressed in many forms their resolve to remain Jews?

Here we are confronted by new apprehensions. Are we not in danger of becoming casualties of our success, victims of Jewish prosperity and affluence?

Although a relatively short time in the sweep of history, recent decades have compressed greater movement and transformation than periods lasting centuries at other stages in Jewish history. Change is of course a constant factor in human experience, but what is new is the rate of change, the rapidity with which our lives have become transformed under our very eyes.

For one thing, American Jewish life has gone "native." The first congregation to which I ministered was largely foreign-born. But immigration is now a thing of the past. Eighty percent of American Jews are native, free of the scars of that desperate struggle for recognition and Jewish rights in the pre-Emancipation period which in Eastern Europe extended to the threshold of our day. Our immigrant fathers did not enjoy citizenship in the Old World; as Jews they suffered disability and deprivation. Their children were free at birth.

These native-born Jews are at home in America. Nobody had to open gates for them; they belong. America is bone of their bone and flesh of their flesh.

As American life becomes the primary force in molding Jews, there is an inevitable movement toward greater homogeneity. Most American Jews, integrated into American life, feel no duality between their Jewishness and their Americanism. They identify themselves openly with assurance and self-respect: Jewish affirmation no longer represents a subtraction from Americanism.

This is not an unmixed blessing. Many Jews today are losing contact with Jewish life as a *force*, though they accept it as a *fact*; the real centers of behavior and motivation in their lives are outside the Jewish community.

From American life they draw not only its virtues, but also its deficiencies and shortcomings. The Jewish family is losing the stability which Jewish life once gave it. Where Jewish divorce used to be a rarity, we are fast rising to the national average. Delinquency, illegitimacy, and other aspects of human misconduct among Jews are also now assuming alarming proportions, tending to blur and dilute our traditional standards.

We are now a middle-class group. In my childhood, Jews in New York were largely proletarian, workers in factories. The two large unions of the time, the International Ladies Garment Workers and the Amalgamated Clothing Workers, had both Jewish leadership and membership. To some extent they still have Jewish leadership, but the membership pattern has changed. They no longer print a Yiddish paper as they used to, or operate a whole host of Yiddish-Jewish educational activities.

The children of the immigrant workers, having entered business and white-collar professions, are no longer to be counted among the proletarians. Jews are economically secure, and because of their industry, intelligence, sobriety, and zeal, have succeeded in the land of opportunity.

But this leads to a new apprehension. There used to be among Jews a questioning, critical approach, a restlessness and social ferment, concern with injustice and inequity in the world. Jews were always deeply involved in movements of social reform.

What happens to the passion for social justice in an affluent society? It is so easy to become smug in prosperity and say, "come weal, come woe, my status is quo," without concern for the centers of anguish in the world and the critical decisions that must be made.

Are Jews losing the capacity of appropriating into their experience the grief, hunger, and need of others? With abundance, are we not becoming, as the Bible feared we might, a people of the calloused heart? "Jeshurun has waxed fat."

Are we doing enough in our collective and personal life to preserve the alert conscience, the sensitive heart, the vital human concern? How do we keep from insulating ourselves with our country clubs, hi-fi sets, trips to Miami? How do we reach out from our comfort into the world-at-large, and open our hearts to its tragedy and needs?

When Jews first came here from Europe, many had dropped the observances and disciplines of Jewish life: those who belonged to synagogues were the merest handful. After the cataclysms of two world wars American Jewry had to mobilize into a dynamic fund-raising mechanism. Jews wrote a golden chapter in the history of human service and philanthropy, calling to the forefront lay leadership that knew how to solicit funds and organize the community so that it could raise large quotas.

Today, however, there is a shift away from defense and a new stress on positive Judaism. Many new synagogues have been built, and many thousands have joined congregations during the last ten or fifteen years. This increased interest has reached such proportions that people speak of a "religious revival."

Here too, as in the case of the material and social affluence of American Jewry, the new prominence of the synagogue is not an unmixed good. What is happening to the synagogue as these masses of Jews, untutored and undisciplined Jewishly, enter it? Will the synagogue be able to maintain itself as a center of religious life, or will it be overwhelmed by the masses and become a secularized social institution with the Jewish motif muted?

Organizations and institutions that rest only on techniques and budgets are likely to collapse of their own weight. And can we rethink our budgets? A budget is not primarily a matter of finance: it is a philosophy, a system of values, a list of priorities, a recognition of what is primary. In our affluent society budgets should reflect the knowledge that Jewish survival is intertwined with and dependent upon the ongoing interpretation and communication of the content of Jewish living.

We cannot rely upon the fact that Jewish survival seems assured. The challenge to our generation is whether we can survive meaningfully. Our need is for a leadership of content and not one merely skilled in administrative and organizational procedures. We must call to the fore artists, thinkers, scholars, men of ideas, interpreters of the tradition so that they can enrich all of Jewish life with something of their spirit.

AN UNFINISHED WALK *

ALFRED KAZIN, in his cultured, sensitively written book *A Walker in the City*, describes an Odyssey to childhood, a pilgrimage to the East Side by one who, so to speak, has for long resided on the West Side, the revisiting of the ghetto by the naturalized dweller of the metropolis. Kazin is one of the finest American critics, and his interpretation of modern American literature, as embodied in his book *On Native Grounds* (the adjective is not insignificant), is highly regarded by students. He has also edited the works of William Blake and F. Scott Fitzgerald.

In his present book he returns to Brownsville in Brooklyn, the scene of his childhood, the place where his immigrant Jewish parents settled. He is an urbane observer as he walks down its streets. Memories are ignited, and often a Yiddish or Hebrew phrase comes out of the past to ring in his ears once again.

Brownsville stirs up many unpleasant associations, though now he is able also to remember much with gentleness. In the opening paragraph he reveals his feelings. "From the moment I step off the train at Rockaway Avenue and smell the leak out of the men's room, then the pickles from the stand just below the subway steps, and instant rage comes over me, mixed with dread and some unexpected tenderness." Brownsville is the home of the old and the poor, of "the old women in their shapeless flowered housedresses . . . their soft dumpy bodies and the unbudging way they occupy the tenement stoops . . . *Urime Yidn*. . . ."

He recalls with vivid painfulness the feeling of fear which like a heavy cloud covered his childhood years in Brownsville. He felt then that he was trapped by the East Side and that he would never be free, "the early hopelessness burns at my face like

---

*A Journal of Jewish Life and Letters, January–February, 1952.

fog from the minute I get off the subway." Brownsville was surrounded by an impenetrable Chinese wall, while beyond lay
America, true America. "We were of the city, but somehow not
in it. . . . We were the children of the immigrants who had
camped at the city's back door, in New York's rawest, remotest,
cheapest ghetto. . . . 'New York' was what we put last on our
address, but first in thinking of the others around us. They were
New York, the Gentiles, America; we were Brownsville—Brunzvil
as the old folks said—the dust of the earth to all Jews with money,
and notoriously a place that measured all success by our skill in
getting away from it. . . ."

Fear and anger give way for a moment to nostalgia. A new
building project has changed the appearance of the streets.
"Brownsville in that model quarter looks like an old crone who
has had a plastic operation and to my amazement I miss her old,
sly and withered face. I miss all those ratty little wooded tene-
ments born with the smell of damp in them in which there grew
up how many schoolteachers, city accountants, rabbis, cancer
specialists, functionaries of the revolution and strong men for
Murder Inc. . . ."

But he cannot shake off the uneasy yearning of his childhood
for America, the America beyond Brownsville. He remembers
wandering into the little church, so strangely out of place in the
Jewish section. "What really held me there was the number of
things written in English. I had associated God only with a foreign language."

Across the horizon of memory the Teacher looms largest
(Teacher with a capital T—not a person but a force). Teacher
spelled the chance of getting out of Brownsville. The road to
freedom ran through the classroom. But "Teacher" also spelled
danger since "Teacher" could cause one to fail. Tenseness and fear
accompanied one to school, for so much hung in the balance. "I
worked on a hairline between triumph and catastrophe." For what
did failure mean? "The alternative was 'going bad'. . . the dangers
of going bad were constantly impressed upon me at home and in
school, in dark whispers of the 'reform school'. . . every refrac-
tory attitude doomed you with the sound of 'Sing Sing.'. . . Anything less than absolute perfection in school suggested to my mind
that I might fall out of the daily race, be kept back in the working

class forever or—dared I think of it?—fall into the criminal class itself."

But there was another motivation for success that added dread to the possibility of failure. "It was not for myself alone that I was expected to shine but for them (my parents), to redeem the constant anxiety of their existence. I was the first American child, their offering to a strange new God; I was to be the monument of their liberation from the shame of being what they were. And that there was a shame in this was a fact that everyone seemed to believe as a matter of course. . . . It was in the sickening invocation of 'Americanism'—the word itself accusing us of everything we apparently were not. . . . "

If one was tense in school, one found escape in the movies. Everyone else might go to movies for relaxation and entertainment. Not the Brownsville immigrant's son. "In the wonderful darkness of the movies there was nothing to remind me of Brownsville. . . . I could never finally leave the movies while the light of Saturday afternoon still filled the streets, without feeling the sadness that Spinoza describes as coming after lust. . . . There was something in the everyday look of the streets that reproached me; they seemed to know I had come back to them unwillingly. But deep inside the darkness of the movies, everything that was good in life, everything that spoke straight to the imagination. . . ."

The movies spoke of the new and the free. The synagogue, on the other hand, kept one rooted in the old. It tied one to "an ancestral world I have never seen." He remembers the forebodings with which he crossed its threshold. "Secretly, I thought the synagogue a mean place and went only because I was expected to. Whenever I crossed the splintered and creaking porch into that stale air of snuff, of old men and old books and saw the dusty gilt brocade on the prayer shawls, I felt I was being pulled into some mysterious and ancient clan that claimed me as its own, simply because I had been born a block away. . . ."

A strange ambivalence marks his attitude to the God who resides in this synagogue. "He was our oldest habit. For me He was horribly the invisible head above the board of superintendents, the Almighty Judge. . . . I resented this God of Israel and of the Board of Superintendents; He would never let me rest."

But despite his resentment he could not turn his back upon God. "Yet I never really wanted to give Him up. . . . He seemed to hold the solitary place I most often went back to. There was a particular sensation connected with this—not of peace, not of certainty, not of goodness—but of depth; as if it were there I felt right to myself at last."

The family relationship was old world, an old world that kept out the new. The parents, however, had advantages denied the children. The children were their parents' America—but where was the America of the children? The parents spoke of the old country as "*der heym*." But to their children "*der heym*" was "entirely dim and abstract . . . alien as the skullcap and beard and frock coat of my mother's father, whom I never saw, but whose calm orthodox dignity stared up at me from an old cracked phtograph at the bottom of the bureau drawer." The children often envied their parents who could talk of a past "with so many private smiles between themselves," while they were bereft of such a past. "It was bewildering, it made me long constantly to get at some past nearer my own New York life, by having to live with all those running wounds of a world I had never seen."

Always there was the lure of the "beyond," the America outside of Brownsville, and the fear and sadness that he may never reach it. Private excursions took you "beyond" your block, but always you had to come back.

There were occasional surges of relatedness to a deepness that "lay under the gloomy obscurities" of his surroundings. Perhaps Jewishness need not be equated with parochialism, poverty, persecution; perhaps somehow this little oppressed minority, so different from others, had laid hold of an idea that the "beyond" with all of its fascination and magnificence had not yet comprehended. Perhaps, "we were a mighty people and He our mighty father. . . . The voice that spoke in that prayer book seemed to come out of my very bowels. There was something grand and austere in it that confirmed everything I had felt in my bones about being a Jew; the fierce awareness of life to the depths every day and in every hour; the commitment; the hunger." But it is a temporary feeling. Nothing in the environment arose to sustain it. The yearning for a deep base to life remained unsatisfied. The stamp of foreigners upon one continued a heavy burden. In his perplexity and

uneasiness he dreams for a time of Jesus and Christianity. Jesus
somehow belonged to the "beyond." Christianity was not a religion that spoke a foreign tongue. It belonged to America. But that
too soon passes. His Jewishness, strong enough to keep him from
"going over," is not deep enough to give meaning and rootedness
to his unanchored life.

The immigrant's son is in quest of a past. Where others enjoy
a sense of continuity, he feels only discontinuity. He seeks it in
literature. He seeks it in American history, with which he tries
to identify himself. But a disturbing residuum of "unbelonging-
ness" persists.

For Alfred Kazin has only walked part of the way American
Jews must walk, if they are to build soundly and creatively. Kazin
is no longer bitter. He is no longer fleeing. He does not resent his
ancestry. He does not despise the roots of his own being.

He has, however, not yet arrived. The negations have not
graduated into affirmations. He does not yet realize that the Jews
of Brownsville were not simply incomplete Americans—but bear-
ers of a culture rich in compassion and sensitivity. He has not yet
grasped the truth that in their individual lives they recapitulated
in no ignoble manner the great story of America. The Revolutionary War was fought and won in their personal life, and the
children of the immigrants emerged no less than Washington,
Adams, and Jefferson as first Americans. Freedom, human dignity, justice, equality, and democracy have a rich spiritual ancestry in their Jewish past.

The Declaration of Independence was inscribed on the parchment of their hearts and minds long before they came here. Indeed, they lived in America before they reached its shores. These
peddlers, tailors, and little shopkeepers were no less heroic than
pioneers celebrated in American history, for did they not cross
frontiers and open new settlements? Their pushcarts were "covered wagons." The hardworking, unkempt, eternally worried
women of Brownsville were daughters of a revolution no less
significant than that in which their genteel sisters of the "beyond"
gloried. The study of Torah turned synagogues into universities,
and Harvard had no higher intellectual standards and traditions.
The Sabbath was no less achievement than the assembly line of
the jet plane. The simple man of faith and integrity of Browns-

ville was an artistic creation by a culture comparable to the most beautiful painting by a Western artist.

Below Brownsville's surface of smells, insecurities, squalor, fears were inspired deeps; and no American Jew comes fully into his own as a personality, as an artist—indeed, as an American—until he has gathered the hidden wealth of his people's tradition.

Someday one will arise who will complete the journey Alfred Kazin has begun. His story will not have the uneasiness, the frustration, the vagueness which characterize Kazin's book. He will be self-assured, clear, rooted. His story or his poem or his painting drawing upon Judaism and Americans will no longer be discontinuous and disjointed. The American tradition and the Jewish will each, like a single parent, contribute to the wholeness of the child.

Then will the flight from Brownsville cease and the civil war within the Jew end. The "beyond" will be within. Then will a new and mighty stream flow from the Jew into American life, into its literature, music, and morality.

ANSWERING WITH OUR LIFE

As an American rabbi, I have unique opportunities to see the fluctuations, the rise and the fall of our private and public lives. Together with my colleagues, our profession places us close to that center upon which the constructive and destructive, the upward and the downward, the outward and the inward pressures of Jewish life converge. And from this vantage point, those of us who have served the community five or six decades have noted three differing eras—each with its own pattern—each marked by its unique dimensions.

The first that I remember from my childhood before I became a rabbi might be called the period of adaptation. The American rabbi was an apostle of acculturation, for he recognized the need of a tradition to be relevant to its environment. The American rabbi of those days stressed the value of integration into American life—integration that would introduce the new immigrants not only to baseball, to social dancing, to movies, but also to Whitman, Thoreau, Emerson, and Emily Dickinson. The rabbis incorporated into their sermons examples of American culture, and often gave lectures upon American ideas and American books. They said to the Jews who came here in such large numbers at the turn of the century: "Enter American life fully; enter it with your tradition; do not remain outside of it; do not isolate yourself from it; overcome the apprehensions which centuries of enforced alienism have bred in you. Do not approach the world here in America with distrust that the Old World aroused in you because society in the past has sometimes held out bright promises only to turn them into dust and ashes once again."

The American rabbi said to his people, "The promises of America are sincere, they are real, they are genuine. You are not exposing yourself to another searing and fearful disillusionment by entering American life fully. The inscription on the Statue of Liberty, symbolically composed by a Jewish poetess, is true. America does say to all who knock at its gate:

> Give me your tired, your poor
> Your huddled masses yearning to breathe free.

We had to tell our people then that Judaism was not a ghetto, a tribal matter at all—that Judaism was a world outlook that can and should live in the broad places of modern civilization; that ghettos were only an accident of history; that apartness was something imposed upon us—it was not a growth from within. We had to arouse a faith in America. How many times have our people encountered lands which seemed to open the door to them only to imprison them later within its walls!

We said to our first-generation Jews: "Have confidence in America. Have faith in America. Bring your Judaism into the highways of the land—integrate it with the rich and fascinating culture of America itself."

Then there arose upon this soil a new generation that equated the acquisition of the new culture of America with the abandonment of the old tradition of Judaism. Like some sabras of Israel in our own time, these American sabras of fifty years ago wanted to close the door on history. They were going to write a new Torah, a new beginning, a new epic, and a new creation. Assimi-

lation and imitation were the order of the day. We saw the deser-
tion of our tradition by multitudes fleeing the altars of their
fathers, abandoning the ancestral way of life.

In his *Autobiography*, Lincoln Steffens draws a picture of
the East Side of those days where he, a Gentile, served many
years as a newspaper reporter. He describes young men smoking
and laughing outside the synagogues on Yom Kippur, while
within the old men were pouring out their hearts in prayer. And
then he, a man far from any religion, reflects sadly: "The tears
hurt. The weeping and the gnashing of the teeth of the old men
who were doomed and knew it. Two, three thousand years of
heroism, devotion and suffering for the cause, lost in one generation."

Indeed, it looked to many of us as though the tradition of
our fathers was rapidly going down the drain. A noble history
seemed to be coming to its abrupt and inglorious end. Sociologists
and journalists were foretelling its disappearance. What an ironic
epitaph could have been written, "Flourished under oppression—
died under freedom."

In their insecurity as Americans, many Jews felt called upon
to renounce Judaism. Judaism was the price they had to pay for
being Americans. Besides Judaism and all it involved was a rem-
nant of a pre-American and premodern period. Judaism had for
so long stamped them as aliens and now that they had arrived, now
that they were Americans, unqualified, unadjectived, unhyphen-
ated, they no longer needed Judaism. It was a barrier to their
entrance into American life.

We were in the midst of a period of assimilation, of escapism,
of flight. We were making for the exits from our community in
those days. The American rabbis tried to teach the people, though
so often they were beyond the reach of our voice, that their conception of America was a travesty, a calumny, and their idea of
Judaism a distortion. America did not want ciphers and zeros.
America was not a "melting pot," though the phrase itself was
coined by a Jewish writer. America, we argued in a hundred
different ways, was more like a symphony, a symphony which
would be impoverished by the muting of any of its strings.

We spoke then of pluralism, of the orchestration of differences, of the union of integration and integrity. This we said was

the real meaning of the American Revolution. It was not simply a political revolution; it was a revolution in the very concept of society. There was to be no heresy in America. Though 97 percent of its population was Christian, the 3 percent of Jews were here as of a right not inferior to that of their more numerous fellow citizens. This was a country in which difference, far from being the focus of conflict and friction, was to serve as an avenue of mutual enrichment and reciprocal stimulation.

We thundered, "You're wrong about America. You can be Jewish without being an alien. This is a new world—a new opportunity."

That second generation was in due course followed by the third. We are presently "American Jew, the Third." This generation is no longer on the defensive. It is rooted in America. Its parents are Americans, and it was brought up in an American home, unlike the preceding generation which, though brought up in America, lived in a home that really embodied the spirit of the *shtetl*. Now we are Americans from birth. This generation heard no discussion across the dinner table about expulsions and ghettos. No painful personal experiences scarred their youthful mind. No pogroms haunted their memories. No prior status of alien and foreigner made them troubled and uneasy. This is a generation, healthy of mind and body; wellborn, coming into freedom and equality with the very first breath of life they drew. They have straight backs and are able to look the whole world in the eye, uncowed, uncringing, and unapologetic.

This generation has publicly proclaimed its Jewishness. It has flocked to the synagogues and has multiplied the number of congregations thoughout the land. It seems to walk the highway of proud affirmation of its ancestry. It buys Harry Golden's books, and reads with interest about grandfathers it never knew, and their heroic trails and efforts as immigrants. It goes to see *Fiddler on the Roof*, and responds sentimentally to the characters, the manners, the strains and melodies of a *shtetl* of which it has only dimly, if at all, heard. It has given the lie to all the prognostication that the American Jew is doomed to disappear.

The sociologists, the writers of articles that analyze the birthrate and project the disappearance of the Jew are no longer popular. Now and then perhaps a magazine, in order to highlight one phase of our weakness, will speak about "The Vanishing American Jew." But the American Jew, by and large, has cast his vote in favor of survival, and has said so that all America may hear, "I AM A JEW." Jewish institutions have never been more visible on the landscape of American life than today. This is not a generation fearful, timid, ashamed of its ancestry.

But, alas, this is only part of the story. This generation publicly affirming its Judaism has throttled Judaism in yet another way. It has reduced its Jewishness to a membership card and to a ceremonialism for stated days and events. It has not yet recognized that Judaism is ethics, morality, prophecy, commitment, the hard way of principle, the determined preservation of identity and continuity. It has not yet recognized that Judaism is a revolt against all that degrades and corrupts, against every unjust coercion, against every conformity that makes the human being less human, against every outrage perpetrated upon man.

Judaism is the enemy of blandness, of compromise, of conformity. As long as there is injustice and war and cruelty, to be a Jew means to be in a state of alienation from a society that permits this. It means to be in a continual condition of protest. It means to reject that which runs counter to our prophetic goals. Ceremonies are not enough to fill a life. They are significant only when they are rooted in an outlook, when they blossom out of a way of life whch one walks devoutly. Otherwise ritual is like thistledown which the wind blows and with which children play. Ritual was important in our parents' life because it was the outward manifestation of an inner life and a way of life which they honored every day.

And so we have this strange and fatal paradox: many Jews have entered into the structure of our community, are carried on our rolls, have expanded our membership figures to unprecedented numbers, yet Jewishly we have assimilated. The Jewish void has been filled with other values. We have allowed the forces of the environment to rush in and occupy the emptiness caused by the absence of Judaism. We have descended to the poor averages of the society about us in the absence of rich standards from our own tradition.

Gone is the character the Jewish home once bred, the loyalties it once fostered, the roots it grew. Jewish affiliation does not mean saying "I'm a Jew," or having your Christian neighbor know that you are Jewish. Jewish affiliation means home-building; it means family-sanctifying; it means a fidelity-honoring life.

The strength of the Jew has always resided in his individuality. He was himself as he strode through all history. Whatever the environment, whatever the circumstances, whatever the temptations, the Jew said proudly, *"Lo yayoseh kain b'Yisroel,"* *"Es passt nisht far Yiden,"* this is not a level to which Jews fall. He resisted single-handedly the pagan world with its shrines and its immorality and its superstitions; he fought the faith of the Persian with his god of light and god of darkness; he rejected the new trinitarian faith which was born on the soil of his own land. The Jew throughout history sought not a good time but a good life.

We must remain true to ourselves at our deepest. We must remain true—not apart from others, not apart from our time and culture—but in their very midst. Then we will find meaning, rich content, and purpose for ourselves. Then indeed will we help America find its way back to moral health and strength. This is a time of maximum demands. Let not the Jews of America lead minimal lives. Archibald MacLeish has written:

> *We are neither weak nor few*
> *As long as one man does what one man can do*
> *As long as one man in the sun alone,*
> *Walks between the silence and the stone*
> *And honors manhood in his flesh, his bone,*
> *We are not yet too weak, nor yet too few.*

PROFILE OF AMERICAN JEWISH YOUTH *

"CHILDREN TODAY LOVE LUXURY. They have bad manners, contempt for authority, disrespect for their elders and they like to talk instead of work. They contradict their parents, chatter be-

*Sixth Annual Evelyn A. Margolis Memorial Lecture, Gratz College, Philadelphia, January 19, 1966.

fore company, gobble up the best food at the table and tyrannize
our teachers."

That this is not the sorrowful plaint of a contemporary parent you will recognize from three omissions. There is no reference to the usurping of the family car, to the penchant for
marching in demonstrations and to rejections of religious practices and beliefs. As a matter of fact, the statement was made by
Socrates, and has undoubtedly been repeated in one form or
another by every subsequent generation of elders.

Clearly, our young are not the first to baffle, confound, and
anger their parents, and we are not the first gray-heads to shake
our heads dolefully and say, "I don't understand what has come
over the youth of our day." The tension between young and old
—which has been called the longest civil war in history—is in the
nature of things, so to speak, and recurs with every new generation.

This perspective, though it may not diminish our concern,
may hopefully keep us from the headlong conclusion that the
young are doomed in themselves, or are acting in such a way as
to doom society. The world is still here, an appreciable interval
of time after Socrates made his gloomy appraisal. Perhaps our
world is doomed, but if it is the entire burden of culpability must
not be placed upon the young.

The young represent either a challenge or a threat to those
of us who have achieved maturity and have settled down in a
firm and permanent position in society. Every generation raises
the standard of newness, of movement, and evidences some measure of disrespect for and repudiation of the venerable fixities
upon which we have erected our adult life. Every child is born
into a world differing from that of his parents because of the
pervasiveness and constancy of the fact of change in human life.
If he is not in conflict with the world in which his seniors have
achieved status and at-homeness, he is nonetheless a product of
a differing environment. It might be said that to be born is to be
fated to dislocation and to qualify for alienation.

In addition, youth represents a phase of development which
is characterized by impetuosity, vigor, dynamism: qualities which
a staid and sober society does not always welcome and for
which it generally fails to provide adequate outlets. In a word,

to be young is to be subversive. The youth collides at many points with the established, the entrenched, the venerable. He demands not only equal rights but policy-making power in a world which, since he did not fashion it, does not conform to his values, purposes, and appetites. He is impatient for an independence which society grants him with a gradualness that can only appear to him as grudging.

This inherent condition is aggravated in our time by additional forceful and compelling contemporary circumstances. Never before in history has change been marked by such a machine-gun rate of speed and by such a comprehensiveness of scope as today. It sometimes seems as if the remaining stabilities are not capable of absorbing the incessant assaults of change. Though we recognize that change is constant in all periods of history, it would be more appropriate in our day to speak not of change but of revolution, and not of one revolution but of multiple revolutions. Norman Cousins has written that into the last quarter of a century we have compressed "more change, more thrust, more tossing about of men's souls and gizzards than was spaced over the human chronicle since the beginning of time." The result has been the proliferation of discontinuities and the escalation of uncertainty in every area of life. Yesterday is part of the distant past, and tomorrow is unimaginable behind the dust stirred up by our rapid movement. Apparently unnegotiable gaps stretch between us and our immediate antecedents, and dark impenetrable curtains hide the sketchiest outline of the shape of things to come in the near future. We have become isolated in time and have lost the elbowroom in which history once allowed us to move freely about and express our own will.

We are denizens of the instant, prisoners of the moment. Orphaned of forebears and uncertain of posterity, modern man falls back on the only reality that seems to be within reach, the self. Parenthetically, it might be observed that the fringe extremisms of our day are the concentrations and intensifications of what exists in more moderate form in the rest of us. It is for this reason that it is necessary to know the pathological in order to understand the normal. The "Beat" movement, for example, represents an attempt to elongate and perpetuate the moment in the absence of both past and future, and to fall back exclusively on the detached self, since there is no stable or meaningful frame in which it can be put. Diana Trilling, the critic, has said that "for the advanced writer of our time, the self is his supreme and even sole referent." The term obsolescence has come into prominence in our current vocabulary, and neither products of the assembly line nor of mind and spirit nor of history and tradition can claim immunity from its engulfing process.

Uncertainty, the concomitant of feverish change, is intensified by the fact that we live in the nuclear age. Not only are we unsure of the character of the future; we lack the assurance that there will be a future. American youth finds itself uncertain of what America represents, where it is going, and what it is seeking. Our national goals and purposes, articulated innumerable times in the past in shining rhetoric, have become nebulous and remote. The new role into which America has been thrust and the global complexities in which it is involved have not been sufficiently naturalized in our concepts, attitudes, and policies to stand out clearly. Nor have statesmen and philosophers emerged among us to give expression to the new dimensions and new realities with which we must as Americans live. Who has the answer to the question "Where are we going?"

Yet for youth, whose unique asset is the future, this is the most basic and vital issue. Detached in time, disoriented from tradition, and uncertain as to goal, the young are compelled to seek the fulfillment of their needs and ambitions and the realization of their idealism in an environment that fails to provide the minimal materials or climate required for the consummation of their rightful hopes and aims.

Since Jews are like everyone else but more so, American Jewish youth live in a universe a hundredfold larger and more intricate than any inhabited by previous generations of Jews. Their universe of thought, feeling, relationships, and interests are not only larger; it is likewise more integral to their life than any collective outside of the Jewish community which Jews may have formerly entered. Life in the larger, integrated society invites the Jew to many areas of experience and involvement and opens to him untold opportunities for expression and fulfillment. Nor need he repudiate his particular community or disengage himself completely from its activities and purposes. He enters a

realm of secularity in which Jewishness is a neutral and irrelevant
accident.

The enlarged circumference in which modern Jewish youth
move exiles their Jewish expression and involvement to a corner
and a margin. The Jew as an individual has grown at the very
moment that Judaism as a tradition and culture has shrunk. The
Jewish education American Jewish youth receive and the sentiment of Jewish attachment implanted in them are not able to
cope with this new dimension. Judaism as a crucial influence and
palpable force tends to become paler and more insubstantial in
the largely increased context of the life they lead. Hence "assimilation" is an effortless, unconscious, natural concomitant of
life in a technological and integrated society.

We have failed in such a transmission of Jewish knowledge
and attitude to counteract the obscuring effect exerted by the
environment in which the American Jew now lives as a member
of the American society. Since America has till now fostered
diverse particularities, the Jew has been impelled by the character
of the larger society to enroll in organized Jewish life. Thus we
have the interesting paradox that though Jewish life in its collec-
tivity has attained a high degree of visibility, if not conspicuousness, on the American scene, Judaism as a personal equation in the
life of its individual adherents has moved toward imperceptibility.

We have failed for a variety of reasons. It may be that we
are casualties of the same process that has blurred Judaism in the
lives of our young. The work of that process is more quickly
evident in the case of the young only because we, their elders,
brought to American life a greater degree of Jewish rootedness
and a strong sense of our Jewish identity. Even our rabbis and
planners, educators and policy-makers do not themselves, whatever their verbal affirmations, possess such a vital centrality of
Jewish identification as to enable them to devise creative Jewish
answers to the problem. Or it may be that we simply do not recognize the unprecedented nature of the new situation as we continue to employ approaches and methods that do not address
themselves to the realities. Or perhaps we no longer attract to
Jewish professional service on all levels men and women of the
skill, vision, and intellectual power requisite for meeting the demands which the pattern of American Jewish life makes.

Now and then, one must confess, there is a sinking feeling that we are caught in a vise of conditions and forces which do not allow of a solution sufficient to them, and we must reconcile ourselves to a blandness of Jewish communal and personal living, devoid of depth, creative power, or vital impact. The breakdown in communicating across the great divide stretching between the generations, coupled with our own vagueness as to what it is we ought to be communicating, constitutes our major problem.

In other words, the problem of Jewish youth must be viewed from the larger perspective of the Jewish community, the Jewish leader, the Jewish school, and the adult Jew generally. In his recent insightful work, *The Uncommitted—Alienated Youth in American Society*, Kenneth Keniston points out that the rejection of adult society on the part of the young is related not only to the psychic inadequacies of the young but also to the facts of adult life in America.

A blurred image of Jewish selfhood is all but universal in American Jewish life, and it would be more than miraculous if our youth had a clear sense of their identity. We are in the throes of a tension between continuity and relevance; between religion and secularity; between the Jewish community and the larger society; between a yesterday that is remote and a future that is inconceivable; between reason and emotion; between the high level of our familiarity with the intellectual disciplines of our time and the low level of our knowledge of Judaism; between the ease and self-assurance which Jews have acquired in the sciences and humanities and the uneasiness and uncertainty with which they talk of Judaism because of their limited knowledge.

Perhaps "tension" is too strong a word. American Jewish youth accept the fact of their Jewishness, since there is general environmental support for such acceptance. To reject implies an emotional involvement that is not felt by them. In the absence of a fervent affirmation or a sharp rejection, it may be inappropriate to speak of a "tension."

The nebulousness of our youth's idea of what "Jewish" means even when they so designate themselves reflects their unsureness of their Jewish identity. One of the central forces in establishing a concept of self is the home. (Psychologists speak of the home as a "crucible of identity.") Through rebellions or emulation the young acquire an awareness of their own identity and selfhood. But the Jewish parent is a shadowy and unclear figure as a Jew, arousing neither great admiration nor intense opposition. He serves neither as "target" nor "model." A young Jew is likely to appraise his father in some such words as "Oh, he's a nice enough fellow," implying that you cannot really hate someone like him, but what is there to love?

Neither is the synagogue effective in helping the young Jew define his role as a Jew in American society and in the contemporary world generally. It represents a religion that is detached not only from the religion of the majority of Americans but also from the young person's life. Indeed, it may not even be related to the life he sees in the Jewish community at large. The organized Jewish community represents a mechanism more than an idea; a system of techniques more than a spirit. Its standards are too often shoddy and poor. Its leadership and programs often do not stimulate a positive response in those who come to it fresh and open-minded.

The fact of Jewishness thus remains undenied and unrejected. It is isolated, incidental, and marginal to the rest of the young Jew's life. It is unillumined by any viewpoint to give it meaning and coherence. It casts no shadow and enkindles no glow.

Yet Jewishness is acknowledged as fact. It is not placed in some subterranean chamber of consciousness. It thrusts itself upward and makes itself felt at family gatherings, in the case of the children's education, in the matter of intermarriage, and occasionally in relations with non-Jews. The fact is deeper and more influential than one would judge from a study of the American Jew's habitual life. It has a subsurface intensity, of which he himself may be unaware.

What is lacking? We have a valuable protoplasmic core in the circumstance that the American Jew sees himself as a Jew and does not feel that this affiliation shuts him out of any other circle into which he would like to be admitted. There is an at-easeness about his Jewishness, an absence of discomfort. He is not plagued by it. He does not live in a twilight zone, Hamlet-like, debating "to be or not to be." He is not looking for avenues of escape. It elicits from him no neurotic responses. It scars him with no depressing memories.

The modern Jew needs a rationale, an outlook which translates his Jewishness into articulated value and genuine significance; a rationale which correlates his Jewishness with the large ambit of his interests and views. Judaism as a world view, meriting intellectual respect, congenial to the values of a free society, contributing to the dignity of the individual, has yet to be presented to the American Jew. For one thing, our scholars and thinkers (with rare exception) have not helped us in the formulation of such a philosophy of Jewish life. For another we have been so busy stressing Jewish education for the young that we have failed to give adequate thought, time, energy and, of course, budget to that period in our young people's lives when we can induct them in a reasoned and compelling rationale.

We who have built Jewish communities must now set ourselves to building Jewish lives.

13 • The Human Comedy

TRUE AND FALSE WIT

HUMOR PERFORMS many invaluable functions. It eases tensions. It joins a group into a closer bond. It relaxes the mind. It brings relief to those who are depressed. It is a lightning rod that draws off anger. In laughing at human foibles, we learn to see ourselves in larger perspective. In poking fun at various social situations and national events, we perform the important task of pointing up follies and wrongs in our collective life. Humor is the best weapon of social criticism and protest.

People without a sense of humor—which means a lack of awareness of the absurdity of one's pretensions and self-impor-tance—are not just bores; they are menaces. The Stalins, Hitlers, and Mussolinis of our time were grossly deficient in a sense of humor. Nor did it ever occur to the Coughlins, Gerald Smiths, the Eastlands and McCarthys to pause and laugh at themselves.

There is, however, a kind of pseudohumor which masquer-ades as genuine and which has none of the virtues and whole-someness of the real thing. It substitutes malice and savagery for wit, and seeks to rouse laughter by tearing down and degrading people. The auditor receives a moment's spirit of superiority by contrast with those who are viciously trampled upon by such oral thuggery. Obscenity and smut are sometimes treated as if they were humorous in themselves, and the mere recounting of pornographic details is expected to be greeted with gales of laughter. There is also the spurious humorist whose witticisms are merely barbs hurled at another race or group. In this instance prejudice and vulgar snobbishness are seemingly garbed as clowns but in truth are vile hatemongers. The mannerisms, appearance, accent, customs, and religion of a whole group become the grist for the mill of such counterfeit jesters.

True humor is never irrelevant, venomous, malice-inspired, or vicious. It may be irreverent, thumbs its nose at the high and mighty, puncture the pretensions of the stuffed shirt, and laugh at the frailties, follies, and fallacies that inhere in man and in the human situation. As such, it plays an important role in our group life.

IN PRAISE OF THE FUMBLER

I WANT TO SING A HYMN for the duffer, the poor shot, the amateur, the butter-fingered, unskilled, but determined participant in the sports or arts who will never set the world on fire. We Americans are an energetic and active people who worship success and venerate achievement. We therefore uphold as an axiom never to be questioned the statement that if a thing is worth doing at all, it is worth doing well.

A golfer who enjoys the game likes the opportunity to be in the open, the exercise and companionship it affords. It is obvious that he will never rival Bobby Jones or Sam Snead or Ben Hogan, or for that matter his neighbor. Should he mobilize all his energies to play a better game and make that a serious goal determinedly to be pursued, golf ceases to be relaxation and becomes responsibility. He will banish play without necessarily acquiring skill or increasing pleasure. Why should he not be content to remain what he is, a "duffer," an "also-ran," twenty-five strokes removed from the man who wins? Why must one excel and turn the practice of the game into solemn and grave routine, like a child playing on the piano keyboard under the supervision of a stern parent? The game has its value and justification precisely because it relaxes and rests the heart rather than burdening and taxing it. Why must the drive to be first prompt every putt we make?

This thought applies with equal validity to the amateur singer who enjoys raising his voice in song, though concert impressarios will never fight over him; to the individual who enjoys a game of bridge though he is no threat to Culbertson; and to the fisherman who finds delight in the sport, though its intricacies and subtleties are hidden from him.

I celebrate the unskilled in this sad age of the specialist; the amateur in an age of experts; the layman in the midst of would-be professionals; the man who enjoys doing a thing despite the fact that others do it better.

TOURISTS IN ISRAEL

Of tourists to Israel there are a hundred varieties. I can only suggest a few types with whom my limited experience has brought me in contact.

My observations are neither academic nor pretentious. They are fruits of a study unfortified by the utilization of such scientific apparatus as field glasses, telescope, spectroscope, range finder, or binoculars. Nor does my report contain the graphs, statistics, diagrams, and charts which make scientific papers appear so formidable. My only credentials: "I see what I see."

There is the tourist who is in a perpetual hurry. The incarnation of impatience, he lives by the principle that time is money and he cannot afford to be a spendthrift. A site may have a four-thousand-year history behind it; he has only swift seconds to spend on it. He begins moving to the next place of interest instantaneously on his arrival at the first. At the end of his trip this tourist's principal boast will be that he covered so many miles, saw so many sights, visited so many places in so few days. He comes back with the illusion that he has really been to the land, though he has only a hazy, murky conception of what he has seen or heard.

Then comes the tourist who is more avid to parade his old knowledge than to acquire new knowledge. He has "boned up" on a guidebook and no sooner does the trained, informed guide begin a description of the history or the geographical characteristics of a place being visited then our erudite traveler interrupts with an ill-digested version of what he has read. His facts are uncertain, his selections injudicious, and his recital incomprehensible.

Another type is the tourist who is interested in places but not in people. He comes to a land rich in historical associations and treats it as if it were uninhabited. The struggles and hopes, the problems and attainments of those now living on the historic sites are of no interest or concern. It almost appears as if he resents the intrusion of the contemporary into the sphere of the historic, the presumption of people to live where once prophets, sages, and warriors engaged in immortal drama. On his return, he will describe the relics of centuries long past, the scenes of ancient battles, the roads which caravans were wont to travel, the stone pillars, and the excavations. The conditions of the present, the nature of the people and the circumstances of their life, fall far outside the purview of his curiosity or observation.

Perhaps the most offensive type is the one who thinks that by flashing a wad of American dollars he can command the obedience of the highest and the lowest in the land he is visiting. His passport is the dollar bill. He is the roving feudal lord, and all whom he sees are serfs bound to jump at the crackle of his American currency.

What then are the traits which characterize the good tourist to Israel?

First, it seems to me, the visitor to these shores should show a respect and regard for the way of life he finds here, however it may vary from the one in his native land. Too many people see the forms and customs of their society as the absolute from which all others are a descent and a deviation. Hence what they find in other places is strange and inferior. The great insight of modern life, one which has made it possible for Jews at long last to secure their rights and positions in society, is that difference is not the antithesis of equality. Parity is not dependent upon identity. The sensible tourist will therefore not feel any sense of supremacy by reason of the wealth of his country, his personal affluence, or the customs he follows and conveniences he enjoys when at home. The people he is visiting are no less gifted, no less human, no less sensitive, no less proud than his neighbors. They are not a lesser breed than his fellow citizens. As the Rabbis long ago instructed us, he who respects others will gain respect for himself.

Coupled with this respect for others should be a personal humility, an openness of mind and heart, a readiness to learn, an eagerness to observe, the feeling that everyone we encounter and everything we experience has something to teach us. The Rabbis said that the world is too small for God and for a man of pride and arrogance. The man who feels that he has reached finality in his own development and lacks nothing in understanding, knowledge, or ability, is doomed to tour a sterile and dreary landscape all the days of his life. But he who recognizes that he has much to learn and is possessed of a zeal for learning and growth will come upon interesting and exciting scenes wherever he goes. The tourist who seeks to learn rather than to teach, to grow rather than to guide, to observe rather than to judge will find exhilaration in every tour.

This humbleness of spirit is a special necessity for the American Jew who comes to visit Israel. No matter how active he is in his own community and no matter how substantial has been his monetary contribution to the U.J.A., no Israeli is required to prostrate himself before him. He must not expect to find a nation of Sir Walter Raleighs putting down red carpets for him to strut upon. The people of Israel have done infinitely more than the American Jews out of their sense of Jewish obligation. At best we are partners.

Nor should the American Jew come to Israel with Utopian expectations. Zion the reality could not live up to Zion the free and unrestrained vision which has for so long informed our lives. The people are human, human in their noble and admirable qualities and human too in their fallibilities and weaknesses. There are Israeli saints and sinners, idealists and materialists, men of lofty spirit and men of gross ambitions and appetites, people of heroic stature and those of microscopic virtue. And the life in Israel too has glorious lights and dreary shadows; peaks, plains, and valleys. One finds the fresh living waters of hope, vision, and learning and the Dead Sea of pettiness, decadence, and selfishness. The landscape of human life is as varied as the landscape of the land itself with its gardens and its wasteland, with its rich green fields and its stony and barren soil.

Yet for all that, Israel is one of the most fascinating and entrancing of the world's places, representing a high-water mark in Jewish history. The tourist who comes with respect, humility, and gratitude will harvest a fascination and exaltation that no other experience can yield in equal measure.

RELIGION THAT COMES OUT ON TOP

ONE OF MY FRIENDS is devoutly Orthodox and is doing his utmost to follow a path consistent with the practice which his beliefs dictate. Yet, it seems to me, he has singled out for special attention and unique emphasis one of the customs regarded as minor by the tradition. He insists on wearing a hat or skullcap at all times, at secular gatherings, interfaith meetings, in the public library. He has made of the skullcap the proud banner proclaiming his adherence to the Orthodox view, challenging and rebuking those who are more lax. His faith and piety have gone to his head; the hat has become for him the insignia of Judaism, its distinguishing symbol and perennial manifestation.

While I do not know where Jewish law decrees the wearing of a hat at all times as a commandment or labels its removal at any time as a sin, I do concede to my Orthodox friend the right to follow this practice as slavishly as he wishes. Yet I am amused by his exaltation of his seeming fear that his religion will fall at the drop of a hat.

Another friend belongs to the Reform wing. Upholding the position that ritual is not an essential or binding element, he has discarded most of the traditional observances. Yet he retains more of them than he recognizes since he attends temple Friday evenings; hears Scripture read from a Torah written by hand; marks by some type of observance the festivals of the Jewish year; calls his spiritual leader rabbi; has restored the rite of Bar Mitzvah; and attends wedding ceremonies and funeral exercises. But he too has a blind spot. My liberal friend is a fanatic about removing the hat. He declaims about it, insists upon it, and is ready to make a *cause célèbre* of it in season and out of season. "If one is a Reform

Jew," he recently burst forth, "one should under no condition wear a hat, whether in the funeral parlor or at the marriage service." Indeed, he scoffed at a fellow member of the temple whom he saw wearing a skullcap. "So you think you're a Reform Jew," he bitingly remarked. While the *yarmulke* is never upon the head of my Reform friend, it seems to be always on his mind.

My Reform friend joins hands at this point with my Orthodox neighbor—with but a minute difference. Whereas the Orthodox Jew makes a fetish of covering his head, this Reform Jew makes a fetish of uncovering it. Both, it seems to me, make of a minor ritual a major issue bordering on the superstitious. I, who recognize the rightful and indispensable role of ritual in the religious experience, refuse to hang my religion on a hat.

NAME-DROPPING

WE HAVE ALL MET THE TYPE described as a "name-dropper." He seeks to achieve importance by association. Apropos of nothing at all, he will introduce the name of this or that celebrity and will intimate, if not proclaim explicitly, that he is on very close terms with the distinguished people to whom he is always alluding. Thus you may hear him say in a studied casual manner, "I was saying to Lyndon the other day . . ." or "Winston once related to me . . ." or "I did not hesitate to say to Nikita. . . ." Though he may never have come within hailing distance of the notables he calls by their first name, he derives great pleasure from imparting to his hearers the impression that he has devoted friends among the mighty. I do not begrudge him his self-delusion, springing as it does from his own vanity or insecurity. The harm he does is small, and his transparent antics lead his more discerning friends to chuckle behind his back.

There is, however, one example of "name-dropping" that is more widespread and more serious. I refer to the easy and thoughtless way in which we use the word God. A contemporary translation of the Biblical commandment "Thou shalt not take the name of the Lord in vain" might well read "Thou shalt not be a name-dropper where the name of God is concerned."

We attend services out of habit or out of conformity with the practices of a particular group or as a sentimental tribute to the memory of parents. We repeat the word "God" or "Lord" many times; submerged and muted in the context, it excites no special interest since it is so frequently used. It does not suggest to us the boldest, broadest, most exciting generalization which the human mind has ever attempted, nor does it suffuse the world and life for us with the warmth and tenderness which the existence of God should inspire.

Most people who say they believe in God are "name-droppers" since their belief lacks the intensity and intimacy of close association and devoted communion. The word, since it does not evoke the reality, is used by us as a magical symbol, a talisman, a verbal amulet. For all our vaunted loyalty to faith and religion, and for all the bulging memberships of church and synagogue, the impact of religion on personal experience, behavior, and social morality is infinitesimal.

FREEDOM MEANS PRIVACY

THE NEWSPAPERS recently carried this item: "Mississippi Governor Ross Barnett said in a speech in Jackson that he was glad to appear before this 'fine Christian gathering.' The audience stirred nervously but the Governor went on, referring several times to the 'Christian' audience. When he finished, Rabbi Perry Nussbaum rose and good-naturedly reminded the Governor that he had been speaking to the congregation of a Jewish synagogue celebrating its centennial."

This incident highlights a self-evident truth: a Jewish gathering stoops to folly when it invites as its guest of honor, or as one of its main speakers, a political figure unfamiliar with the significance of the occasion or the background of the sponsoring group. The mania for "a big name," the hope that the fame of the speaker

will draw a larger crowd than would otherwise be attracted, or
the feeling that the importance of the occasion will be augmented
by the presence of a well-known figure (despite the fact that he
is completely indifferent to and uninformed about the event or
the institution) represents a scale of values that is shabby, calcu-
lating, and unworthy.

Jews do not have to dramatize their integration with the
larger society. It should be beneath our dignity to seek the approval of others for activities and purposes which our faith has
upheld through a long history. A scholarly non-Jew, who has a
fine and sympathetic understanding of our past or of our current
challenges and problems, may appropriately be asked to a meeting
of Jews assembled to celebrate a milestone in the Jewish community or to confer on immediate Jewish concerns.

Unfortunately, program chairmen, in planning a Jewish
gathering, are often more intent upon obtaining as speaker a
non-Jew who is a celebrity rather than one who has something
to contribute to the deliberations. Political figures, knowing of
this weakness, prepare a stock address which they believe to be
suitable for all Jewish occasions. Such an address generally contains two or three Jewish or Hebrew words (gleaned by the
great man from one of his Jewish subordinates and mispro-
nounced with gusto at the time of the delivery of the speech);
a reference to the monumental contributions of the Jewish past;
an account of one's Jewish friends, and a glorious peroration
about the need for goodwill. Sometimes the address is couched
in terms of condescension; sometimes the speaker is so obviously
bored that his pathetic efforts to appear gracious and interested
arouse pity; at other times the remarks of the guest are so full
of gaucheries that they prove embarrassing.

The Jewish community, like any religious or ethnic group
within the framework of American life, has a right to its "private"
moments when it discusses its problems or marks its festivities
within its own "family." It does not need to borrow importance
by inviting an outstanding non-Jew who, however significant his
contributions to the general good may be, must of necessity feel
and talk as an "outsider" at an occasion devoted exclusively to
Jewish affairs.

HONORS UNLIMITED

A JEW WITHOUT A SCROLL for distinguished service is as rare as a private in Kentucky. Jewish universities, yeshivots, colleges of higher Jewish learning, and seminaries seem to have far outstripped their non-Jewish counterparts in conferring honorary degrees, not only at the usual commencement exercises in June but also at special midsemester winter and spring convocations. A study may well reveal that some of our institutions of learning have given out more degrees *honoris causa* than "in course." In addition to the free distribution of doctorates, scrolls, medallions, statuettes, a host of varied titles—including patron, benefactor, defender, disciple, and builder—are bestowed upon the fraternity of the favored and the congregation of the commended.

Our fund-raising national organizations have developed their own hierarchy of honors. "Woman of Valor," "Man of the Year," "Public Friend Number One," "Lover of His People," and similar designations are handsomely engraved on bracelets, charms, Bibles, bronze, parchment, and watches and are publicly given out with great pomp and unrestrained rhetoric to small armies of people.

Nor have synagogues lagged behind. To show their involvement in the current scene, they confer honors on those generous with their support at Hanukkah Dinners, Purim Balls, *S'lichot* Soirées, *Pesah* Jamborees and Sukko Serenades. *Slishi, Shishi,* and *Maftir,* the traditional *aliyot* which were the tributes formerly paid to respected men, are sometimes given to persons who find difficulty with the benedictions to be recited.

The most virulent manifestation of the honors epidemic is the testimonial dinner. He is undoubtedly far down in the scale of leadership (for there is no such person as a Jewish non-leader) who has not at one time or another been given a tribute in the form of a dinner. Indeed there are *machers* in every Jewish community whose exclusive function and talent seemingly is to sponsor and organize testimonial dinners.

It all starts with a phone call by one such *macher* to his buddy. The proposal is generally introduced thus: "You know Jack is going to be fifty (or sixty, as the case may be) next

month. It will be nice if the boys run him a testimonial dinner."
A list is readily drawn up (or since this is not the first similar
dinner inaugurated by this active individual, he simply asks his
secretary to bring in last month's list of people called to Irving's
dinner) and twenty people are telephoned to act as cosponsors.
History has yet to record that one of the invited asked: "Jack?
Why, what has he done?" (There is so much strife in the world,
why antagonize anybody?) Stationery is printed with an im-
posing list of members of the committee. Invitations are sent
out. The response to the printed notices are usually feeble, for
only a handful of the guest of honor's relatives reply. It is then
that the enterprise goes into high gear. People are buttonholed at
meetings, on the golf links, at lunch in the restaurant, or in the
course of a card game. "It will be a really nice affair. You know
Jack—he's a grand guy. Give me ten dollars and promise me you
will come." A committee closes itself in and makes frantic tele-
phone calls. The refrain is, "You must not let me down!" Since
many people have a hidden hope that some day they may be
tendered a testimonial dinner, they quickly succumb.

I was recently at one such affair where about a hundred and
fifty of the guests had been given testimonial dinners and hence
were obligated to attend, and the other hundred and fifty, hoping
for a dinner in their honor in the near future, regarded their
presence as an investment. Of the three hundred reluctant in-
vitees, not one was interested in the guest of honor. As one guest
was heard to say to another, "Which of the men at the head
table is the fellow for whom this dinner was arranged?"

This passion for distributing honors is a curious development in the case of a group whose early literature was written
for centuries by anonymous men who were more interested in
communicating their message than in receiving personal recognition and plaudits. What has become of the outlook on life in
accordance with whose tradition we recite on festivals, "Not unto
us, O Lord, not unto us, but unto Thy Name give glory." We
seem to have forgotten the comment of a great sage to his
disciples, who, in their modesty, were reluctant to accept office,
"You are not chosen for distinction and dominion but for service
and servitude." What of the prophetic definition of the good life
which includes as an indispensable condition, "to walk humbly?"

To be sure, the largest number by far of such occasions marks not the exaltation but the exploitation of an individual for a charitable campaign, an agency, a fund-raising effort for Israel. The "guest of honor" is incidental, and the tribute is a gimmick, for all is fair in fund-raising. The synthetic spontaneity of the affair is evident to all.

In truth, nothing is cheaper in our organized Jewish activities than "honor." It honors neither the man receiving the tribute nor the community bestowing it. In some places, the real honor is to him who has escaped being honored.

A HEALTHY INSANITY

A GRANDPARENT who is not insane should have his head examined. The arrival of a grandchild should stimulate a kind of euphoria which borders on madness. You should relax and enjoy the justified and delightful aberration associated with the status of grandparenthood.

For one thing, to witness your progeny burdened in turn with a child is to revel in a mild type of retaliation. Since there is a tension in the parent-child relationship, the fact that the offspring who inspired tension in us is now the object of tension breeds the satisfying reflection that though justice is often delayed, it ultimately prevails.

For another, grandparenthood comes at a stage in life when you have all but resigned yourself to the thought that life holds no further thrills. You are now living in a subdued state of middle-age blandness. Along comes a child and excites a jubilation which you believed yourself no longer capable of experiencing. The greater leisure enjoyed in your latter years affords the opportunity to spend more time with your son's or daughter's baby than you were in a position to do a generation earlier with your own infant.

You approach your grandchild out of a serenity and ease not known when your own children were growing up. The upbringing of the grandchild does not impose the same severe obligations and heavy responsibilities that a father and mother must inescapably bear. You are by now a kind of Senior Statesman, a Visiting Elder, a Sage Counselor, a Parent-Emeritus. Only on the larger issues and the more important decisions is your advice sought. In addition, the grandchild provides an inexhaustible subject. No conversation need lag, no party grow dull if a grandparent is present. Then too there is not only oral elaboration but also visual demonstrations. Breathes there a granddad with soul so dead that his wallet is not choked with photographs!

But the greatest fascination is the opportunity in your mellow years to be an intimate witness of the miraculous and entrancing process of growth. Every day brings a new discovery, new skill, additional knowledge, and greater facility of movement and action. Electric with vitality, dynamic with a restlessness and power which refute every philosophy that opposes change and seeks to endow the status quo with permanence, a child is the largest argument against personal conservatism.

RESPECT FOR THE WORD

I HAVE A FEELING of love and tenderness for words. I cannot forget that they are among the greatest gifts the past has given us.

There are words wrung out of some unknown heart long ago during a sad and harrowing experience. There are words that leaped from a man's lips in a moment of rare ecstasy. There are poems into which a man compressed a mood, a story, an outcry which we unfortunately can no longer decipher. Who first said, "alas," and what occasioned it? Who first spoke of "the break of dawn," and did he leave any other poetic legacy? Which forgotten genius uttered for the first time "innocence," "heaven," "twilight," "love," "family," "joy"? Who was the ancient philosopher who first said, "I," "mankind," "idea"? Which anonymous immortal first ended a sentence with an upward inflection to indicate he was seeking an answer to a question?

Language is, if not man's greatest creation, certainly his most indispensable. Yet it is daily abused. Millions of words are carelessly uttered in daily conversation, from platforms and pulpits. Who can count the words we mispronounce or those to which we give incorrect meanings? We apply noble words to trivial things and cheapen the value of significant terms by overuse and overapplication.

We start a sentence with "I think," though our mind is unemployed and only our tongue is at work. We have become skilled in business and at social gatherings in the art of using a multitude of words to say nothing. Our children, aping us, learn to slur the words they speak and never go beyond the surface meanings which we, their elders, give to the words we pronounce in their hearing. We denude words and pauperize ourselves by draining them of their deeper significance.

"Talk is cheap" we say, and we do our part to keep it so.

Perhaps this frivolous treatment of words, so characteristic of our talkative age, is symptomatic of the greater crisis of values and purposes which runs through so much of modern life. Responsibility in our use of words may be a good beginning toward a return to a more mature and serious understanding of ourselves and our world.

IN PRAISE OF WALKING

WHEN ROBERT FROST visited Detroit a short time ago, he remarked that he never feels that he has really been in a city until he has walked in it alone. The octogenarian poet wryly added that he had walked for a time on our streets and had met only two men on the way.

Walking has joined letter-writing and conversation as arts lost to our day. Our upper extremities—mind and heart—are being homogenized by the mass media to which they are exposed while our lower extremities are being mechanized by Detroit's unique contribution to comfort and status—the automobile. We are a nation of sitters-before-television, of riders, of reducers, followers-after-diet-fads. But we are definitely not a nation of walkers.

Does one really see the landscape who flies over it or races across it? Appreciation is the fruit of observation and a degree of unhurried lingering reflection. The automobile thus becomes the enemy of nature appreciation.

Like the poet, philosophers too have recognized the virtues of walking. Indeed, in ancient Greece, the mother of philosophy, there was a school of walking thinkers—the peripatetic philosophers. As one walks one enjoys a detachment which stimulates reflection. One turns a subject over and over in his mind, reviewing it from every angle. But is a school of "riding philosophers" thinkable? Is a new system of thought likely to arise from those who rush about in their automobiles?

I therefore raise my voice in behalf of walking. The promenade, relaxed, aimless, easygoing, might provide the therapy

that many of us vainly seek in pills, in trips to resorts or at the
card table.

The slow long walk induces an easing of tension, a calming
of nerves, and a soothing feeling that no other hobby can. In
golf the walk is subordinated to a little ball and counteracted by
a concern about one's score. We have only entered another kind
of race. The purposeless stroll, on the other hand, is free of all
competitiveness. We do not seek to outstrip anyone—we are not
intent upon proving anything, achieving anything, or arriving
anywhere at an appointed time. We simply, in the words of Walt
Whitman, "loaf and invite our souls." We break the stranglehold
of the activism which our civilization seems determined to force
upon us, and refresh ourselves with a leisureliness and calm that
escape us in our daily round of duty. We are neither in pursuit
nor are we being pursued. In entering into a peace pact with
our surroundings, we find peace within ourselves for ourselves.

"O House of Jacob," said the prophet, "come ye and let us
walk in the light of the Lord." As we walk we shall find the
world revealed to us under an aspect we had not recognized
before. We shall become aware of stirrings of appreciation and
thought within us which we had not experienced before. In the
communion beween our deeper self and the world as it appears to
us, we shall have stronger intimations of the presence of God
above the din and madness of our times.

LETTER FROM JERUSALEM

IT HAS BEEN SAID that cities have faces, some angry, some volup-
tuous, some arrogant, some drowsy and lethargic, and some soft
and gentle. Sometimes travelers speak of the "voice of the city,"
and picture cities that speak in strident and assertive tones; others
with a voice, measured, moderate, restrained; and a few memorable places that seem to caress one with their whisper.

Tonight, as I walked for hours through the streets of Jerusalem, the city struck me as being full of echoes. All about me I

seemed to catch the present echoes of voices of long ago. A famous Hebrew phrase, literally translated, refers to the "daughter of a voice."

In Jerusalem one's ears become increasingly attuned to the grandchildren and great-grandchildren, so to speak, of sounds that were spoken in a far past. The noise of contemporary life has not stilled them, nor have they become spent with the passage of many centuries. They have miraculously survived and continue to strike one's ear gently, yet audibly. The clamor of motorcars and hurrying buses; the many who rush past you as you slowly stroll through the city; the new and impressive buildings, self-conscious both in their newness and impressiveness, that forcibly seek to capture your attention and subdue you in your admiration of them—all of these cannot dispel or mute the persistent echoes that live in the atmosphere of the city.

Here a prophet spoke rich and intense words, and the echoes of those words move on evermore through time like waves rolling to a far shore. Here a seer, exalted and inflamed by an overwhelming vision, gave such expression to his ecstasy that, like a mighty hammer striking an anvil with infinite force, it sent forth sparks that time and wind will never be able to extinguish. Here a sage taught with a wisdom deep as a great sea, and sent forth streams and rivulets that will never cease to flow. The remembrance of past words is here—no escape into the past, no pilgrimage to the ancient and bygone. Here the past overflows into the present, becoming reborn and restored, endowed with the vital and vigorous reality of the presently living.

Awakened for a moment out of your reflections and yet dominated by the mood they inspired, you see the people on the streets of the city, walking, selling, buying. But now they have undergone a transformation and are no longer like people of any other city in the world. They, too, are part of the great and deathless Book in which the words whose echoes you have been hearing are imperishably recorded. And you are not dreamily sauntering the streets of a city but are instead moving through the pages and chapters of that selfsame Book, for you, too, are part of its chronicle.

The city, its echoes and its people, and you, no longer a beholder, are all now verses and phrases of the Book, imprinted on its pages, drawn into its contents. A people is a Book, and each of its members, in addition to his own individuality and voice, is a sound, an echo, an overtone of the Book's immortal message. We came out of that Book, and its words are intermingled with ours, and its spirit is upon us. Here one feels as if all the world were a sacred ark and Israel the Torah housed in that ark.

The Book will speak again so that all of mankind may hear, through the people that have marched out of its pages into the world of men and things, of movement and noise, of sorrow and hate, of conflict and fear. And the voice in which it speaks will bring healing and peace to men bruised and tormented. The still small voice will be heard above the fire and the storm and the earthquake. Its echo resounding in the hearts of men will instill the wisdom and compassion which have been lost in the world and which they cannot find on their way to the morrow that has been foretold by the Book.

MORDECAI M. KAPLAN

THE OBSERVANCE OF THE seventy-fifth birthday of a great and distinguished Jewish scholar and thinker should be marked by all Jews, irrespective of ideology, who are interested in Jewish thought, learning, and who revere human greatness. Such an occasion is now being celebrated in the life of Mordecai M. Kaplan. Those of us who have known him as teacher, as guide and friend, have been immensely enriched by his profound and fruitful mind, his lofty spirit, his uncompromising integrity, his intense devotion to Judaism, and by the example of his lifetime of service and leadership. Every Jew in America who is informed and concerned has absorbed, knowingly or not, impulses of influence that have emanated from Dr. Kaplan.

Mordecai Kaplan calls upon us to meet the revolutionary impacts of modern life. He wants Jews to integrate their Jewish faith and loyalty in the pattern of thought and the outlook upon life which characterizes them as twentieth-century men. Judaism must not become a mere heirloom or an outer adornment hanging

by the thread of sentimentality. It must enter the life-stream of
thought and motivation of our entire personality. Hence it must
be reexamined and reinterpreted so that it can function in the
context of our present intellectual and emotional life and experience. Dr. Kaplan writes and teaches out of a profound faith that
Judaism, rightly understood, is not only relevant to modern life
but can greatly contribute to it.

His restless mind ranges over the large tradition of the Jew
as well as over the vast field of modern philosophy and thought.
He has enlarged the horizons of our conceptions of Judaism and
has deepened our understanding of the realities of the modern
world. Like no one else in our time, he is the great bridge-builder
between Judaism and the thought of our day; between the pre-
Emancipation outlook and the new and vastly changed universe
of ideas in which we now live, between the Jew of yesterday and
the Jew of tomorrow. He refutes the "intellectual" who asserts
that we have outlived all need for Judaism. He opposes the "tradi-
tionalists" who believes that a tradition can remain inert and static
while life moves on. He chides the timid who, in an age calling
for bold thought and imagination, are trapped by their own inertia
and hesitancies. He opposes the innovator who acts as if one
should or can wipe the slate clean and start anew without maintaining vital continuities with the richness of past insight and experience.

Mordecai Kaplan challenges each Jew alert to Jewish needs
and zealous for the creative survival of the Jewish community and
its heritage. Whether one accepts fully his conclusions or not, one
must recognize the indebtedness of every intelligent Jew to the
stimulating and incisive analysis of the problem which he presents
and to the heroic and significant attempt to meet it which he has
made.

MAN OF BURDENS AND OF HOPE

THE RABBI LEADS MANY LIVES. He seeks intimately to enter into
the lives of his people and understand their needs and aspirations.

He attempts to identify himself with the young collegian, the professional, the businessman, the parent, the idealist, the man of affairs so that he may present the tradition in terms meaningful and relevant to his congregation. He seeks to know the conflicts of the adolescent, the perplexities of youth, the pressures and problems of the man of business, and the challenges and difficulties which confront the doctor, lawyer, or engineer.

The rabbi dies many deaths. His relationship with his congregation is not formal and external. His people become members of his family, to whom he is bound by ties of affection and concern. Their sorrows become his sorrow. The tragedies that overtake them register painfully upon his heart. In their bereavement he feels grief and pain. Constantly exposed to participation in the anguish of others, he is often visited by sadness. The circle of his love and the area of his sorrow are large, and grief is a frequent companion.

The rabbi knows many joys. The marriage of one of his young people, the academic achievements of another, the professional success of a third, joyous milestones in the lives of his families—all have a place in his personal calendar. Births, weddings, anniversaries become happy experiences in his individual life.

The rabbi is heir to many frustrations. Many gaps yawn between the ideals he envisions and the realities in the midst of which he lives. The fact that the sources of influence and power in society are far removed from the spiritual evaluations and standards to which he is dedicated leads to recurring attacks of disillusionment. His messages often fall echolessly into an oblivion of indifference, inattention, and preoccupation. The sovereign hold which "practical" men—administrators, promoters, organizers, men of action—have upon our communal structure is a fertile source of disappointment. The evils which lurk beneath the cloak of respectability and which come to view in his counseling bring anxiety and concern in their wake.

The rabbi, to borrow a prophetic phrase, is the "prisoner of hope." His frustrations and recurring moods of disillusionment do not end in a philosophy of despair. From faith in God and from the large perspectives which a long and profound tradition opens to him, the rabbi draws sustaining nourishment and strength for the performance of his daily duties. Though he may be tired and

spent at the end of a day, he is not bereft of faith and resolve.
Renewed, he awakes fortified and invigorated to teach and to
guide men, interpreting to them those values and ideals which
alone can restore men to serenity and society to peace.

THE RABBI: 1966 *

UPON NO ONE ELSE in the Jewish community have the hammer-
blows of change and mutation fallen as forcefully as upon the
American rabbi (excepted are those who live in the few communities of refuge from modern life to be found in Brooklyn and
Long Island—the Mea Shearim of our continent). None has been
more exposed to the "acids of modernity" than he; none as storm-
tossed by the multiple revolutions that have worked such havoc
with the inherited and hallowed.

It is small wonder that he appears to himself as standing at a
crossroad of uncertainty and ambiguity, without a clear conception of his function and baffled as to direction. He does not define
himself either as prophet or priest, philosopher or mystic, communal leader or administrator. He may be something of each, and
the result is a blurred portrait that is not easily recognizable, and
that except for the designation "rabbi" bears little similarity to
that of his predecessors. How easy it is to pick upon the weakness
he betrays, the inner contradictions he unites within him, the corrosions his profession has suffered.

He provides a ready target for those who delight in making
ironic thrusts at the vulgarities of the organized life over which
he presumably presides in their desire to exculpate themselves
from their noninvolvement in matters Jewish. He has attained a
high degree of conspicuousness, a condition which invites critics
to heap upon him the guilt for the shallowness of so much of communal activity. (There may be a psychological basis to the need
or desire to level criticism at the rabbi.) Yet he is more victim
than culprit, more the object than the shaper of the forces of Jew-

---

* *Jewish Heritage*, spring, 1966.

ish collective endeavor. The real power in the community rests in other hands, while his own influence is more apparent than vital. The Jewish community itself is in the vortex of powerful circumstances that have their origin and focus outside of it.

But it is not to defend him that leads one to speak of the rabbi, current vintage—though obviously one should appraise his position and work in proper perspective. Understanding should be prior to judgment. What claims our attention here is an aspect that goes unnoticed in the novels in which he is a character—chief or subsidiary—and in the essays which treat their readers to a philosophical or sociological analysis of the rabbi on the American Jewish scene. It is an aspect that lies hidden beneath the surface of his prominence and success and seems to be denied by the adulation accorded him and the comfortable livelihood granted him.

His is essentially a life of pathos. He suffers a score of alienations and must daily battle for his faith and hope. For he is isolated at the very center of the community he "leads" and serves as the spokesman of a group tradition at a time when the group has become all but traditionless.

The rabbi is the heir and teacher of the longest continuous history and tradition in the Western world. From early childhood he has trained to look at life from the vantage point of a millennial history. In his father's home, he had become rooted in a faith and background, and its symbols, institutions, and rhythms are deeply intertwined with his personal attitudes and beliefs. History-oriented and tradition-centered he now sees himself a stranger in a land not his.

For ours is an age of a receding if not disappearing past, in which yesterday quickly joins antiquity in the mounting heap of the obsolescent. Daily are we witness to the proliferation of discontinuities and the escalation of transitoriness. Modern man is "isolated" in time since change, vast, constant and relentless, cuts the ground of the past from under his feet and allows him but the immediate moment in which to move about. Life no longer proceeds from precedent to precedent but rather from the novel to the unprecedented.

Not for our day the admonition, "remember the days of old, consider the years of ages past." Today we feel no continuity with our antecedents and sense no kinship with the days ahead, for both the past and the future are separated from us by profound and all-encompassing changes. The rabbi, scion of a tradition and heir of a culture, must now function in the midst of a technological setting in which cultural differentiations are obliterated and traditional modes discounted. After all, computers have no particular identity and reflect no specific culture. They are neither Western nor Eastern, Jewish nor Christian, Hebraic nor Hellenic. The rabbi now lives with his congregation in an increasingly homogenized world, encapsulated in the moment, thus denying history, and undistinguished in substance and form, thus negating culture.

Jewish tradition defines the rabbi as a layman, yet to his parishioners he is a clergyman and pastor, and he has not yet grown comfortably into the new role that has been thrust upon him. A teacher of a tradition, he is now in the service of an institution; an interpreter of a history, he has in fact become the executive of an agency. By calling and temperament a student, he has been turned into an official, a steward, a member of a staff. Interested in ideas and disciplined to study in privacy, the logic of surrounding circumstances has led him to serve as an apostle of affability and conviviality. He knows and is known by more people than any other leader in the community (save the political boss) and yet at the heart of him there is an unsureness of self in the midst of the crowd. Often a consciousness of apartness grips him, for which he quickly compensates with simulated exuberance. He is a frequent guest at testimonial dinners, receptions, and the multiple bizarre festivities that clog the calendar of American Jewish life, and yet in the brief moments when he is not "socializing" he finds himself agonizing over the question, "What am I doing here?"

The issues around which his organized thinking revolves— God, Torah, moral values, social goals, the crisis of faith, theology —are remote to the people to whom he ministers. They are good and friendly men and women who, in moments of his detachment and introspection, seem to be a pre-Sinaitic tribe which has not repudiated a covenant but rather has not yet accepted one.

He sees himself shipwrecked on an uninhabited island, far from centers of life and movement. He sadly concludes that he is a member of the world's loneliest profession. He is modern and advanced, but the background he brings to his modernity stands in the way of his full integration into contemporary life. He is liberal and recognizes not only the inevitability but the desirability and value of change even within the tradition which he represents. He recognizes an irrefutable truth in the words of Whitehead, "The art of free society consists first in the maintenance of the symbolic code and secondly in the fearlessness of revision. . . . Those societies which cannot combine reverence of their symbols with freedom of revision must ultimately decay." Yet he is restrained by the inhibiting apprehension that the stabilities needed to absorb the changes (Whitehead's "symbolic code") are lacking in Jewish life, and change that is not made in a frame of reference of the continuing becomes dissolution rather than revision. He responds to a devoutness to which he cannot give full expression at the services of which he is the officiant. Compelled by the convention of our times governing the clergy to make many public addresses, he worries constantly whether the fluency and felicity of expression he has developed are not the enemies of his thought and reflection.

As a rabbi he has not inherited a structured system of doctrine and is therefore given to a constant quest and reexamination. Yet it is expected by those who seek him out that he dispense certitudes and teach finalities. Himself of intellectual inclinations, he is looked down upon by the academic intellectual fraternity as the upholder of the discredited, outlived, and irrational. Eager for dialogue, he engages for the most part in monologues from pulpit and platform. He censures himself for sinking into the middle-class ethos from which he is striving to raise his people. He is a teacher of ends and goals at a time when techniques are in the saddle and means are supreme.

While religion is respected, it is not invoked. Though he is honored as a "man of God," he is not taken seriously. He has become a symbol on a par with other symbols—the ark, Torah, menorah, altar—and like them revered at a distance but not profaned by involvement in daily life and crucial decisions. (He wryly muses that the traditional reference to the enkindled lights of Hanukkah reflects, ironically, the contemporary attitude, "One is not permitted to make use of them, but only to behold them.")

The rabbi recognizes that what his generation needs, perhaps above all else, is a rationale, a reasoned exposition of Judaism that would not only serve as its intellectual justification but would also naturalize it in the larger universe of discourse and thought in which educated modern Jews move. But he is too fragmented, too diffused, to attempt such a synthesis, and the age too greatly in flux to permit such a structure. He is perforce a dealer in fragments, fugitive texts, disparate insights. The context to enclose them seems to have dissolved. Unity and wholeness are neither in him nor in his teaching.

The rabbi is not infrequently troubled by his own inadequacies. He has not resisted what should have been resisted. He has not devoted himself to basic matters with the inflexible single-mindedness they deserve. He has permitted himself to walk for too long on surfaces and has lived too much with the peripheral and incidental. He has not sufficiently ignored the dais and the limelight. He has failed his tradition and his people. He sometimes feels this most keenly when he is being feted, or complimented.

In the rabbi are concentrated the frustrations, ambivalences, confusions, and uncertainties which bedevil the modern Jew, intensified by his greater rootedness in Judaism and magnified by the representative nature of his position.

WHEN THOU CALLEST ME

GOD, THOU HAST GIFTED ME with blessings beyond my merit and hast shielded me times without number from evil and hurt. Thou hast guided me through many years of life and hast caused it to be enriched by the love dear ones have given to me. Thou hast enabled me to serve my fellowmen and my community and hast not withheld from me evidence of the regard and friendship in which others have held me. Thou hast set my lot in a land of freedom and justice and hast spared me the indignities and torments which so many of my brethren have endured.

O God of truth and mercy, it is in disregard of the many rich bounties Thou hast showered upon me that I approach Thee for yet another manifestation of Thy infinite and divine love. Thou who hast made me in the past the object of Thy care and concern, grant me one more plea.

O God, when in Thy wisdom Thou callest me to leave this earthly life I shall come uncomplaining and unafraid, since it is Thou who calls. But let Thy command that I depart this life be sharp, clear, and decisive. Remove me, O God, quickly and do not let me journey with lingering slowness and halting steps from life here to whithersoever Thou wouldst lead me. Spare me a long interval of helplessness, the delaying period of a slow illness before my breath ceases in fulfillment of Thy wish. Allow me, O God, to leave in instantaneous compliance with Thy decree and bestow upon all whom I love that healing solace which Thou alone canst give. May but a quickly passing moment separate life from death so that I may serve Thee in whatever realm awaits me, with unimpaired strength of body and vigor of mind. Take me unto Thee, O Father, in wholeness, not broken and wracked by suffering and illness. Graciously grant me the great joy of coming to Thee with reverent gratitude for Thy many blessings in this life and with unfaltering trust and faith in the life beyond, to which Thou hast summoned me. Amen!

FAREWELL *

"SPEECH," WROTE GEORGE ELIOT, "is but broken light upon the depth of the unspoken." I must rely upon the friendship and understanding you have so abundantly extended to sense "the depth of the unspoken" gratitude which fills Goldie's and my heart at the moving demonstration of your interest and regard on the occasion of the twenty-fifth anniversary of the assumption of my rabbinical duties at Shaarey Zedek. Words can only suggest but not exhaustively communicate the many feelings which clamor and surge within me. I am proud of your friendship and humbled by the affection and trust you direct to me. I am fortified in my responsibility to serve and teach, and distressed by my inability

*Address on occasion of celebration of his twenty-five years of service as rabbi of Shaarey Zedek, January 10, 1964.

to measure up to the stature which your affection has stimulated
you to ascribe to me. I am uplifted by your confidence and dis-
quieted by your kind and high expectations. I am gratified by
your expressions of appreciation and concerned by your friendly
glossing over my limitations and frailties. I am enriched by your
generous thoughts and I am overwhelmed by my sense of indebtedness to so many who have instructed, guided, and inspired me.
You have made me the sole object of your commendations at the
Service of Tribute, and yet I am the humblest member of the
company that deserves the honor accorded me.

There are the parents whose imprint of love and example has
not been weakened by the passing of many years. There are teachers whose scholarship and wisdom have inspired me and whose
friendship elevated my spirit. There are friends, rabbinic and lay,
who have taught me serenity and gentleness and through their
companionship imparted to me a strength I could not otherwise
have achieved. There are the books whose words have opened
windows for mind and soul and enabled me to glimpse a universe
made large by their beauty and creative imagination. And in this
human circle of those whose debtor I will always be, there is the
beloved life partner who shares my life and dreams; the daughter
who has illumined my life with her radiance, and my dear son-in-
law whose understanding and loyalty knit him to me as closely as
one's own son; and of course the incomparable grandchildren,
Judith, Jeremy, and Joel, whose laughter brightens the heart when
it is heavy and banishes the darkest mood.

Beyond and above all, I am thankful to God whom I have so
inadequately served but who has nonetheless given me blessings
beyond my desserts. The moments when I have most vividly felt
His Presence have flooded my entire life with their glory.

• About the Author

• Rabbi Morris Adler

MORRIS ADLER, the son of an immigrant rabbi, was born in 1906 and brought to the United States in 1913. He was educated in New York's public schools, and later graduated from both the College of the City of New York and the Jewish Theological Seminary of America, which ordained him.

After serving briefly in pulpits in St. Joseph, Missouri, and Buffalo, New York, he became Rabbi of Detroit's Congregation Shaarey Zedek, a post he held until his death in March, 1966, the victim of bullets fired by a deranged student. During World War II, he served as chaplain in the Southwest Pacific and Japan.

Rabbi Adler's numerous civic and cultural endeavors won him national renown. In 1960 Wayne State University conferred upon him the honorary degree of Doctor of Law; in 1965 he received an honorary Doctor of Philosophy degree from his alma mater, the Jewish Theological Seminary of America; and in 1966 he was awarded, posthumously, an honorary Humane Letters degree from the University of Detroit. He was frequently called on by national and state bodies to speak on matters relating to church and state, interfaith and intergroup relations.

Rabbi Adler held many high communal offices. He served as chairman of: United Automobile Workers Public Review Board; B'nai B'rith's Commission on Adult Jewish Education; Rabbinical Council, United Jewish Appeal; and Law Committee, Rabbinical Assembly of America. He also served on boards of Michigan's Cultural Commission, its Commission on Problems of the Aging, its Fair Election Practices Commission, and its Commission on Ethics in State Affairs. He was an officer of Detroit's Round Table of Christians and Jews, its Community Health Association, and many other civic groups.

In addition to numerous periodical articles, Rabbi Adler was the author of *Selected Passages from the Torah* and *The World of the Talmud,* and co-editor of *Jewish Heritage Reader.*

239